CORRUPTION AND POLITICAL REFORM IN BRAZIL:

The Impact of Collor's Impeachment

EDITED BY
KEITH S. ROSENN AND RICHARD DOWNES

North·South Center Press
UNIVERSITY OF MIAMI

The publisher of this book is the North-South Center Press at the University of Miami.

The mission of the Dante B. Fascell North-South Center is to promote better relations and serve as a catalyst for change among the United States, Canada, and the nations of Latin America and the Caribbean by advancing knowledge and understanding of the major political, social, economic, and cultural issues affecting the nations and peoples of the Western Hemisphere.

© 1999 North-South Center Press at the University of Miami.

 Published by the North-South Center Press at the University of Miami and distributed by Lynne Rienner Publishers, Inc., 1800 30th Street, Suite 314, Boulder, CO 80301-1026. All rights reserved under International and Pan-American Conventions. No portion of the contents may be reproduced or transmitted in any form, or by any means, including photocopying, recording, or any information storage retrieval system, without prior permission in writing from the North-South Center Press.

All copyright inquiries should be addressed to the publisher: North-South Center Press, 1500 Monza Avenue, Coral Gables, Florida 33146-3027, U.S.A., phone 305-284-8912, fax 305-284-5089, or e-mail mmapes@miami.edu.

To order or to return books, contact Lynne Rienner Publishers, Inc., 1800 30th Street, Suite 314, Boulder, CO 80301-1026, 303-444-6684, fax 303-444-0824.

Library of Congress Cataloging-in-Publication Data

    Corruption and Political Reform in Brazil: The Impact of Collor's Impeachment / edited by Keith S. Rosenn and Richard Downes

    p. cm.

    Includes bibliographical references and index.

    ISBN 1-57454-065-3 (hardcover: alk. paper)

    1. Brazil—Politics and government—1985- 2. Political corruption—Brazil. 3. Collor de Mello, Fernando Affonso, 1949- —Impeachment.

    I. Rosenn, Keith S. II. Downes, Richard, 1947- .

    F2538.3.C67 1998   98-49839

    320.981'09'048—dc21   CIP

Printed in the United States of America/TS

03 02 01 00 99   6 5 4 3 2 1

Table of Contents

Preface and Acknowledgments

This work is designed to contribute to the understanding of Brazil's ongoing political development and to informed dialogue on the interaction between corruption and political reform in Latin America's democratization process. It reviews the dynamics of the impeachment of Fernando Collor de Mello and subsequent efforts at political reform within the Brazilian political system to shed light on the progress of Brazil's political modernization effort and, by implication, on the fate of similar efforts in other major Latin American nations.

The analyses of the Collor episode presented here are elements of a work in progress, contributions to understanding the broad institutional and personal dimensions of Brazil's and Latin America's quest for effective governance. Like all others in the near future, this effort will remain limited by the yet incomplete and conflicting accounts of the existence and extent of corruption within the governments of Collor and his successors. The unfinished nature of the investigation into the 1996 assassination of Collor confidant Paulo Cesar "P.C." Farias and the lack of detailed accounts of the behind-the-scenes maneuvering of the impeachment process suggest that new evidence may influence any final evaluation of the Collor presidency. Collor's own continuing efforts to embellish his actions as president while debunking corruption charges in an effort to regain his political rights before 2000, in defiance of the Supreme Court judgment to that effect, may raise doubts among some about the nature and motivations of the charges that forced him to resign the presidency and then become the first Latin American president ever to be impeached.

The incomplete historical record is but one of the serious analytical barriers confronting efforts to identify corruption and its effects in this case and others. The interdisciplinary nature of the analysis of corruption, the absence of a widely accepted definition of corruption, the culturally bound notion of what constitutes corrupt behavior, and the pervasive deceit and mendacity practiced by corrupt politicians and their co-conspirators challenge those who would analyze its impact on a system of governance. Scholars admit that the study of corruption requires "a confrontation with the most fundamental questions of political economy in a society" but lament the lack of a "body of theory ready made for the problem at hand" (Rose-Ackerman 1978, 2-3) and the deficiencies of a literature that is "tentative and thin, with few theoretical frameworks, international comparisons or careful case studies" (Klitgaard 1988, ix). Further complicating analysis of the role of corruption is the burden incurred by analysts of one cultural background when examining the practices of another. The penchant to identify corruption primarily within other cultures, while ignoring transgressions at home, is universal. English visitors to the United States at the end of the nineteenth century were asked by their compatriots upon their return, "Isn't everybody corrupt there?" (Little and Posada-Carbo 1996, 2-3). Today the Third World is often seen as a crucible of corruption even while modern democracies practice kickbacks, influence peddling, and questionable campaign financing arrangements. This work seeks to avoid that pitfall by balancing Brazilian and non-Brazilian viewpoints.

Such limitations do not allow the issue of corruption to be easily dismissed or discounted as a critical factor in Latin America's continuing democratization process. The excesses of Collor and others in the face of an expanding free press and pressures for increased transparency in business transactions have been instrumental in spawning broad interregional efforts to prevent and ferret out corruption. The hemisphere's leaders gathered at the 1994 Miami Summit stressed the need for "effective democracy" to launch a "comprehensive attack on corruption as a factor of social disintegration and distortion of the economic system that undermines the legitimacy of political institutions," and four years later at Santiago they pledged to give "a new impetus to the struggle against corruption." The Organization of American States (OAS) has been aggressively focusing attention on corruption's ills, evoking a commitment from its members to "make every effort to prevent, detect, punish, and eradicate corruption in the performance of public functions and acts of corruption specifically related to such performance" through the Inter-American Convention Against Corruption, signed in March 1996. OAS Secretary-General Cesar Gaviria has judged combating corruption as essential to sustaining the credibility of economic reforms, noting, "It would be pointless to move forward in economic and market reform if democracies are crumbling because of corruption" (Gaviria 1996, 2). Directors of the World Bank and the International Monetary Fund (IMF) stated in 1996 that recipient countries will be held accountable for their practices. Governmental pressures against journalists who have exposed corruption have lead to immediate outcries by human rights groups and press associations who recognize the threat to democratic governance represented by corruption unchecked by civil society. Transparency International, a nongovernmental organization founded in 1993 by former World Bank official Peter Eiger, has established chapters throughout Latin America to heighten public pressure for accountability in government. The days when Latin American presidents enjoyed such power that the president's wife and daughter could regularly draw the first and second prizes in the National Lottery, "all without shame" (Whitehead 1983, 148), have clearly receded into the darker days of Latin American history.

A new emphasis on the pernicious effects of corruption on democratic systems with Latin America's transition from "bureaucratic authoritarian" regimes of the 1960s through the 1980s to democratic forms of government has complemented multilateral efforts to expose corruption. Many developmental economists and political scientists of the 1960s and 1970s considered corruption an unavoidable byproduct of the modernization process. Samuel P. Huntington argued in 1968 that "modernization breeds corruption" by changing the basic values of society, creating new sources of wealth, and expanding government authority and regulation (Huntington 1968, 59-71), and Nathaniel Leff suggested that criticism of corruption represented the political, economic, and ideological interests of particular groups and that governments could acknowledge corruption "as an aspect of their societies and try to optimize policy-making within this framework" (Leff 1978, 518-520). Far from accepting corruption as inevitable or even necessary to economic development, contemporary analysts of the transition to democracy have focused attention on the tension between democratic principles and political corruption, "the use of political power and office to benefit some individual or collective self in ways that are illegal and/or considered corrupt, improper or self-serving" (Knight 1996, 220). The focus here is on whether the liberalization process will result in protection for "both individuals and social groups from arbitrary or illegal acts committed by the state or third parties" and allow the citizen to exercise the access and accountability essential to a functional democracy (O'Donnell and Schmitter 1986, 7-9).

Addressing the issue of whether the new Latin American democracies have become more or less corrupt has become intertwined with considerations of reform of the state, an integral element of processes of democratization, liberalization, and globalization shaping contemporary events in the region. Many Latin Americans (and Latin Americanists) remain convinced that "government is unresponsive and at times an obstacle, traditional political leaders deserve no support, and political reform is an illusion because those who promise change are likely to change only the beneficiaries of corruption" (Dominguez and Giraldo 1996, 1). A recent survey indicated that political corruption remains the most significant problem in Latin America in the judgment of 303 officers or presidents of Fortune 1000 companies, commercial banks, and debt investment firms (Manzetti 1997, 3). Liberalization has increased the opportunity for rent-seeking behavior, requiring new reforms to protect the *"res publica* against the greed of powerful individuals and groups" (Bresser Pereira 1996, 5).

Contemporary efforts to combat corruption have focused on administrative and legal reform, consistent with the recent recommendation of Venezuelan President Rafael Caldera that "the problem should be seen mostly as one of corrupt systems rather than corrupt persons" (Caldera 1996). Transparency International urges "changes in the government and its methods of assuring accountability and changes in moral and ethical attitudes," along with greater public involvement, especially the private sector and civil society (TI Source Book, 2). For many, the task remains to mount a "sustained effort to reduce corruption and clientelism" and build up "a core of permanent civil servants" (Roxborough 1997, 64), an effort well-rooted in numerous previous efforts to improve public administration and reform Latin America's civil service. Recent efforts at reform include commitments by the governor of Argentina's province of Mendoza to create "islands of integrity" by holding public hearings and requiring anti-bribery pledges; modernization of Bolivia's tax, financial, and accounting systems; institution of inspectors- general within each Brazilian ministry; creation of a Department for the Prevention of Corruption in the Dominican Republic; financial disclosure by Nicaragua's president; greater transparency in the procurement process and the initiation of judicial proceedings against several allegedly corrupt officials in Panama; and the creation of a code of ethics for public employees in Venezuela (Transparency International 1997). However, without effective enforcement and an end to impunity generally enjoyed by senior officials, especially presidents, such efforts may well constitute modern versions of the nineteenth-century Brazilian practice of passing laws designed "para o Ingles ver," legalisms designed mainly to impress foreigners with little intent of enforcement.

The case of Fernando Collor de Mello can be instructive and illustrative of the dilemmas facing Latin America today as nations attempt to construct modern democratic states. Even though Fernando Collor was no ordinary civil servant, his actions were intimately related to electoral reforms that reduced incentives for cooperation and party discipline while giving preference to pork-barrel politics. After Collor was sworn in on March 15, 1990, as the first popularly elected Brazilian president in 30 years, his stormy presidency temporarily ended on September 29, 1992. The Chamber of Deputies took the unprecedented action of impeaching him on charges of corruption, and Vice President Itamar Franco became Acting President. The Collor presidency ended definitively at the end of December 1992, when Collor formally resigned, just as the Senate was about to begin the impeachment trial. Itamar Franco became the president of Brazil to serve the remainder of Collor's mandate. While the Senate formally convicted the ex-president and his political rights were abolished until after the year 2000, he was judged innocent of criminal charges.

Despite the strength of his initial image as a new-age politician devoted to reform, Collor proved to be yet another corrupt leader milking his lofty position to squeeze contractors and other favor-seekers for his own personal gain and attempting to use the state's resources to cover his misdeeds. The lifting of bank secrecy revealed a flow of funds through checks made out to the bearer destined to support a luxuriant life style for the first family replete with regal automobiles and an imposing "Babylonian garden." As Collor soon found out, his assumptions that he could honestly justify the resulting extravagant life style to the Brazilian public and that, if discovered, he could rely upon the collaboration of the usually deferential Brazilian public servants whose names were appropriated for false bank accounts and of politicians willing to trade favors for support proved egregiously unsound and faulty.

The perspectives provided here on these events and their aftermath represent insights gained from cumulative decades of analyzing events in Brazil through historical, legal, and political templates. They explore several themes related to the linkages between corruption and political reform: the range of corrupt activities by individual rent-seekers dedicated to maximizing their personal returns, the incentives for corruption spawned by institutional and legal processes that impede financial accountability, the prospects and limitations of the campaign to create meaningful reform, how institutional struggles for power impact upon the public's perception of corruption, and the clash between democratic and patrimonial forces within Brazilian society as part of a process of societal modernization.

The ways rent-seekers attempted to maximize their personal returns become apparent in Chapter 1, "Collor's Downfall in Historical Perspective," by Thomas Skidmore, and in Chapter 2, "Institutional Sources of Corruption in Brazil," by Barbara Geddes and Artur Ribeiro Neto. Both chapters highlight the disfunctional systemic and personal dynamics of the failure of the Collor government and those that followed. Thomas Skidmore explains how Fernando Collor was the product of both the traditional and modern world of Brazilian politics and an authentic product of Brazil's political system. The type of political presence he created drew from efforts to introduce an accountability into Brazilian politics that had been missing during the authoritarian era. It was also a byproduct of the colossal economic problems that arose during the presidency of José Sarney from 1985 on. Finally, the Constitution of 1988 created further difficulties for effectively governing Brazil by excessively diffusing power away from the central government in an overreaction to centralized military rule.

For Skidmore, Collor's exceedingly ambitious nature hopelessly complicated his efforts to govern. His extensive use of provisional decrees, failure to seek consensus, and lack of recognition of the power of public opinion within a democracy, his arrogant nature, and a reinvigorated press had already pushed Collor toward the edge of a political precipice. When revelations about corrupt dealing involving an Alagoan businessman named Paulo Cesar Farias came to light, Collor's "Indiana Jones" image faded quickly. Actions Collor took to contain the crisis only generated more tinder for a political bonfire, as improbable explanations produced political ridicule. Even lavish patronage could not hold back the waves of political rejection.

Skidmore illustrates how the Collor episode manifests certain constants within Brazil's political culture. Like Jânio Quadros, Collor was able to build upon the messianic hopes of the Brazilian people. The return of legal and judiciary powers to the political process with the fading of authoritarian rule, along with the military's unwillingness to intervene based upon their own experience in government, became important factors in Collor's demise.

On balance, Skidmore judges the Collor episode to have shown the strength of Brazil's democracy while simultaneously exposing the depths of its social, economic, and political problems. Only an electoral system that allows for far fewer parties and more party discipline and accountability will allow Brazil to sustain a functioning system. A combination of reforms and enlightened political leadership is needed to transform Brazil into a functional democracy and to avoid resurrection of the frequently exercised authoritarian option.

Geddes and Ribeiro Neto concentrate upon the environment that facilitates corruption and collusion. They raise the specter of the Brazilian nation drowning in a sea of mud — corruption so widespread that it jeopardizes Brazil's chances for economic and social development. They highlight the depth of corruption within the Brazilian political system and its growth with the onset of privatization. They address systemic causes of corruption within the post-1985 Brazilian political system, the increased benefits of corruption, the decreased likelihood of being caught, and the low probability and cost of punishment to those who are caught.

Investigations of Collor's government and the Congressional Budget Committee discovered highly sophisticated corruption schemes designed to provide influential insiders with kickbacks or illegal campaign contributions. Contractors conspired with politicians and among themselves to obtain specific public works contracts or divide the work among themselves, regardless of which company received the winning bid. Officials of the executive branch, members of Congress, and even state bank officers participated in the scheme, allowing enormous amounts of money to be extracted from the public till.

Geddes and Ribeiro Neto cite changes in electoral rules and the Constitution as responsible for the growth in corruption. Under the new political system, the president is unable to build stable coalitions and ensure the loyalty of supporters in Congress. Meanwhile, Congress has gained in power and incentives for exchange-based and corrupt practices. Corruption has grown as the executive seeks political support by distributing projects to the districts represented by supporters, and congressional influence over the budget process has grown, even while the need to generate funds for reelection campaigns has become an imperative. Contributing to rampant corruption is the perception, prior to Collor's impeachment, that punishment for corruption is unlikely because it depends on congressional and court action.

Geddes and Ribeiro Neto then explore in detail the varieties of corruption practiced in Brazil, defined as "abuse of control over the power and resources of government." These primarily involve the exchange of resources for political support and designed to enrich the participants at the public's expense. Fundamental causes of corruption in Brazil include the high levels of state intervention in the economy and electoral rules that promote exchange politics. The latter helps promote a broad range of corrupt practices because of the consequent weakness of political parties and the overrepresentation in the legislature of "backward" parts of the country.

Within an institutional framework that promoted corruption, Collor instituted radical economic reforms designed to reverse the economic crisis. These also offered insiders unprecedented opportunities for graft. Corruption flourished not only among Collor and his confidants but also at the hands of appointees who were conducting "free-lance operations."

Only an unlikely concurrence of events led to Collor's impeachment. While holding corrupt government officials accountable is a function of the public's desire and ability to end the political careers of corrupt office holders, it was only the massive public attention given to the Collor case, the Supreme Court's refusal to allow members of Congress to vote secretly on the case, and the impending municipal elections that convinced members of Congress that they would be held accountable. Aside from allowing subsequent presidents to focus on economic reform, the successful impeachment of Collor may signal a willingness to implement important reforms within the political system. Such political reforms are essential to the formation of stable executive-legislative coalitions that would allow the nation to sustain economic reforms and resolve long-standing social and economic problems.

Efforts to overcome personal and institutional failings are thoroughly discussed in David Fleischer's Chapter 3, "Beyond Collorgate: Prospects for Consolidating Democracy in Brazil Through Political Reform." Fleischer argues that the revelations of the Collor impeachment process and the subsequent "Budgetgate" scandal have had important effects on the consolidation of democracy in Brazil. After reviewing congressional actions that led to the impeachment and resignation of Collor, the failure of Collor's appeal to the Supreme Court, and then his acquittal on corruption charges for lack of evidence, Fleischer explains how Brazil has made important, if qualified, gains in consolidating democracy.

The liberalization of the political system since the mid-1970s permitted a high percentage of the Brazilian electorate to become involved in the democratic process. Elections, mass mobilizations, and deliberations for the 1988 Constitution provided vehicles for popular political expression. Unfortunately, the electorate itself has not been prepared to exercise an informed role in the democratic process. High levels of illiteracy and semi-literacy leave the electorate subject to manipulation by clientelism or by clever television campaigns. Other South American nations have done a markedly better job of preparing their populace to exercise effective roles as an electorate by offering more educational opportunities and broader deconcentration of political and economic goods.

Nevertheless, political reform in Brazil has made important headway since the Collor impeachment. Brazilian voters agreed to sustain the presidential form of government in a 1993 national plebiscite. Even though reforms designed to impose a minimum level of 3 percent representation of a party in the Chamber of Deputies or the respective state assembly to qualify for presenting candidates for president or governor in 1994 were circumvented by a Supreme Court decision, they represent a recognition of the ills of the fragmented party system. The most powerful generator of reforms was the Budgetgate scandal of late 1993 and 1994 that unearthed a chain of corruption linking Congress, bureaucrats, and government contractors. The final report's recommendation that 18 legislators be expelled for alleged corruption indicated important progress on holding corrupt politicians accountable.

Additional reforms are considering modifying the proportional representational system that encourages divisions within parties instead of competition among them. Various options include the possible adoption of "mixed" or "pure" proportional representation systems that would hold elected officials more accountable and strengthen the party system. Fleischer explains in detail other reforms that would install a "one-person, one-vote" concept, overcome the underrepresentation of the more populous South-Central states, change campaign financing to curb the incentive to expend huge personal fortunes (often gathered through questionable means), make voting optional, increase accountability of elected officials, eliminate political immunity for members of Congress, discourage formation of "dwarf" political parties, increase transparency on bidding for public contracts, reform the 120-member Joint Budget Committee, and reorganize public service.

Fleischer concludes that the Brazilian public continues to suffer from an inadequate understanding of democracy while at the same time remaining skeptical about its chances for success in Brazil. Without an improvement in Brazil's educational system, new institutional arrangements, and a deconcentration of Brazil's political, economic, and social wealth, Brazil's journey along the path to developed nation status will continue to be tortuous. The adoption of Fernando Henrique Cardoso's economic reforms should improve the prospects for the economic component of a brighter future for Brazil, but the outcome of the process of reforming Brazil's constitution and the rules within Brazil's Congress will also play an important role in determining the long-term fate of democracy in Brazil.

The next two chapters explore legal and institutional ramifications of the Collor episode. In Chapter 4, "The Impeachment Process and the Constitutional

Significance of the Collor Affair," Fábio Konder Comparato offers suggestions for improving existing systems of determining the political responsibility of government leaders. He addresses the legal complexities of the impeachment decision, discusses the history of impeachment provisions within Brazilian constitutional history, and offers a comparative perspective on U.S. and Brazilian constitutional law concerning impeachment.

He highlights the differences between U.S. and Brazilian legal systems regarding the impeachment process. While the framers of the U.S. Constitution intended impeachment to be a political rather than a criminal proceeding, the drafters of Brazil's original Republican Constitution in 1891 adopted an opposite interpretation, based upon practice during the monarchy. This interpretation that an impeachable offense has to have occurred has been largely sustained, even though there is disagreement within Brazilian legal doctrine about the real nature of impeachable offenses. Konder Comparato argues that impeachable offenses within the Brazilian system are indeed crimes, but they are tried before a political branch and not before the judiciary and have a political sanction. Another major difference between U.S. and Brazilian practices is the disposition of the president while the impeachment process is underway. Within the Brazilian system, an impeached president is suspended from duty pending the outcome of his trial. A third difference involves the precedence of trials of a president for an impeachable offense. While U.S. practice calls for trial and judgment by the judiciary only after conviction by the Senate, in Brazil the president can be tried concurrently.

Konder Comparato argues that the course of the impeachment process revealed the weakness of Collor's defense and the strength of legal arguments against him. Collor's argument that the charges were too vague and that he was the victim of a prejudicial attitude by more than one-third of the senators who either had served on the initial inquiry committee or who allegedly were political enemies failed to persuade senators thrust into the public spotlight. Even Collor's abrupt resignation in the midst of the proceedings failed to deter the senators from impeaching him.

In Konder Comparato's opinion, the Collor affair generates important suggestions for judicial and administrative ways of enhancing the accountability of political rulers, especially chief executives. Clear distinctions should be drawn between criminal and noncriminal liability and the differences between ordinary and political crimes made clearer. The procedures for conducting the impeachment process should also be reviewed, with deference given to individuals who wish to present impeachment writs to the legislature. Allowing a president to continue to exercise office while under impeachment is a dangerous situation, given the powers to influence the process that may remain within his grasp. Finally, disqualification from office of an impeached president should be permanent, rather than temporary as is currently the case in Brazil. It is essential to ensure that top executive officers are liable for a breach of public responsibility as previously defined by the representatives of the people.

Closely related to Konder Comparato's suggestions are the observations of Amaury de Souza who examines the role of domestic political institutions and processes in the Collor affair in Chapter 5, "Collor's Impeachment and Institutional

Reform in Brazil." He asks whether this episode attested to the capability of the political system to deal effectively with its own transgressions, serving notice to future presidents about the power of the rule of law, or whether it was the product of an unpredictable and highly unlikely configuration of events, leaving untouched or even aggravating the underlying causes of ungovernability.

His fundamental answer is that "Collorgate" was the product of unsettled institutional rivalries between Congress and the presidency that crystallized in the transition to civilian rule. The conflict between Congress and the executive branch that dominated the political agenda during the military period carried over into the 1980s. The Constitution of 1988 only sustained the controversy because it failed to separate clearly the powers of parliament and government. Collor exacerbated the conflict by trying to assert supremacy over the Congress even while support was growing for a parliamentary form of government. In the wake of the Collor fiasco, institutional reform remains a high priority of the Cardoso government as a means of halting the political system's drift toward institutional polarization and crisis.

Parliamentarism emerged in the mid-1980s as a pivotal element of institutional reform, as Brazil's political elite searched for a democratic model that would strengthen the Congress and the party system. Parliamentarism was brought to a vote during the 1987-1988 Constituent Congress but became entangled in an attempt to shorten President Sarney's term of office. While the overall proposal was defeated, the constitution did strengthen the role of Congress even while reinforcing the role of the president. Other features seemed to counterbalance the power of the presidency, including maintaining the system of proportional representation, amplifying the representation of smaller states, imposing no restrictions on party formation, and increasing the power of state and local governments. This institutional arrangement challenged the president to serve as a unifying force in the face of a powerful but divided Congress and a fractionalized party system.

Unfortunately, President Collor's popularity and his credibility with Congress quickly eroded as his first two years in office witnessed continuing high inflation, declining real wages, and a string of scandals involving cabinet members, leading to the resignation of his entire cabinet on March 30, 1992, on the eve of "Collorgate." As he sought to refurbish his government with new faces and policies, rumors of his personal involvement in scandalous behavior surfaced in late May. Further complicating his fate were the fragility and political ineptitude of his support within Congress. As the details of the scandal were revealed, the public and then the Congress lost faith in his government, stripped him of his political power, and commenced the impeachment process.

This process should be understood as an effort of Congress to turn the presidential system into a quasi-parliamentary regime in which impeachment would serve as the equivalent of a vote of confidence. Even under normal conditions, it would have been difficult for the president to muster a stable congressional majority, but the difficult economic conditions confronting Collor removed the possibility of popular support. Congress began to veto his policy initiatives or demand prohibitively high retribution, eventually forcing the president to resign or be removed from office. The constant reference to the Congress's disillusionment with Collor's performance in its investigatory reports lends further support to the notion that his impeachment was effectively equivalent to a vote of no confidence.

Today the controversy over the impact of the impeachment process on the overall political process remains an important question. Investigations into corruption prospered in the immediate aftermath of Collor's impeachment but became less salient as the 1994 presidential election approached. With the acquittal of Collor in 1994, the issue of ethics in politics was moved to the back burner. No push toward reforming presidentialism followed the defeat of parlimentarism in the 1993 plebiscite. However, Collorgate did coalesce liberal and social democratic forces in favor of reevaluating the public sector and carrying out structural reforms. The 1994 presidential election gave this ideological coalition the opportunity to act. Fernando Henrique Cardoso was the beneficiary, as his party coalition and alliances have provided him with enough votes to pass constitutional amendments.

Nevertheless, the need for substantive institutional reform that would supplant the conflictive nature of the current executive-legislative relationship persists. The presidency should be strengthened, and sweeping changes in the electoral and party systems should be promulgated to allow the president a means of forging enduring majorities in Congress. Unreformed presidentialism can neither hold presidents accountable nor make the Congress act responsibly. A clear definition of the respective prerogatives and competencies of the executive and legislative branches and an overhaul of the electoral and party systems is essential for the creation of a functional political system. Such reforms would prevent the impeachment of Collor from serving as an incentive to transform presidentialism into a dangerous alliance of populist, messianic believers in a grand salvation plan under the leadership of an energized plebiscitary presidency.

Leonardo Avritzer views the Collor episode as part and parcel of a continuing struggle between modernizing and patrimonial elements within Brazilian society. Borrowing from Max Weber's concept of patrimonialism, Avritzer notes that the conflict between modernization and societal organization has persisted throughout Brazil's twentieth century. Especially in the mid-1960s, authoritarian modernizers attempted to isolate the economy from the political process but found that they had to allow limited functioning of the political system. When their efforts at legitimation through electoral processes proved unsuccessful, they sought refuge in patrimonial politics. This effort ignored the possibility of the creation of modern and democratic forms of social relations, a reality that soon took place through three strong social movements: the "new unionism," the challenge of urban social movements, and the emergence of middle-class neighborhood and professional associations.

These movements not only "gave the final blow to authoritarian modernization," they also set the stage for eventual conflict with President Collor. The transition process resulted in the strengthening of traditional politics, especially after President José Sarney decided to create a patrimonial network of support based upon a conservative alliance of former supporters of the authoritarian regime in Congress and recently elected governors of the Partido Movimento Democrático Brasileiro (PMDB). Despite his rhetoric against the excesses of patrimonialism, Fernando Collor de Mello kept most of its mechanisms intact and personalized their use. In doing so, he seriously underestimated societal reaction to his practices and the influence of nonpatrimonial politicians who felt themselves accountable to the press and social movements. Public opinion became a crucial element in the impeachment process, fortifying the actions of social movements and the legal system to result in Collor's ouster. While Collor's impeachment does not herald the end of patrimonial practices in Brazil, it represents an important turning point in the process of modernization as understood by the country's social actors. A new societal consensus is being formed in Brazil about the rule of law and accountability.

Finally, the concluding chapter sets the debate about corruption and political reform within Brazil in the context of events and processes within other Latin American countries by citing legal and political factors that have shaped political accountability in Argentina, Mexico, Peru, and Venezuela. It argues that the process of accommodation between the authoritarian heritage of the region and a rising consciousness of the need for fundamental reform has yet to create institutions capable of sustaining pervasive and enduring change. A struggle for Latin America's future is shaping up between those who advocate "politics as usual" and those who see the region as truly on the verge of a new era of transparency and accountability in its political life.

This volume would not have been possible without the unceasing cooperation of the authors of each chapter and their generous willingness to update papers originally presented at a conference in Miami in February 1993 on the impact of the Collor impeachment. Their unfailing good humor and faith in the editorial process have sustained this project from the beginning, and we shall forever be indebted to them for their assistance. The support of the North-South Center Press, especially Kathleen Hamman, editorial director; Jayne Weisblatt, free-lance copy editor; Mary Mapes, publications director; and Susan K. Holler, free-lance indexer, has been crucial to maintaining the work's quality throughout the production process. We are also indebted to Professor William C. Smith of the School of International Studies, University of Miami, and Jeffrey Stark, Director of Research and Studies at the North-South Center, for their continual encouragement and advice.

Richard Downes and Keith S. Rosenn

CHAPTER 1

Collor's Downfall in Historical Perspective

THOMAS SKIDMORE

The downfall of Brazilian President Fernando Collor de Mello was such a dramatic process that one is tempted to be caught up in the personal details.[1] A telegenic young president (called the Brazilian "Indiana Jones" by George Bush), a brother determined to expose him, a sinister influence peddler with a plane called the "black bat," a politically savvy but emotionally distraught mother, a wife who went on multi-thousand-dollar shopping sprees in the best European boutiques — this is the stuff of Brazilian television soap operas, not serious politics in the world's ninth-largest industrial economy.

The ouster of Collor had authentic Watergate-style overtones. It was almost as if the Brazilians had studied the script of Richard Nixon's decline into disgrace and resignation. On center stage was a president whose basic honesty was in question. Hounding him were the investigative reporters, keeping the story alive with their periodic revelations. Surrounding him were the loyal aides, whose own honesty soon became suspect. Watching him was a public, at first indifferent (corrupt politicians being no novelty in Brazil), but soon drawn into the drama. Stalking him were the opposition politicians, who yearned to depose him but feared they could not get enough public support. Finally, there was the vast majority of politicians, who dreaded a confrontation because it might expose their own questionable ethics or threaten the system over which they presided.

As with Nixon during Watergate, Collor was drawn to the television camera. Nixon had once saved his career with an infamous television appearance — the 1952 "Checkers" speech. Nixon later thought he could save himself again by repeatedly using television to explain to the U.S. public how he had withheld no information about the Watergate burglary and its follow-up. Collor had an even greater debt to television. He owed his meteoric rise in national politics to his skill in television appearances aided by some manipulation by TV-Globo, the leading network.[2] Now, under siege from the media, he thought he could again use television — this time, like Nixon, to proclaim his honesty.

As Brazilians and foreigners watched this drama, they became mesmerized by its power. In the last six months of 1992, Brazilian comedians and news commentators talked of little else. As in the case of Watergate, the media intensified the attention of a public accustomed to allowing television a central place in its daily routine. Few Third World countries of Brazil's size and level of development can match the penetration of television into more than 75 percent of the nation's homes.

1

Television news brought the "Collorgate" scandal (as it was inevitably called) into virtually every household. Suddenly, Brazil had become "first world" in the sophistication of media coverage of its political crises.

In fact, the Brazilians outdid the Americans. Nixon had cut short his final scene by resigning before the House of Representatives could vote impeachment. Collor refused that solution (until after his impeachment by the Chamber of Deputies and on the eve of his conviction by the Senate), although it was repeatedly urged on him. Instead, he defied his tormentors almost to the end. By transforming the drama into a test of wills, Collor further raised the stakes and turned the contest into a demonstration of empty machismo. Here again, television magnified the denouement. When the Chamber of Deputies finally voted to impeach, the scene was captured on television. One by one, the deputies approached the podium to register their votes and (for those voting yes) emotionally declare their commitment to democracy and honest government.

This political drama was far more than a media sideshow. It was also an unhappy chapter in Brazil's search for democracy after the longest period of military rule in its history. Collor was Brazil's first directly elected president since 1960. He was also governing under a new constitution, approved in 1988. Collor's ability to govern was a key test of Brazil's newest attempt at democracy. The military had earlier justified its imposition of authoritarian rule on the grounds (among others) that democracy could not work in Brazil. Was the military now proved right by Collor's failure?

COLLOR: THE PRODUCT OF A SYSTEM

Fernando Collor was no political outsider, despite his efforts to present himself as such. In his virtues and vices, he was an authentic product of Brazilian political culture. His father's family came from Alagoas, one of the poorest states of the impoverished Northeast. The family was a textbook example of the local northeastern oligarchies that had grown rich on sugar but for decades had depended on federal government subsidies while continuing to dominate their states' economy and politics. Collor's father, Arnon de Mello, had been a federal senator from Alagoas. The violence long typical of politics in the Northeast found its way to the national capital in the early 1960s when Arnon de Mello, in attempting to shoot a rival senator from Alagoas, killed by mistake a visiting ex-senator on the Senate floor. His son Fernando was also said to have a violent temper and to be of unpredictable temperament.

This was the old Brazil — the regime of "colonels," who controlled the nation's political machinery between the fall of the Empire in 1889 and the first launch of mass democracy in 1945. Yet this Brazil was fading. The dynamic section of the country was now the Southeast, especially São Paulo. Here the gunmen and political clans were gone. Political networks were more modern, depending on extensive organizations and media efforts.

In fact, Collor bridged these two worlds. He had spent most of his youth outside the Northeast, in Rio de Janeiro and Brasília. His education had been almost entirely outside Alagoas. Furthermore, he was no stranger to the world of mass media. His father had been an early partner of Roberto Marinho, owner of TV-Globo, Brazil's most powerful national television network. The Arnon de Mello family got in on the ground floor of TV-Globo by winning the concession for the network station in Alagoas. Thus, Fernando's family had connections to both the old world of political clans and the new world of mass media.

There was another sign of Collor's attempt to link the two worlds. For his first marriage he had chosen a beautiful Rio socialite whose powerful family typified the sophisticated South where Fernando had spent much of his youth. Yet, once he returned to Alagoas to pursue his political ambitions, he divorced his Rio wife and married a young woman from the Malta family, known for its clout in Alagoas clan politics. Thus, Collor projected a schizophrenic political identity: part the scion of an old-fashioned northeastern political clan, part the dynamic young representative of a "modern" Brazil (the latter largely a product of his public relations team).

Collor was a product of the system in another sense. He had entered politics during the military government (1964-1985). Yet, he did not do so in opposition to the generals. On the contrary, he was appointed to his first post, mayor of Maceió, capital city of Alagoas. Thereafter, he assumed and discarded party identities at his convenience. He was a good example of those politicians who chose to cooperate with the authoritarian regime rather than embrace the more uncertain fate of opposition.

Collor's ability to change parties so readily was another proof that he was an authentic product of the system. Brazil's electoral legislation, as amended in the 1980s, created the most permissive system in terms of party creation among the major democracies.[3] He had taken advantage of that in numerous ways. First was his shuffling of party labels as he made his way up in Alagoas politics. Second was his use of radio-TV time in early 1989, when the presidential campaign was beginning. The campaign law allotted free radio-TV time to all political parties, even the tiniest. Collor legally bought the time of several small, largely unknown parties, combined them, and made highly effective national television addresses, exploiting his extraordinary telegenic appeal. Under more stringent party (and, therefore, media time) legislation, Collor would never have been able to emerge so quickly on the national scene.

There is a final aspect in which Collor was a product of the Brazilian political system, or, more accurately, Brazilian political culture. Collor based his presidential campaign on appearing as a political messiah.[4] He was the miracle worker who would sweep away corruption, inefficiency, and an archaic economy.

Here Collor was tapping into a long tradition. Brazilian belief in messiahs had its roots in Portuguese *Sebastianismo* — the faith that Prince Sebastian, who disappeared in battle in North Africa in 1578, would one day return to lead Portugal to greatness. Brazil had had its own political messiahs in such figures as Padre Cicero, the northeastern priest who became a regional political power in the 1920s and 1930s. More recently there had been Jânio Quadros, elected president in 1960 only to resign abruptly after seven months in office, an action as mysterious as Dom Sebastian's disappearance four centuries earlier.

COLLOR IN THE CONTEXT OF DEMOCRATIC TRANSITION

Fernando Collor assumed the presidency as his country was completing Latin America's longest transition from an authoritarian regime. Brazil's challenge to build a functioning democracy was not easy, and previous experience offered an uncertain guide. The 1945-1964 political system had been put to the test and failed. In retrospect, analysts of all political views agreed that there could be no simple return to pre-1964 conditions. That reality had been irrevocably changed by the work of the military and by the increased complexity of Brazilian society. The new constitutional structure had already been crafted in the Constitution of 1988, and such areas as electoral legislation had been defined earlier in the 1980s. However, it was by no means certain that this new structure would correct the defects that helped end democracy in 1964 or would deal adequately with the demands of the post-military era.

The political alignments created by the existing rules seemed to guarantee an unworkable government. The highly permissive electoral legislation, written in the late 1970s and early 1980s, had led to the rapid creation of 40 political parties, of which 17 were represented in Congress. This exaggerated tolerance for party proliferation could in part be explained as a delayed reaction to the military regime's earlier manipulation of electoral legislation to guarantee the victory of the government party. What the electoral rule authors had forgotten, however, was that even democratic governments have to govern. Without a firm political base, policy cannot be adopted and effectively carried out. In a democracy, such a political base must normally be furnished by the political parties. More on this point later.

The balance in question is between governability and accountability. The military regimes had justified themselves by saying they could govern, when the democrats had failed (or worse) in the early 1960s. On the other hand, the military lacked accountability, the deliberate result of its interference with the press, the courts, and the legislatures. Accountability had been largely restored with the new constitution, although one key arbitrary executive power—the decree-law (*decreto-lei*) — had reappeared under a new label, the provisional measure (*medida provisória*) and in less powerful form. Whether the new system would produce governments able to govern was still a question.

The problem had already become clear through the economic debacles of the presidency of José Sarney (1985-1990). Trouble began in 1986 during the colossally mismanaged Cruzado Plan. The failure to adjust the stabilization measures or to formulate an adequate successor plan led to a surge of hyperinflation (approaching 100 percent a month) as the presidential term ended in early 1990. Sarney used gross political payoffs to retain power and left the federal government in chaos. He had achieved neither governability nor accountability. It was an inglorious beginning for civilian government but the perfect backdrop of failure for Collor to wage his campaign as miracle worker and savior of the Brazilian state.

Collor took office at an especially difficult moment in Brazilian economic history. Like most of Latin America, Brazil had been experiencing difficult economic times since the onset of the foreign debt crisis in 1982. Over the course of the 1980s, Brazil had seen its per capita gross domestic product (GDP) fail to grow significantly, while the distribution of income became steadily more unequal. It was the worst record for the Brazilian economy since the late nineteenth century. The immediate scene was intimidating: inflation approaching 100 percent a month, the world's largest foreign debt still not renegotiated, perilously low investment rates in both public and private sectors, a ballooning domestic debt (much of it financed on a daily basis), and an endemic federal budget deficit.

Adding to the burden were the economic problems bequeathed by the 1988 Constitution. Most important, the states and *municípios* had been given a greatly increased share of federal tax revenues without an equivalent shift in responsibilities. Here was an example of overreaction to the military era, when the federal government had greatly reduced state and *município* shares. A second constraint in the constitution was the guarantee of lifetime tenure to federal employees after only a short probation, thus greatly limiting any effort to reduce the federal payroll.

At least one bright spot on the economic horizon gave Collor room for maneuver. It was the significant trade surplus Brazil had enjoyed since the mid-1980s. On the one hand, this surplus meant that, with the resulting foreign exchange reserves, Brazil could continue servicing enough of its foreign debt to avoid losing leverage with creditors and therefore possibly having to turn to the International Monetary Fund (IMF), which would require commitment to a tough stabilization program. On the other, the surplus gave politicians a greater opportunity to procrastinate on facing the need for stabilization.

Another source of strength for Collor was his effective cultivation of public opinion. Collor's high-powered presidential campaign, fueled by his high standing in the polls (which he led throughout the campaign), had created the impression of an unstoppable new political force. This perception was aided by the run-off between the top two candidates, which guaranteed the winner the moral boost of having gained a majority of voter support. Collor was further blessed with an extremely favorable foreign press. Thus, his election victory and messianic style were initial assets that lent him the aura of success and the guarantee that the Congress would respect (at least, at the outset) his popularity. Yet, at the same time, they created very high expectations. Collor would have to deliver on his promises, especially in the crucial arena of economic policy. Brazilians had been battling inflation for decades and wanted results. Any new government would have to produce results on the inflation front or pay a steep price in popularity.

THE SOURCES OF FAILURE

Despite Fernando Collor's triumphal start in the presidency, fed by an almost totally favorable media, he soon began to endanger his political position by resorting to a device to bypass Congress, the *medida provisória*.[5] Decree-type powers had been a favorite of the general-presidents, and the *medida provisória* had been used liberally by President Sarney.

Collor depended upon this device for many of his most important measures in 1990, such as, for example, his economic stabilization programs, which included the freezing of savings accounts. It was used 141 times that year, arousing much anger and numerous court challenges. Reliance on it, therefore, proved increasingly difficult. According to the Constitution, a *medida provisória* immediately takes effect when issued. Moreover, it is also sent automatically to Congress; if not approved by Congress within 30 days, it lapses. When Congress began failing to approve his *medidas*, Collor reissued them. The Supreme Court declared that procedure unconstitutional with respect to *medidas* that had been specifically rejected by Congress. A congressional revolt forced Collor virtually to give up his use of this instrument by February 1991. He had lost what had been a valuable weapon after less than a year in office.

Collor's failure to seek consensus for controversial changes attests to weaknesses in his approach to the enormously complicated task of governing a democratic Brazil. Successful democracy, even in Brazil, seldom consists of the executive being able to issue uncontested unilateral decrees. The essence of democracy lies in negotiation. Differing interests have to be conciliated, opposing parties convinced, and a sense of mutual concessions achieved. In a presidential system, the head of government must serve as a constant negotiator or at least have someone who can do so reliably in his name. The leading Brazilian example of such success, albeit in different times, was President Juscelino Kubitschek, who sought to make "fifty years of progress in five" as president from 1956 to 1961, although Getúlio Vargas also played the role skillfully during his various tours at the helm of the Brazilian state until his suicide in 1954.

Collor also should have realized that new political forces were requiring him to perfect his skills in democratic persuasion. State and *município* politicians had begun to feel their oats in the democratic transition. They had not waited for a new constitution to begin spending at a higher pace (especially by expanding payrolls) than the military governments had allowed. Upon taking office, Collor was confronted with a major crisis in federal-state financial relations, brought on by massive overspending by the states, which they had covered by resorting to state banks. The latter, in turn, had covered these accounts by borrowing from one or another federal authority. As a result, the federal government held large unpayable loans, which were simply rolled over. Only a strong government in Brasília could stop this practice.

The Brazilian public was also determined to play a political role consistent with modern democracy. Any elected politician struggling to reduce inflation soon learns that the public may differ in its initial understanding of the issues at stake. After a period of relative price stability, for example, the public may not immediately perceive the effects when mild inflation sets in. This "money illusion" can lead to thinking in nominal rather than real terms. Insofar as that perception persists, the public may be slow to defend its interests. For the policymaker attempting stabilization, this "money illusion" can give room for maneuver in the short run.

The Brazilian public of the early 1990s, however, could hardly be accused of suffering from any such illusion. On the contrary, Brazilians were among the world's most sophisticated financial actors. Television told them every day how each indicator—the dollar, the stock market, the savings bank interest rate, and gold — was doing against inflation (sometimes expressed in more than one index).

This public understanding of anti-inflationary measures and the media's role in it was no accident. The military governments had made a crusade of teaching the public to think in real terms. From the moment the Castelo Branco government (1964-1967) introduced indexation (automatic adjustment for inflation) in government mortgages, it had a stake in educating the public on the need to maintain the real value of capital stock such as housing. That meant monthly mortgage payments went up along with inflation (they had not on pre-1964 federally financed mortgages). At the same time, the military governments introduced indexed savings accounts, where the depositor's principal was adjusted for inflation, as well as a real interest rate paid.

These innovations had made the Brazilian financial system of the 1970s one of the most closely studied in the world. Admirers argued that Brazil's technocrats had devised a way to live with inflation (which remained in the range of 20 percent a year in these years) and achieve real growth as well (which averaged over 11 percent in the early 1970s). Critics argued that Brazil had merely institutionalized inflation.

In any case, the Brazilian public became a sophisticated consumer of financial news and an unforgiving judge of economic policymakers. They had plenty of news to consume, and most was not encouraging. Through the 1980s, inflation had returned to rates that seriously distorted relative prices, eroded capital values, and virtually eliminated long-term financial markets. Governments had tried repeated "packages" and "plans" without success. As a result, the Brazilian public in 1990 was a difficult sell on anti-inflation policy. The policymakers would be watched carefully.

Still another trait of Brazilian public psychology raised levels of expectations and watchfulness. Brazilians have long believed their country is different from the rest of Latin America — not only because they are the only Portuguese-speakers but also because they see their land as uniquely endowed. Constituting one-half of South America, and almost twice as populous as the second-largest country, Brazil has virtually every natural resource (except oil) in quantity. The average urban Brazilian can be counted upon to articulate this belief in Brazil's unique natural gifts. Strengthened by this faith in their country's capacity to become a major economic power, the Brazilians tend to downplay the impact of short-run crises. Their faith holds that, despite the incompetence of government, Brazil will muddle through and, equally important, can afford to muddle through.

Admittedly, this traditional optimism had been battered by the dismal economic record since 1982. It had been further eroded by such disappointments as the death of President-elect Tancredo Neves on the eve of his inauguration in 1985 and the scandals leading to President Collor's impeachment. Nonetheless, an underlying belief in Brazil's uniqueness persists. This faith was powerfully exploited by the military governments, especially those of the 1970s. They accompanied their massive public investment projects with a propaganda campaign to glorify "Brasil Grande." From the Transamazon Highway in the north to the world's largest hydroelectric project at Itaipú in the south, the generals claimed they were finally realizing Brazil's potential.

Collor rekindled those hopes with his campaign rhetoric and his initial economic plan, promising to return Brazil to its previous rise toward "First World" status. While this vision neatly meshes with the average Brazilian's feeling about Brazil, it easily leads to shallow optimism because it obscures Brazil's fundamental social and economic weaknesses. Without a frank discussion of the challenges involved, Collor had not prepared the public for a supportive role in difficult but necessary policy choices.

The most difficult choices in the early 1990s were, not surprisingly, economic. Collor's initial economic stabilization plan, which included a massive freezing of savings accounts and the end of indexation, was breathtaking but oversold as a quick fix for Brazil's endemic inflation. When it failed within less than a year, the widespread public belief that Brazil was different was ironically reinforced. Economic formulas tried elsewhere simply could not apply to Brazil, and frequent newspaper columns and congressional speeches explained why the apparent economic success of Chile ("a population smaller than São Paulo") or Mexico ("proximity to the United States makes it noncomparable to Brazil") were irrelevant for Brazil. All the features of Brazil's differentness — its larger internal market, its greater industrial base, its continental dimensions — were cited to explain why orthodox stabilization plans could never work there. This widespread belief in Brazil's "uniqueness" has made it ever more difficult for governments to sell tough stabilization measures based upon their success elsewhere in the hemisphere.

Added to Collor's problem with the economy was the aggressiveness of the press — both print and electronic — which played a crucial role in his fall. For a variety of reasons, many journalists got a relatively free hand in covering the Collor demise. By the beginning of the Collor presidency, many journalists were living with an intense sense of frustration. They had watched corruption flourish during military rule, when censorship prevented its exposure. Even in the later years of the military, when censorship was lifted, exposés seemed to have no impact. The Sarney administration engaged in large-scale, blatant corruption, such as favoritism in awarding contracts for the North-South Railway, an ill-planned political boondoggle, but exposure in the press had little effect. A motion for Sarney's impeachment was presented in Congress without any proof of personal corruption, but few took it seriously. Sarney survived because he was a shrewd manipulator of the old-fashioned patronage system and because he was sensible in his relations with the press. There were also several other factors in Sarney's favor. He was a genial personality completely lacking Collor's arrogance. Furthermore, it was widely said that the payoffs extracted in the Sarney era were within traditional limits, unlike the unprecedented percentages demanded by the extortioners of the Collor government.

Press revelations accelerated Collor's political demise, and the last six months of the Collor impeachment crisis assumed an uncanny resemblance to Watergate. Although no one has suggested there was a Brazilian "deep throat" to feed information to sustain public interest, insider stories appeared at critical moments. Whenever Collor appeared to have regained the initiative, as after several of his early television addresses, a new press story (his personal car bought by P.C.

Farias, or his $2 million garden paid for by the same source) put him back on the defensive.

As the Collor crisis grew, the investigative reporters did their work well. The spirit of Woodward and Bernstein, the famous *Washington Post* journalistic duo, was in the air. Reporters came up with extraordinary exposés, such as the July 1992 interview with Eriberto França, the driver for P.C. Farias' Brasília office (which appeared in *Istoé*) and the sensational May 1992 interview with Pedro Collor de Mello and follow-up revelations on the distributions of payoffs within the government (which appeared in *Veja*). The *Folha de São Paulo* designed a special logo and used the heading "Collorgate" for its coverage of Collor's troubles.

While the print media ignited the political brushfire, the winds of competition within the electronic media transformed it into a nationwide firestorm. TV-Globo, the dominant network and the one that had played a key role in giving Collor his initial visibility, tried initially to ignore or downplay the scandals. Only when the public had gotten strongly interested did TV-Globo begin to cover the story. If TV-Globo had entertained the absolute monopoly that Televisa enjoys in Mexico, Collor might well have escaped the final media pressure. However, three other television networks were competing for Brazilian viewers' attention, and all covered the story heavily from the beginning. Successive revelations of corruption and deceit not only aroused the public, they were paths to good ratings, advertising revenues, and respectability as well.

COLLOR: THE PERSONAL FACTOR

D espite the influence of ambient and institutional factors, there would have been no impeachment without Fernando Collor de Mello's personal qualities. Whatever the structural defects of the political system, the conventional politicians who made up the Congress were not likely to have voted to remove the president. They were forced into acting by presidential behavior that can only be called politically suicidal.

Collor's first problem was his personal manner. His good looks and bent for adventurous sports had made him the most telegenic Brazilian politician in decades. That television appeal had given the little-known provincial figure instant national visibility in early 1989, thanks to the help of TV-Globo.

Yet Collor's good looks could not conceal an attitude of arrogance befitting an earlier era of Brazil's politics. This quality is common among public figures, but Collor made little effort to disguise it. He was used to making few concessions in dealing with other politicians. He seemed the modern incarnation of the infamous "colonel" of northeastern politics, accustomed to giving orders ("mandando") rather than negotiating.

Collor's style was shown in his choice of Claudio Humberto Rosa e Silva, also from Alagoas, as his press secretary. The role of press secretary is normally to cultivate favorable press relations, giving background information and supplementary briefings that will improve the government's image. It is also normally to clarify presidential statements or actions to put them in the best possible light.

Claudio Humberto not only did not follow this "normal" pattern, he proved to be one of the most abrasive press secretaries ever seen in Brazilian politics. He routinely descended to abusive language, personally attacking journalists and their editors. His letters to the editor became classics of invective. None of this would have mattered in itself (and Claudio Humberto eventually left to become cultural attaché in Lisbon), except that it reflected the president's own lack of judgment by establishing an ugly atmosphere for public debate.

Claudio Humberto's belligerent style epitomized Collor's politically myopic decision to bring Alagoas to Brasília. Every president brings friends and associates from his home state. However, Alagoas is a poor, northeastern state that incarnates the old-style politics regarded condescendingly by Brazilians of the more developed Center-South. Collor failed to realize the need to mute the provincial air of his government to become politically effective on a national scale. He could have followed the example of his predecessor José Sarney, who was from the equally poor northeastern state of Maranhão. Sarney had taken much greater care with his public relations, especially in his government's early years, and, unlike Collor, had presented a much more conciliatory face to the public and other politicians.

The Alagoas native who proved most damaging to the Collor presidency was not Claudio Humberto, however, but a hitherto obscure minor local businessman and fixer named Paulo César Farias (soon known as "P.C."). As treasurer for Collor's 1989 presidential campaign, P.C. Farias was rumored to have raised a minimum of several hundred million dollars. (In the absence of reliable records and accounting requirements, this is based on journalists' estimates.)

P.C.'s corruption was matched only by his indiscretion. He set up an elaborate scheme, including computer spreadsheets, for extorting kickbacks from firms having financial dealings with the federal government, especially contractors. He was apparently not the only Collor government official engaged in such a scheme, but he was the most ambitious and the one who was subsequently proved to have given proceeds from his scheme directly to the president. Most important, his operations were documented by the congressional commission whose report led to Collor's impeachment. No less damaging than his extortionist activities was his indiscretion. He let drop not so subtle hints about how much he was doing for the president and his wife and openly bragged of his power within the Brasília bureaucracy.

Collor's oligarchical origins also carried a potent agent of betrayal within the personal world that he brought to Brasília: his family. At the outset this seemed to be an asset — his family's links to TV-Globo, his mother being the daughter of one of Getúlio Vargas's most famous ministers. The Achilles' heel proved to be his brother, Pedro. The rivalry between the two brothers escalated to the point where Pedro gave his interview to *Veja*, revealing the kickback schemes and the president's direct involvement. This was the fatal trigger that started the impeachment process. Without these charges from Pedro, Collor might have escaped a full-scale congressional inquiry, as had Sarney, but in a Latin American culture such as Brazil's, accusations from a brother carry far more weight than those from an opposition politician.[6]

As these personal factors became obvious to the public, they transformed Collor's image from that of "Indiana Jones" to a Brazilian version of Spiro Agnew, the disgraced ex-U.S. vice president. Collor's arrogance and provincialism reduced his potential support among the public and the politicians, should a major crisis arise. The kickback scheme and his angry brother combined to make him especially vulnerable to an aggressive press.

Looking back on the Collor presidency, one cannot escape the feeling that Collor had been on the path to political self-destruction for some time. Especially after the 1992 vote authorizing a congressional inquiry into the charges against him, it seemed as if Collor were following a script consisting only of errors and gaffes. The opening scene included the early decision in 1990 to change banking regulations for check writing. Previously, Brazilians could write checks "to the bearer" (*ao portador*), which meant that there was no record of the payee. The newly elected Collor government eliminated this practice, thereby requiring recipients to be named on the check. The change came back to haunt the president when the congressional investigating committee succeeded in lifting bank record confidentiality. Among the 40,000 checks they obtained were a number written by P.C. Farias's employees for the benefit of Collor (for a car, for the "Babylonian Garden" at his house, and so on).

As the investigation unfolded, it seemed that P.C. Farias had been extraordinarily careless in leaving such a trail of evidence. One would have expected more from perpetrators of large-scale corruption in Latin America. In his defense, if one can use the term, it should be noted that the congressional commission's lifting of bank record confidentiality was unprecedented. Thus, Collor's larcenous associates were faced with a surprise their predecessors (of the Sarney era, for example) had not had to worry about.

Collor provided more wood for his own political coffin by showing a stubborn loyalty to P.C. Farias, with whom he was publicly claiming to have broken all ties, even after the revelations began. Collor's brother Pedro had warned that the price for stopping his own revelations was P.C. Farias's abandoning a plan to launch a newspaper in Alagoas that would rival the Collor de Mello family's paper, now managed by Pedro. Apparently, Farias wanted to build his own political dynasty in Alagoas, with the paper as an anchor. Was Fernando to be a partner in this new dynasty — rivaling his own family's — or was he unable to put sufficient pressure on P.C. Farias to drop the scheme? Or, perhaps more likely, Fernando mistakenly did not believe his brother would carry out his threat.

Collor also misjudged his ability to influence the Brazilian public through its favorite medium, television. He had first gained national prominence through television. When the impeachment crisis hit, he looked once again to television. He gave four different television speeches, reminiscent of Richard Nixon's attempts to save himself via television as the Watergate net grew tighter. Like Nixon, Collor had to explain away the continuous revelations. Also like Nixon, he was increasingly on the defensive.

Most important, and again like Nixon, Collor was driven to give improbable explanations that were soon disproved. As the appearances became more desperate, Collor, like Nixon, lost his air of authority. In appealing to the public, both eroded their own legitimacy. Prime examples in Collor's case were his claim that he had never benefited from P.C. Farias's scheme (soon contradicted by evidence of purchase of his Fiat car) and his claim that his personal expenses had been covered by a loan from Uruguay (soon revealed to be based on forged documents). Collor's most sensational miscalculation was his August 1992 appeal to Brazilians to show support for him by wearing green and yellow, the national colors. The response was startling: Vast crowds appeared all over Brazil wearing black. This was the start of a series of major anti-Collor demonstrations in the larger cities, often led by middle-class teenagers sensitized by watching a then-current telenovela about student protest marches that had occurred during the military dictatorship of the late 1960s. Collor had become, ironically, the target of the same kind of civic mobilization that was instrumental in undermining the military regime.

Collor's personality and use of television had transformed his fight to remain in power into a psychodrama. It was the kind of spectacle that periodically occurs in Brazil, as in the electrifying rallies for direct election of the president in 1984 or the vigil for the dying Tancredo Neves in 1985. This time the president had turned himself into the evil (the corrupt politician) he had promised to banish.

As the impeachment vote neared, Collor desperately resorted to a familiar device: dealing out lavish patronage. His aides feverishly polled Congress to find any undecided votes. Collor then offered lavish government prizes (funds for public works and the like) in return for loyalty in the impeachment vote. The press followed these efforts closely, making the members of Congress solicited by the president self-conscious in the glare of publicity. Collor's blitz became counterproductive. It was as if a shaft of light had fallen on the seamiest sides of Brazilian politics. Collor's effort symbolized what the critics said was worst in Brazil's political system: bartering away public money for short-term partisan gain.

Collor in the Light of History

B razil lacks a record of stable democracies. Since 1945, only two directly elected civilian presidents have finished their mandates. Among them, one committed suicide, one resigned, and another was ousted in a military coup. Vargas killed himself in 1954 rather than face removal by military coup. João Goulart, his political heir, was deposed by the men in uniform in 1964. Both involved full-blown confrontations between populist presidents and an anticommunist military. The ideological climate was heated in both cases, fed by radical nationalists on the left and conservative anticommunists on the right.

Collor's fall lacked the drama and potential for conflict of either of those cases, but it does resemble one case of resignation: Jânio Quadros in 1961. Quadros's abrupt departure from office has remained difficult to analyze because the sources are thin. Quadros himself never satisfactorily explained his action, although he repeatedly promised to do so. He claimed to have been blocked in carrying out his program, but seven months in office were not enough to substantiate that claim. Apparently, Quadros was maneuvering to increase his powers and thought his resignation, submitted to the Congress, would be refused. If so, his miscalculation was worthy of Collor, since the Congress rapidly accepted his resignation. His bluff had been called.

In any case, Quadros's demise as president offers some interesting parallels with the case of Collor. First, as noted earlier, Collor assumed a messianic role, as had Quadros. His campaign appeal was similar, an emphasis on morality as the essence of government and an attack on his opponents as the incarnation of immorality. Collor was also like Quadros in his "loner" stance. In addition, Collor, like Quadros, had switched parties frequently and relied on his direct, personal appeal, not on any identification with a party or ideological tradition. Both thought they could impose their will on the political scene by force of their personalities. Both harbored a strong sense of arrogance.

Jânio Quadros, however, had better political instincts. He had come up through a difficult political world, becoming mayor and then governor of São Paulo in the 1950s. He had a brilliant feel for public relations, which kept his enemies on the defensive. In his seven months as president, Quadros faced the difficult economic problems of inflation, foreign debt renegotiation, and federal government deficits. Given this economic mess and the existing constitutional structure, it is indeed possible that Quadros had decided he could not govern successfully and would therefore gamble, by means of his resignation, to win greater executive powers from a Congress he hoped would reject his resignation. If so, his gamble failed, and the country's ungovernability, given the ideological polarization, was soon demonstrated by the presidency of João Goulart who, as vice president, succeeded Quadros in September 1961. Goulart's overthrow in 1964 was precipitated by the left-right confrontation and the Goulart government's decision to carry out radical change, such as land reform and nationalization of foreign-owned firms. Another significant factor was the paralysis in economic policymaking in the face of record-breaking inflation, dwindling foreign exchange reserves, and an unpayable (on the terms then prevailing) foreign debt.

The military government that seized power in 1964 promptly strengthened the powers of the executive to deal with all those problems and to make itself immune to popular opposition. During the years 1968-1974, those executive powers were increased and used for systematic repression. They were used also to carry out an ambitious economic program that any pre-1964 government would have found difficult to bring off. The military governments gave themselves the sweeping powers that Quadros evidently believed he needed in 1961. Meanwhile, important changes had occurred in Brazil's political landscape. The continuous *abertura* after 1974 had slowly rehabilitated the legislature and the judiciary. They forced Collor to seek laws through the normal legislative process, a strategy for which neither his temperament nor his political style prepared him. Another important change since the pre-1964 days was the Brazilian military's steadfast refusal to intervene during the Collor impeachment crisis. With the Cold War over and the threat of a "red menace" implausible, the higher military told the politicians *they* had to solve the crisis in a constitutional manner. Nor was any segment of civil society calling for military intervention, which was important as significant civilian support had been essential to every successful coup since 1945.

Arrogant, politically adrift, and forced to rely upon discredited tactics of patronage, Collor remained blindly confident that he would win any impeachment vote in Congress. After all, it required a two-thirds majority, and the parties hostile to Collor at the outset of the crisis (in March 1992) did not constitute even one-half of the deputies. Unlike Getúlio or Jânio, Fernando was going to see it out to the end. His political judgment proved monumentally poor. The Chamber of Deputies impeached him by a vote of 441 to 38, and the Senate voted by 76 to 5 to convict, even though Collor had resigned hours before.

Fernando Collor de Mello's downfall was more than a personal failure. His personal defects, which were many, proved politically self-destructive in a crisis. Yet, this flawed president was acting within a political system that itself made effective government extremely difficult.

A glance around Latin America illustrates the problem. Of those countries that had suffered military regimes like Brazil's, Chile was the most successful in emerging from the economic stagnation of the 1980s. However, President Patricio Aylwin inherited a far sounder economy than Collor did and, at least as important, a much stronger and more disciplined party system. In the case of Argentina, President Carlos Menem was able to capitalize on the loyalty of the Peronists, the largest single party, and he had at his disposal a wide-ranging decree power that he used liberally in economic policy. Mexico, which had not suffered military government, presents an even more striking contrast. There the technocrats, under Presidents Miguel de la Madrid and later Carlos Salinas de Gortari, pushed through a tough, though subsequently mismanaged in 1994-1995, stabilization-cum-privatization and economic opening similar to that of Chile, and, to a lesser degree, Argentina. Yet, Mexico was hardly a democratic system, as was dramatized by the fraudulent vote count in the 1988 presidential election. The Mexican president had a range of power more comparable to Brazil's early military presidents than to that enjoyed by Collor. In shedding its authoritarian past, Brazil produced a central government weaker than any others among the Latin American countries that had achieved economic success (measured by greatly reduced inflation and a resumption of growth).

From one standpoint, though, the Brazilian system can be judged a success. It succeeded in removing a president in a constitutional, nonviolent manner — a first in Brazilian history. It led many political commentators and ordinary citizens to cite it as evidence of their country's new political maturity. The successful impeachment of Collor offered further reassurance to those who saw the process as evidence of a strengthened Brazilian democracy. The crisis mobilized Brazil's democracy by raising the stakes of accountability and involvement. Campaigners in the local elections (mayor and city council) set for October 1992 soon found the public wanted to know their stands on Collor's impeachment. Many candidates from the center and center-right parties expected to support Collor. As the public movement against the president picked up steam, these candidates found themselves under increasing pressure to declare their positions on the Collor scandal. Sensing that their local political fortunes were at stake, many became part of an anti-Collor force, relaying their concerns to their colleagues in Congress. Here, at least, the political system was producing accountability.

The second form of popular involvement was the series of anti-Collor marches that erupted across the country as the charges and Collor's denials piled up. Although not as large, these demonstrations had the flavor of the 1984 rallies for direct election of the president. The anti-Collor press printed a daily score card of how each deputy was expected to vote on impeachment. This directed pressure on those undecided deputies. National television coverage of the vote was continuous. Each deputy's vote became, in the Brazilian manner, a civic ritual.

Whatever it may have symbolized as a democratic triumph, however, Collor's impeachment also signaled a serious breakdown in Brazil's ability to deal with its most pressing problems. Inflation that had reached 25 percent per month, deteriorating social services such as crumbling schools and nonfunctioning health posts, and a serious lag in the country's productivity and technical capacity could not wait. Collor's government represented another two and one-half years lost in facing up to many of Brazil's unmet needs. The "Land of the Future" had once again failed to confront the demands of the present.

Collor's failure also meant that Brazil was still unable to mount a government equal to those of Argentina, Chile, and Mexico. On the international scene, Brazil had become the odd man out. Its rating on the scale of international competitiveness, for example, landed it almost at the bottom.

Collor was right when he claimed his impeachment was not simply a personal defeat, but he gave the wrong reasons. He claimed that his enemies wanted him out because they feared his policies of economic modernization, such as tariff reduction and privatization of state enterprises. This charge was aimed at the São Paulo industrialists who benefited from protectionism and the economic nationalists who defended a large state role. Yet, neither group could come close to influencing two-thirds of the deputies. Furthermore, the economic nationalists were on the defensive, since much of their support traditionally had come from the left, now disorganized in the wake of communism's collapse in East Europe and the former Soviet Union.

WHAT THE COLLOR ERA TELLS US

What grounds are there for saying that by late 1992 Brazil had become ungovernable? A number were suggested earlier in this chapter. First is the political system. Since the French Revolution, political parties have proved to be the most reliable vehicle for transmitting popular opinion and for organizing governments and holding them accountable. Outside of Chile, Colombia, and Uruguay, Latin America offers few examples of long-lasting, stable, competitive party systems.

Brazil does not furnish an example of such a system. It might be argued that between 1946 and 1964 a relatively stable party system emerged, but the military buried it in 1965, opting for an artificial two-party system. Moreover, toward its end, the military regime resorted to fragmenting the party system to increase the chances of victory of the government party. The politicians, happily reinforcing this trend, passed highly permissive electoral legislation that led to a Congress with 19 political parties. The three largest party delegations did not add up to a majority.

Even if Collor had been a more subtle, statesman-like president, he would have found it difficult to patch together majority support in Congress. Collor had discovered the realities of dealing with the fragmented party system in 1992, when he attempted to negotiate with congressional leaders in an effort to project a more mature political image after a major cabinet reshuffle. The moral of Collor's rise and fall from political power is that the electoral legislation needs to be radically revised to encourage the creation of a system with far fewer parties and far more party discipline and accountability.

A second reason for the system's nonviability was the distortion written into the allocation of seats in the Chamber of Deputies. The Constitution of 1988 perpetuated overrepresentation of the smaller states (primarily in the North, Northeast, and West), first established by the military government. This had been done by granting every state, regardless of size, a minimum of eight and a maximum of 70 deputies. The military government's purpose was to increase the political weight of the states likely to support it. The odds were greatest in the smaller, mostly poorer states, where the traditional political machines were pro-military, partly by ideology and partly by readiness to trade votes (which could still be delivered by old-fashioned manipulation) for patronage.

The result is that these small and underpopulated states exercise a disproportionate weight in the Chamber in comparison with more populous states. One serious consequence is that presidents are tempted to use the clientelistic tactics most effective with the old-style politicians, who usually predominate in the less-developed states. This device helped Sarney to deal with the Congress, as he liberally distributed such favors as radio station licenses, always reliable moneymakers and instruments of political influence for the recipients. Finally, provisions in the 1988 Constitution regarding federal-state-*município* relations badly need an overhaul. Here the politicians were clearly reacting to the excesses of the military government, which had subordinated states and *municípios*, especially in finances, to Brasília.

CONCLUSIONS

By the end of Collor's presidency, Brazil's economic problems had become painfully obvious: endemic inflation, lagging competitiveness, insufficient investment, decaying infrastructure, and deteriorating social services. The social consequences were equally obvious: rampant street crime, continued high rates of illiteracy and ill health, and one of the world's worst distributions of income. The psychological consequences may have been the most serious: growing cynicism and an unprecedented rise in the ultimate social indicator, out-migration.

There were also some pluses to the Collor presidency. Most important was the start on transforming Brazil's "inward oriented" economy into an economy that competes on worldwide terms. That meant significantly lowering tariffs (to the 10 to 20 percent level from many that were the world's highest), abolishing government subsidies to industry, and promoting competition among firms producing for the domestic market. It also meant privatizing notoriously inefficient state enterprises. Finally, it meant reducing the costly federal payroll that had been greatly increased by patronage appointments during the Sarney presidency. Yet, the only solution to the overriding problem of economic stagnation at the heart of Brazil's crisis was political leadership. That leadership had appeared elsewhere in Latin America, whatever one may think of the solutions adopted. How could Brazil gain the necessary leadership to attack successfully the problems on whose nature there was a virtual consensus among economists? It is here that the debacle of the Collor government has played both a negative and a positive role. It was negative in that it allowed the politicians and the public to fix on the drama — with its elements of carnival and civic ritual and even Brazilian soap opera. Unfortunately, however, the debacle was reality.

That is why one needs to look beyond the personal dramas to see the structural defects they revealed. While it is true that Fernando Collor did almost everything wrong from a political standpoint in his final six months, what would his chances have been had he done everything right? Would he have been able to provide the leadership Brazil needed? Given his political style and priorities, and for reasons suggested earlier in this chapter, the answer is no. Was Brazil approaching ungovernability under its existing constitutional and political structure?

The odds against success of the new efforts seemed high. The reversal of inflationary expectations, the basis of any successful anti-inflation program, would be especially difficult in a country where indexation had been institutionalized so widely and for so long. Furthermore, public skepticism about all government efforts was rife — understandable given the five failed plans since 1986. That experience made it hard to change expectations and set up a struggle of wills that only a very strong government could win. Nonetheless, Cardoso's team succeeded. By mid-1997, his government had reduced the inflation rate to less than 1 percent per month, with growth averaging a respectable 4 percent per year. Meanwhile, Cardoso had gone on to be elected president in his own right in 1994, capitalizing on the public's favorable reaction to the Plano Real. His government then succeeded in carrying through numerous privatizations of state enterprises, consolidating the bloated financial sector and attracting massive foreign investment.

On the other hand, the Cardoso government made little progress on such key issues as national pension system reform, administrative reform, and electoral reform. Not coincidentally, these measures all required congressional approval, a challenge that had proved too much for the Collor regime under similar circumstances. Cardoso did, however, resort to one device Collor had used to bypass Congress: the *medida provisória*. He experienced a different result.

Cardoso was either able to gain explicit congressional approval of his *medidas* or, when they expired without congressional action, reissue them. In fact, Cardoso's use of this exceptional legislative device was far more frequent than Collor's. How, then, does one explain his greater ability to gain apparent acceptance of such a quasi-authoritarian instrument? In the past, it was because the success of the Plano Real (enacted by *medida provisória*) gave him greater political legitimacy. Yet, it was also because he sought to negotiate with virtually all the political actors, thereby eschewing the arrogant, imperial style of Collor.[7]

Moreover, the relative success of the Cardoso government also reveals an important continuity with the Collor presidency. Cardoso, despite his greater political experience on the national scene as a multiterm senator, has run into the same structural barriers: the fragmented party system, the ill-fated division of federal revenues, and the intransigent congressional defense of corporative interests. These all reflect the legacy of both Getúlio Vargas's dictatorship of 1937-1945 and the reaction to the military dictatorship of 1964-1985.

Collor's unsavory presidency in its own way had dramatized these roadblocks to building a modern democracy in Brazil. Unfortunately, that lesson was obscured by the manner of Collor's fall. By focusing on his corruption, his opponents capitalized on the issue on which he himself had campaigned. By the end, it was not stabilization or economic adjustment through tariff reduction and privatization that occupied the limelight. It was personal morality. Morality in politics is certainly an important issue. Yet, even honest politicians eventually have to deal with difficult major policy issues.

What, in the end, was the significance of Fernando Collor de Mello's unhappy passage through the Palacio Planalto? It was both morality play and soap opera. It was also a throwback to the days before the military seized power. Collor was the Jânio Quadros of the 1990s. Just as Quadros ended up not governing, Collor also failed. Political messiahs may come and go, but the hard tasks remain.[8]

The stakes are high because Brazil's enormous "social debt" demands action. Collor's arbitrary and unprincipled presidency should remind observers that Brazil's patience with democracy is not infinite. After all, authoritarianism is no stranger to Brazil's twentieth-century political deadlocks.

Notes

1. I wish to thank Lincoln Gordon, David Fleischer, Robert Levine, Mac Margolis, Richard Newfarmer, Joseph Tulchin, and an anonymous reader for their helpful suggestions. The views expressed are, of course, my own.

2. Collor's election campaign and victory stimulated scorn from the left, as can be seen in de Oliveira (1990) and Goldenstein (1990). For a booklet promoting Collor's candidacy during the campaign, see *O Fenômeno Collor*, which includes the campaign platform. Typical of the adulatory treatment Collor received right after his election is Nery (1990).

3. For a review of these issues, see Brasil de Lima Júnior (1993). Scott Mainwaring offers a complete analysis of the issues surrounding the electoral system in his "Politicians, Parties, and Electoral Systems: Brazil in Comparative Perspective," *Comparative Politics* 24(1): 21-43 and in Mainwaring and Scully (1995). For an angry attack on those who blame such institutions as the electoral system for Brazil's political crisis, see dos Santos (1994).

4. For a deft treatment of this theme, see Velho (1990).

5. For an analysis that differs from mine, see the detailed discussion in Power (1994). I am grateful to Professor Power for making available a copy of his paper.

6. Pedro told his story in Collor de Mello (1993).

7. For an overview of the political and social scene at the outset of the Cardoso presidency, see Dagnino (1994). For interim assessments of the Cardoso record, see Purcell and Roett (1997) and Woodrow Wilson International Center for Scholars (1997).

8. For another retrospective look at the phenomenon of Collor, see Weyland (1993). For a generally favorable view of Collor's first year, see Schneider (1991).

CHAPTER 2

Institutional Sources of Corruption in Brazil[1]

BARBARA GEDDES AND ARTUR RIBEIRO NETO

"In Brazil, the contractors define the priorities of the State."
Adib Jatene, Minister of Health in the Collor government

At 7:30 every weeknight during fall 1992, millions of Brazilians gathered around their televisions to watch a soap opera called *God Help Us*. The opening credits began with shots of an up-scale party. Elegantly dressed men and women exchanged small talk while waiters served champagne and canapés. A little mud appeared in a corner of the large living room. A few seconds later, the mud had spread through the room. The mud rose until it submerged first the furniture and then the guests, without anyone appearing to notice. Finally, a vortex appeared. Houses, boats, planes, television sets — everything was sucked down into the vortex while "phantom" checks fell from the sky. The image shifted suddenly: Brazil disappeared from the South American map as a flow of mud went down the drain.

The soap opera began airing just after a Parliamentary Inquiry Commission (Comissão Parlamentar de Inquérito — CPI) found strong evidence of then-President Fernando Collor de Mello's involvement in corruption. Its opening captures the generalized perception in Brazil that the country was drowning in a *mar de lama* (sea of mud) — that corruption had become so deep and widespread that it jeopardized Brazil's chances of economic and social development.

Another major corruption scandal hit Congress in late 1993. A new CPI, formed to investigate this case, concluded that 18 deputies should be expelled from Congress and stripped of their political rights for eight years. The CPI also found evidence of involvement in corruption by two ministers and three state governors and listed 22 additional deputies as possible suspects for further investigation (*Veja* 1994, 28-35; *Istoé* 1994, 39-53; Krieger 1994). Three years after the attorney general began legal proceedings against nearly 50 legislators, only one deputy, who ironically had been acquitted in the CPI, had actually been tried. Cases against other deputies remained mired in a host of legal quarrels. As of late 1997, the Supreme Federal Tribunal had yet to determine whether former deputies were entitled to the same immunities given to sitting legislators. Proof obtained by the CPI by breaking the rule of banking secrecy had been successfully objected to in the courts. As a result, the government had to begin new court actions to try to obtain bank records in a proper manner (Carneiro 1997; Baltazar 1997).

Commissions of Inquiry and court cases have multiplied, but punishment of offenders has been uncertain and erratic. Collor himself was acquitted of passive corruption, along with several of those indicted with him, by the Supremo Tribunal Federal in December 1994. Paulo César Farias, architect of the corruption scheme, was also acquitted of passive corruption, though he was found guilty of falsification of documents in setting up the bank accounts under false names that were used in the scheme. For this crime, he received a fine and a sentence of seven years, but, because he was a first offender, he was sentenced to spend only nights actually in custody. The difficulty in proving corruption charges and leniency in sentencing added uncertainty about whether corruption would be punished.

The massive distributive operation mounted by former President José Sarney to "buy" support for a five-year presidential term, the centralized system of "mediation taxes" organized by Farias, the corruption-induced increase in public spending associated with the schemes of the Congressional Budget Committee since 1988, and several other scandals reported by the press suggest that corruption had been more extensive since 1985 than it was during the previous democratic period (Pompeu de Toledo 1994, 80-93). A CPI inquiry into illegal capital transfers found that 40 percent of government investments in infrastructure and public works goes astray. Irregularities were discovered in every project or contract examined in the transportation and social welfare ministries. Investigators estimate that US$40 billion a year of public money ends up in overseas tax havens. An inquiry into the financial affairs of the National Medical Assistance Institute reported that 25 percent of government spending on health is pocketed by corrupt officials, costing taxpayers an estimated $1.6 billion per year (*Latin American Regional Report* 1995, 7).

Corruption cannot be measured accurately. Those who engage in it naturally attempt to hide it. When instances do come to light, one can never be sure they are representative of what remains hidden. Those who expose corruption — journalists, political opponents, disgruntled friends and associates — have their own reasons for doing so, and thus one cannot assume that an increase in exposés reflects an increase in corruption. For all these reasons, one can never prove beyond doubt that corruption has increased.

Nevertheless, we believe that corruption did increase in Brazil during the 1980s and early 1990s. We base this belief on our own observations of Brazilian politics over a number of years; interviews with knowledgeable Brazilians, especially during the summer of 1992; and comparisons of the reports of Parliamentary Committees of Inquiry over time. The amounts of money described and numbers of people implicated in corruption schemes investigated recently are substantially greater than those described in earlier inquiries (Bruzzi Castello 1989; Petersen Mendes 1992).

A new pattern of corrupt practices seems to have emerged in the 1980s with the creation by politicians of organizations aimed at accumulating private wealth by manipulating the distribution of public resources. In addition, the cost of corruption apparently increased. According to Cecílio Rêgo de Almeida, president of one of the country's largest contracting firms, the percentage demanded by public officials for choosing a firm to carry out a public works project jumped from 4 percent during the government of General Ernesto Geisel (1974-1979) to 18 percent during Collor's government (*Folha de São Paulo* 1993a, A1).

This chapter seeks to explain these changes in the practice of corruption in Brazil. In particular, it tries to identify the systematic factors that have made high levels of corruption possible — even perhaps likely — in post-authoritarian Brazil. Although idiosyncrasies such as the personal morals of presidents and members of Congress, their family and regional backgrounds, and their past experiences affect levels of corruption, this study focuses on more systematic causes. Corrupt individuals can achieve power some proportion of time in any political system, but some systems enhance both the usefulness of corruption to individuals engaged in politics and their ability to get away with corrupt practices while in office. This study, therefore, seeks to identify the characteristics of the Brazilian political system that increased the benefits available through corrupt practices, decreased the likelihood of being caught, and reduced the probability and cost of punishment for those caught during the first 10 or so years after redemocratization.

DEFINITION OF CORRUPTION

V.O. Key defines corruption or graft as follows:

> ... the abuse of control over the power and resources of the government for the purpose of personal or party profit. This profit ... may be in the form of power or control within the political organization or in the form of political support from various individuals. . . (Key 1936, 5-6).

This study concerns two forms of "abuse of control over the power and resources of government." The first — the exchange of resources for political support — is often legal but violates norms of fairness and efficiency, may dissipate scarce state resources on frivolous projects, and creates opportunities for corruption in the strict sense. The second — the sale of government contracts, services, privileges, exceptions, information, and so on to individuals or firms by government officials — is illegal and, therefore, corrupt in a strict sense.

EXCHANGE POLITICS

The exchange of resources for support involves the manipulation of public power by officials for the purpose of "buying" political support in Congress, financial support from the business community, or either from other interest groups. Such exchanges occur in all political systems and have a long and celebrated history in Brazil. Although such exchanges have been a common feature of Brazilian politics, reliance on them varies, depending on other political circumstances (to be elaborated below). When reliance on exchange politics increases, so does clearly illegal graft.

Exchange of public resources for support can involve the distribution of either public or private goods. Public goods allocated for this purpose, such as hospitals, schools, roads, sewage plants, and so on, are usually referred to as "pork." Although congressional control over pork has increased since the devolution of budget powers to Congress by the 1988 Constitution, most pork is still provided by the executive. Presidents offer public goods to legislators in exchange for support of key legislation. Legislators, in turn, offer pork to municipal and state leaders in return for support at election time.

Legislators are elected by proportional representation from multimember districts coterminous with state boundaries — so one would not expect the emphasis on pork-barrel politics found in single-member district electoral systems — but a large part of the vote is mobilized by *cabos eleitorais* (local political bosses) in towns and neighborhoods.[2] In order to maintain their followings, *cabos eleitorais* have to be able to provide material benefits. Local public goods have a high value to citizens and, hence, to *cabos eleitorais* because municipalities in Brazil historically (that is, before the 1988 Constitution) have had little power to tax and thus little capacity to provide such goods. Most local improvements came from the central or state government through the political exchange network, and municipalities continue to rely on higher levels of government for large-scale public works and projects.

Presidents also exchange private goods for support. The distribution of private goods occurs through clientele networks. Individuals who control significant political resources, such as seats in a constituent assembly or legislature or the ability to deliver large blocs of citizen votes, can demand high prices for their support: radio or television licenses, jobs for relatives and supporters, subsidized loans from state banks, favorable rulings on questionable tax deductions, or special consideration when contracts are awarded. Ordinary citizens who have only their own votes to exchange receive less, but, if they are lucky, benefits can still be significant: coupons for free milk for pregnant women or free lunches for children, materials for building a minimal dwelling, or help in activating pensions.

Although many of these exchanges are not illegal, most are seen as illegitimate and unfair. All citizens are entitled to pensions under certain conditions, but only those with political connections can get payments initiated expeditiously.[3] All needy pregnant women and all children in certain areas are supposed to be provided with coupons for service, not just those whose families support the right political group. The selective distribution of what are supposed to be entitlements constitutes an abuse of the power of government for political profit.

CORRUPTION IN THE STRICT SENSE

Corruption in the strict sense refers to illegal actions undertaken by government officials to enrich themselves, raise campaign funds, or "buy" support among legislators, executive officials, or interest groups. This definition covers, for instance, the provision of privileged information in exchange for support or money; the acceptance of kickbacks from firms awarded contracts, loans, and other subsidies; the changing of regulations for the purpose of supporting or protecting criminal activities; and the facilitation of tax evasion. The most publicized forms of corruption during the Collor administration included the following:

1. *Overpricing* — artificially increasing the prices of goods or services sold to the government in order to provide extra profits for businesses in exchange for kickbacks;

2. *Expediting payments* — speeding up payments to contractors for services rendered in exchange for kickbacks (because the government is notoriously slow in paying its debts and the value of money depreciates rapidly with high rates of inflation, contractors have often been willing to pay bribes to expedite payments);

3. *Facilitating contracts* — extracting a commission or "mediation tax" as a necessary condition for obtaining a government contract;

4. *Rigging public bidding for contracts* — ignoring technical and price criteria in the selection of contractors to carry out public projects or firms to supply goods and services to the government;

5. *Manipulating regulations* — changing regulations to provide tax breaks, fiscal incentives, or other subsidies for particular firms or individuals in exchange for support or kickbacks;

6. *Selling information* — trading privileged information about government decisions regarding exchange rates, interest rates, anti-inflationary policies, and the policies of international organizations that regulate Brazilian exports, for money or support; and

7. *Illegal fund raising* — collecting illegal campaign contributions from businesspeople.

We argue that corruption, both in the strict sense and in the gray area of exchange of resources for support, was more pervasive during the first 10 years after redemocratization than during the previous democratic period. Certainly, no president before Collor faced substantiated charges of comparable magnitude — though the scandal of the North-South Railroad and the exchange of radio and television licenses and development projects for votes regarding the length of the presidential term during Sarney's term seemed impressive at the time. Although corruption scandals erupted now and then during earlier democratic governments (especially during the last years of both the Vargas and Goulart administrations), past episodes lacked the magnitude and pervasiveness of recent ones.

The perception of corruption as a problem began to rise during the last five to 10 years of military rule. It is difficult to be sure how much of this rise was caused by an actual increase in peculation and how much by decreasing censorship. Censorship hampers any effort to compare the current period with the situation during military rule, but this is not really the relevant comparison. The lack of accountability characteristic of authoritarian regimes can be expected to increase the incidence of corruption. Nevertheless, the free press and open elections of democracy are supposed to limit corruption by increasing the probability of discovery and punishment. This chapter seeks an explanation for why corruption failed to decline after redemocratization in Brazil.

CONTEMPORARY CORRUPTION IN BRAZIL

According to congressional inquiries, both Collor and his associates and the group of politicians who controlled the Congressional Budget Committee created organizations aimed at accumulating large amounts of cash through kickbacks or "mediation taxes." Although the range of the Collor group's dealings was wider, by virtue of the scope of the president's powers, the country's major contractors played a prominent role in both schemes as "buyers" of the "services" offered by the two corruption rings.

These schemes for bilking Brazilian taxpayers relied on simple techniques that have been used at many other times and places. The Federal Police found at the office of Collor's campaign fund-raiser, Paulo César Farias, a computer file named "Collor," basically a Lotus 1-2-3 spreadsheet, that contained the names of several public works projects, indications of whether deals had already been made, a code representing the name of the contractor involved, and a percentage that police believe indicated the president's share of profits (*Folha de São Paulo* 1992a, 7).

In the course of investigating the "Seven Dwarfs," as the group that controlled the Congressional Budget Committee is popularly known, the Federal Police found a series of documents at the house of Airton Reis, a director of Construtora Norberto Odebrecht, one of Brazil's major contractors, listing the names of members of the Budget Committee and other politicians who had received kickbacks or illegal campaign contributions in exchange for appropriating federal funds to projects that interested the contractor (*Folha de São Paulo* 1993b, A1).

Also turned up in the search was a document showing that 17 of the largest contractors had formed a cartel to circumvent the rules governing competition for public works projects. The document, called "Normas de Consenso" (Consensus Norms), shows that the contractors divided the pool of public works among themselves regardless of the results of public bidding. If the firm assigned a particular contract by the contractors' cartel failed to win the public competition, the winning firm would simply subcontract the loser to do the work (*Folha de São Paulo* 1993c, E1). The graft revealed by subsequent investigations was widely known, but the level of sophistication of the operation was unexpected. Contractors, according to the president of one large firm, had a "corruption kit." They selected the public works they wanted to carry out and obtained the signatures of the relevant mayors or governors on project requests in exchange for a percentage; they lobbied for approval of the allocation of federal funds for the project with executive officials and members of Congress, again paying kickbacks; they even arranged financing, working with state banks where necessary, and paid more kickbacks (*Folha de São Paulo* 1993a, A1).

Both corruption schemes involved enormous amounts of money and a brazen disregard for appearances. Members of the first CPI estimated the total amount of money collected by Farias and his associates at about $2 billion (Neumane 1992). Most of the money that ended up in Collor's personal account took the form of "phantom" checks. These were checks drawn on bank accounts opened by Farias's employees, including secretaries and servants, using false identities (Petersen Mendes 1992, 135-156). Ironically, it was an early Collor reform outlawing checks made out to bearer that made it easy for investigators to amass evidence against Collor. One of the checks, for example, was used to buy Collor's car (*Folha de São Paulo* 1992b, 1-18). Evidence indicates that Collor spent $2.5 million to construct a spectacular garden at his home and that he withdrew at least $63,000 from bank accounts, circumventing the freeze he had imposed on the accounts of other Brazilians (Petersen Mendes 1992, 214; *Veja* 1992a, 16- 18; Brito e Policarpo Jr. 1992, 16-25; Krieger 1992, 9).

Deputy João Alves, the leader of the scheme in the Congressional Budget Committee, has claimed that his sudden wealth resulted from winning the lottery 333 times in two years (*Folha de São Paulo* 1993d, A6). He has indeed owned winning tickets many times. According to the police, however, Alves used the lottery as a money-laundering scheme, in very much the same way that drug dealers and other criminals do. He spent $25 million on tickets, winning $9 million that could be claimed as legitimate income. Alves invested so much money in lottery tickets that his purchases alone accounted for 85 percent of gross lottery receipts between 1988 and 1993 in Brasília (*Folha de São Paulo* 1993e, A6), home to 1.6 million inhabitants in 1990.

EXPLANATIONS OF CORRUPTION

Most discussions link corruption in Brazil to aspects of political culture and traditionalism or backwardness. Brazil is seen as a dualistic society divided between an urban, modern sector in the south and southeast and a traditional and backward sector in the center-west, north, and northeast (Hirschman 1958; Cardoso and Faletto 1969). Within each area, different types of voting behavior are said to prevail: issue-oriented and ideological in the modern sector and elite-dominated and exchange-oriented in the traditional sector (Lamounier and Cardoso 1975).

Whatever the merits of these arguments in other contexts, they do not explain the recent increase in corruption in Brazil. Corruption has increased while the political culture has changed little; traditionalism has, if anything, declined. The formative experiences of two of the men who have occupied the presidency since the end of military rule in the clientele-based politics of the backward parts of the country no doubt help to explain their personal values and norms of behavior. Yet, these experiences do not explain how they were able to transfer practices developed in backward areas to the national arena, nor do they explain the behavior of members of Congress. One has to consider other explanations, especially features of the political system itself.

In broad comparative perspective, high levels of corruption are associated with extensive state intervention in the economy, state ownership of the primary export commodity, and single-party rule or personalist dictatorship. With this sketch of the general causes of corruption in mind, high levels of corruption in Nigeria, Indonesia, Venezuela, and Mexico are not surprising. The moderate level of corruption in Brazil between 1946 and 1964 also conforms to general expectations. The first 10 years after redemocratization, however, do not. It is this deviation that motivates the search for causes in recent Brazilian institutions and circumstances.

Our central argument, elaborated more fully below, is that changes in the electoral rules and in the Constitution have increased the likelihood of corruption by 1) decreasing the ability of the executive to build stable coalitions and to assure the loyalty of its supporters in Congress and 2) increasing both the power of Congress and its incentives for exchange-based, corrupt practices.

The weakening of the political capabilities of the executive has created strong incentives to exchange material benefits for congressional support. Deteriorating economic conditions have put strong pressure on executives to exert policy leadership. The high political cost to legislators of supporting unpopular economic measures, however, has created insurmountable problems for a president trying to build a stable political base of support in Congress. Practices that have always been common in Brazil, such as the exchange of public works projects in legislators' bailiwicks for votes, have become more frequent, as other methods of securing support have been eroded and economic conditions have worsened. To give just one example, by the end of July 1992, the Secretary of Regional Development had distributed about Cz33 billion for projects in the districts of deputies supporting Collor, while the districts of members of the opposition had received only about Cz2 billion.[4] Collor's widely respected second Economy Minister, Marcílio Marques Moreira, admitted that he had to trade an increase of 1.5 percent in overall expenditures for the approval of the budget by the Congressional Budget Committee in 1992 (*Folha de São Paulo* 1994, A1). As is now widely known, this increase in spending was allocated to projects that the contractors' cartel had "bought" from mayors, governors, and members of Congress in exchange for kickbacks.

The increase in congressional influence over the budget mandated by the 1988 Constitution, the overrepresentation of backward areas, and changes in electoral incentives have increased both the potential for pork-barrel politics and corruption in Congress and the need for them. Changes in the electoral and constitutional rules, along with the economic crisis, have transformed running for office into a highly risky gamble. The reelection rate has decreased from 50 percent to only 30 percent during the last few years.[5] As Susan Rose-Ackerman demonstrates, if the fear that detection would reduce their chances of reelection deters officials from enriching themselves at public expense, corruption will rise as the likelihood of or desire for reelection declines (Rose-Ackerman 1978).

Finally, as participation has increased, so has the cost of electoral campaigns. The cost of delivering pork to targeted areas and particularistic goods (such as clothes, food, medicine, jobs, and the like) to voters during campaigns has risen, as has reliance on costly television advertising. Knowledgeable observers estimated that it cost $1 million to mount a winning congressional campaign in 1990 (Petersen Mendes 1992, 177). As a result, members of Congress have greater incentives than in the past to strike corrupt deals for the purpose of obtaining an extra influx of cash to use in their campaigns. Most of the deputies whose mandates were canceled as a result of investigations by the Budget CPI were not charismatic vote getters; they needed to spend heavily in order to insure reelection. Former Chair of the Congressional Budget Committee João Alves, for example, was reelected in 1990 after the 93 municipalities in his Bahia district received grants equal to federal spending in the whole state of São Paulo (*Latin American Weekly Report* 1993, 508; *Veja* 1994, 29).

Meanwhile, as the revenue base of the federal government has deteriorated, politicians have not been able to rely on federal largesse to pay for support, as in the past. They have had to find new sources of income, both for personal consumption and for use in the political game. In response to these needs, both the Collor government, to judge by testimony before the CPI, and the Congressional Budget Committee had developed pervasive systems of informal taxation affecting all entrepreneurs doing business with the federal government.

Thus far, discussion has focused on circumstances that make corruption, broadly defined, more important to politicians. Meanwhile, at the same time that corruption had become more useful, punishment for corrupt acts seemed until recently to have become less costly and less likely. The instruments for detecting and punishing corruption are the press, the public prosecutors (Ministerio Público), the Accounting Tribunals (Tribunais de Contas), the Treasury, the Judiciary, Congress itself, and, ultimately, the public. Since redemocratization, the press has performed its role. Astounding details of presidential and congressional peculation have appeared in print. In fact, neither Collor's impeachment nor the probe into the affairs of the Congressional Budget Committee would have occurred without the press.

Punishment, however, depends on congressional and court action. The Congressional Budget Committee scandal exemplifies the legislature's hitherto lackadaisical response to corruption. In 1991, a CPI was requested to investigate the Congressional Budget Committee. The then-president of the Chamber of Deputies, Ibsen Pinheiro, used a procedural expedient, however, to avoid acting on the request (*Folha de São Paulo* 1993f, A1). Pinheiro was subsequently accused of corruption himself, had his mandate revoked by Congress, and withdrew from politics. Congress finally took action only after the economist José Carlos Alves dos Santos denounced the scheme in an interview with the magazine *Veja* in October 1993, in an apparent effort to sidetrack a police investigation of his involvement in the murder of his wife (*Folha de São Paulo* 1993g, A1). While the resulting CPI recommended cancellation of the political rights of 17 deputies and one senator, only six deputies had their mandates revoked. Four of those cited resigned prior to revocation, and eight others either had their cases archived or their cases were not discussed because of lack of a quorum. Former President José Sarney escaped punishment entirely, though several of the shady deals involving him were exposed in the press and investigated by a CPI (Bruzzi Castello 1989). Collor came remarkably close to escaping impeachment, considering the weight and nature of the evidence against him, and was then, as noted above, acquitted of criminal charges by the Supreme Federal Tribunal.

Congressional ability to punish presidents is undermined by the possibility that presidents might buy congressional support during corruption investigations in the same way that they have bought it for other issues. According to press reports, the president of the Banco do Brasil, Lafayete Coutinho, personally offered deputies willing to oppose Collor's impeachment the opportunity to choose the municipalities that would receive investments in health projects worth up to Cz150 million

(US$1,977,587 at the commercial exchange rate for August 13, 1992) each. For senators, the price of projects was reported to be Cz200 million ($2,636,783) (Mossri and Krieger 1992, 1). Coutinho admitted that government backers had priority for such loans (*Veja* 1992b, 13; Dimenstein 1992, 1).

An informed and mobilized public that made clear its intention of defeating legislators who failed to vote for impeachment could, of course, persuade them to stand firm against the president's blandishments — as in the end happened with Collor. Several enforceable circumstances, however, contributed to the effective public mobilization against Collor. Severe economic distress attributed to his policies reduced the public's tolerance for other failings. The timing of municipal elections, scheduled almost immediately after the vote on impeachment, greatly increased the likelihood that voters would still be thinking about impeachment at their next opportunity to sanction politicians. Many legislators were candidates in these elections, and parties linked to Collor in the public mind feared that voters would take this opportunity to vent their wrath. The decision by the Supreme Court to allow the broadcast of deputies' votes on television removed the possibility of secret votes for Collor.

The factors that increased the weight of public mobilization against Collor also affected the outcome of the investigation of the Congressional Budget Committee. In the spring of 1994, the economy had not yet begun the turnaround associated with the Real Plan, and outrage at the conspicuous disregard for public welfare shown by the "Seven Dwarfs" and their allies was again reinforced by economic distress. Moreover, all deputies and one-third of senators faced reelection in 1994, which made them sensitive to constituents' feelings. Finally, as a result of the success of Collor's impeachment hearings as a media event, the television networks decided to broadcast live most of the critical hearings and votes in the investigation into the Congressional Budget Committee's affairs.

These circumstances could not have been predicted by a careful politician calculating the odds of being sanctioned for corruption. Were it not for these factors, it is unlikely that two-thirds of Brazil's deputies would have voted to begin impeachment proceedings or that the most prominent members of the Congressional Budget Committee scheme would have lost their seats in Congress.

STABLE CAUSES OF CORRUPTION

Traditionally, exchanges have played an important part in Brazilian politics, linking voters to politicians through *cabos eleitorais*. Certain characteristics of the Brazilian political system and economy underlie traditional reliance on machine politics. This section discusses the institutional underpinnings of traditional exchange-based politics in Brazil. Arguably, these are the institutions responsible for the traditional level of corruption. The following section suggests explanations for recent changes.

STATE INTERVENTION

Both pork and most of the private benefits that cement relationships within clientele networks are products of state intervention in the economy. State intervention creates opportunities for officials to profit from their role in allocating scarce goods (Krueger 1980; Bates 1990). These profits along with resources, such as jobs and contracts, drawn directly from the state itself are the goods that politicians offer in exchange for political support. Where state intervention is extensive and the state is large relative to the private sector, politicians have more to offer, and citizens have fewer alternative sources of benefits.

In addition, state intervention in the form of extensive regulation and subsidization makes businesspeople dependent on state policies and administrative decisions and, thus, increases their interest in influencing decisions and their willingness to spend money to do so. All else equal, corruption can be expected to increase as the dependence of the private sector on the state increases, as the number of interactions between businesspeople and officials increases, and as intervention becomes more detailed and discretionary. In Brazil, many firms long depended heavily on the government to maintain their profitability. Especially obvious and prominent during recent scandals are the large public works contractors who have played a crucial role in campaign financing (Neumane 1992; *Folha de São Paulo* 1992b and 1993c).

Traditionally high levels of state intervention in the economy thus underlie both exchange-based politics and corruption in the strict sense. The state has intervened in the Brazilian economy for many decades, with an especially dramatic increase during the military regime from 1964 to 1985. The intensified intervention bequeathed to the new democratic government by the military has had its effect on contemporary Brazilian politics.

A comparison among different regions of Brazil offers some evidence in support of the argument that state intervention provides opportunities for politicians to use state resources in politically useful ways. If this argument is true, one would expect greater state intervention to be associated with more political advantage for politicians with access to these resources; consequently, one would expect to see larger proportions of candidates with careers that have given them such access elected in states with high rather than in those with low intervention.

To measure careers providing access to state resources, we used the percentage of deputies elected to the Constituent Assembly who had previously held administrative positions in federal, state, or municipal government (Rodrigues 1987). These are positions publicly identified with the politically motivated distribution of pork and private benefits. To measure the state's role in the economy, we used the average value of the public sector share of the gross economic product of the states in each region (north, northeast, center-west, southeast, and south). We then used standard ordinary least squares (OLS) regression to test the relationship between the two. Table 1 shows the results. The relationship between state intervention and the importance of state resources in politics is positive and statistically significant. The R-squared equals 0.435, which seems quite strong considering the poor quality of the measure of the dependent variable.

Table 1.

**Effect of State Intervention in the Economy
on the Importance of Exchange Politics**

	Intercept	Log (State Share of Gross Economic Product)
Coefficient	1.46	0.32
T-Statistic	4.19	2.20
Significance	0.005	0.05

R-squared = 0.435

Dependent variable: Importance of exchange politics (indicated by number of members of delegation to Constituent Assembly with prior experience in municipal, state, or federal administration).

Sources: Background of members of Constituent Assembly, L.M. Rodrigues, 1987, *Quem É Quem na Constituinte* (São Paulo: Oesp-Maltese); Economic data from Instituto Brasileiro de Geografia e Estatístico, 1991, *Anuário Estatístico do Brasil.*

ELECTORAL RULES

Certain characteristics of the Brazilian electoral system have also contributed to the traditional reliance on exchange politics both to secure citizens' votes for politicians and to secure legislators' votes for presidents' policy proposals. Brazil's open-list proportional representation system has accentuated the importance of exchanging public resources for support. In open-list systems, a candidate's position on the candidate list is determined by the number of individual votes received. Thus, candidates run against members of their own parties as well as members of other parties at the same time. As political scientist and defeated candidate for the Constituent Assembly Francisco Weffort remarked to one of the authors, the open-list system pits candidates of the same party against each other. Candidates can distinguish themselves from candidates in other parties on the basis of programmatic and ideological appeals; to distinguish themselves from competitors within their own parties, however, they must rely on charisma and their records as distributors of largesse.[6] Consequently, the open-list system increases the pressure to use clientelism and other forms of exchange.[7]

The open-list system also contributes to the low levels of party discipline that are characteristic of Brazilian parties. In most proportional representation systems, one of the main levers party leaders use to enforce party discipline is their control over candidate placement on the list and, hence, electoral chances. When legislators fear that a particular vote will reduce their chances of being placed high on the list, they rarely break ranks. Brazilian legislators, in contrast, usually have little reason to fear the retribution of party leaders. Rather, legislators have strong incentives to sell their votes dearly to those offering the most in pork and private goods to distribute to supporters back home.

Open-list proportional representation, like state intervention in the economy, has characterized the Brazilian system for many decades. Both have contributed to traditional levels of corruption but cannot be blamed for the recent increase. The next section considers institutional factors that have affected recent corruption practices.

POLITICAL CAUSES OF THE RISE IN CORRUPTION

The basic problem facing the executive in a presidential system is securing the support of enough legislators to pass key legislation. This problem looms especially large if the president's party does not control the legislature or if the president's party is small. The problem is also acute when many parties have seats in the legislature, and, thus, many different deals have to be negotiated, and when lack of party discipline requires negotiating arrangements with many individual legislators rather than relatively few party leaders.

An economic situation that demands unpopular measures from the executive, such as that confronting recent Brazilian presidents, exacerbates these difficulties, especially when accompanied by high uncertainty about the likelihood that the measures proposed will actually overcome the economic crisis. Since it becomes more politically risky for legislators to support the government in such circumstances, they can demand a higher price in terms of pork and private goods for their support of key legislation, especially if other party inducements such as discipline and loyalty are weak. Uncertainty about overall government performance in dealing with economic problems leads legislators and parties to avoid negotiating long-term agreements to support the government. If the economic situation deteriorates further, legislators can either command an even higher price for their support in the next round of bargaining or move into the opposition if that seems likely to result in electoral benefits.

Presidents José Sarney, Fernando Collor, Itamar Franco, and Fernando Henrique Cardoso have faced all these problems to a greater extent than did most of their democratic predecessors. Most notably, all but Cardoso have had to deal with unprecedented rates of inflation and economic turmoil, and even Cardoso faces an uphill battle over economic reform. None of them could even be sure that the parties represented in their cabinets would support their legislative initiatives. In consequence, all but Cardoso have relied on the exchange of material goods for support to a greater extent than did previous democratic presidents.[8]

The causes of this change in the relationship between the president and the legislature can be lumped into three categories: increased party fragmentation, decreased party discipline, and increased representation in Congress of parts of the country in which politicians rely most heavily on the politics of exchange.

The increase in party fragmentation in comparison with the previous democratic period can be seen by comparing Tables 2 and 3. Not only has the number of parties represented in the legislature increased, but the proportion of seats controlled by the top three parties also has declined markedly. On average, the top three parties controlled 77.9 percent of the seats between 1950 and 1962 but only 49.8 percent

Table 2.

Distribution of Seats in the Brazilian Chamber of Deputies, 1946-1962

Party	1946	1950	1954	1958	1962
	(percent seats)				
PSD	52.8	36.8	35.0	35.3	28.8
UDN	26.9	26.6	22.7	21.5	22.2
PTB	7.7	16.8	17.2	20.2	28.4
PSP	0.7	7.9	9.8	7.7	5.1
PR	2.4	3.6	5.8	5.2	1.0
PST	0.0	3.0	0.6	0.6	1.7
PDC	0.7	0.6	0.6	2.1	4.9
PCB	4.9	0.0	0.0	0.0	0.0
N of Other Small Parties	3	5	6	5	6
Total Parties	10	12	13	12	13
Top Three Parties (percent seats)	87.4	80.2	74.9	77.0	79.4

Source: W.G. dos Santos, 1986, *Sessenta e Quatro: Anatomia da Crise* (São Paulo: Editores Vértice, 68).

during the 1990s. (The first legislature in each democratic period was excluded from calculations because the distribution of seats in each case had been influenced by electoral manipulations of the outgoing authoritarian government.)

Party fragmentation reduces the probability that the president's party will control Congress, increases the probability that a president will come from a small party, and increases the number of parties represented in the legislature. Although party fragmentation leads to greater coalitional flexibility, in the Brazilian context of low discipline, this flexibility must be paid for with material goods. Several changes in Brazilian electoral rules have contributed to increasing the fragmentation of the party system: run-off elections for president, governor, and mayor; changed requirements for registering parties; and the *Horário Eleitoral Gratuito* (free time for candidates on prime-time television and radio).

Run-offs in presidential, gubernatorial, and mayoral elections were introduced in Brazil by the 1988 Constitution. Run-offs reduce the likelihood of electing extremist candidates, but they also help to preserve party fragmentation. First-past-the-post electoral systems tend to reduce the number of parties in the system, all else being equal (Duverger 1954, 239-240). Since only the largest two or three parties have any chance of winning in races decided by pluralities, smaller parties tend to form pre-election coalitions with larger parties. Over time, there is some tendency for parties that cannot compete for the top offices to fade away, as they have in

Venezuela and Costa Rica, which have tended toward two-party systems despite proportional representation in legislative elections. The existence of run-offs, however, gives small parties an incentive to field candidates in the first round. The better they do in the first round, the more they can demand in return for their support of a larger party in the second. Run-offs thus encourage the survival of small parties.

To run for office in Brazil, candidates must be supported by a party or coalition of parties. Rules that ease party registration tend to increase the number of parties because they reduce the political costs of forming new parties and party splits. Rules for registering parties have been altered several times in Brazil. Table 4 shows the major changes in requirements for legal recognition. As can be seen, each reduction in the stringency of the requirements has been accompanied by a

Table 3.
Distribution of Seats in the Brazilian Chamber of Deputies, 1987-1995

Party	1987	1990*	1991	1995
	(*percent seats*)			
PMDB	53.2	26.5	21.5	21.4
PFL	23.8	18.2	17.3	17.7
PSDB	0.0	12.3	7.4	12.3
PDT	4.9	7.7	9.3	5.8
PDS	6.6	6.5	8.5	0.0
PRN	0.0	6.3	8.0	3.0
PTB	3.7	5.7	7.0	6.0
PT	3.3	3.4	7.0	9.6
PDC	1.0	3.0	4.4	0.0
PL	1.2	2.6	2.8	3.5
PSB	0.2	1.6	2.2	3.3
PPR	0.0	0.0	0.0	10.1
PP	0.0	0.0	0.0	6.6
N of Other Small Parties	2	10	8	7
Total Parties	11	21	19	18
Top 3 Parties (percent seats)	83.6	57.0	48.1	51.4

Sources: 1987-1991, *Folha de São Paulo*, October 29, 1990, special edition, 1-4; 1995, "Devagar e Sempre," *Veja*, October 19, 1994, 29-30.

*Brazilian congressional elections occurred in fall of 1986, 1990, and 1994. New members take their seats early in the following year. The 1990 figures shown here reflect changes in the party affiliations of members between the time when they were elected in the first post-authoritarian vote and the time just prior to the 1990 vote.

sharp increase in the number of parties. (The decrease in the number of parties shown in 1965 resulted from the military's decision to create an artificial two-party system as a support base for the regime.)

Another change in electoral rules that has affected the number of parties is the institution of two hours of free time on television and radio for candidates during electoral campaigns. The two hours are divided among the parties in proportion to the percentage of seats they hold in the legislature, with a small fixed length of time going to parties without legislative representation. This rule was initially established in 1965 by the military government to give free air time to the candidates of its own party, Alliance for National Reform (Aliança Renovadora Nacional — ARENA). Due to the constraints on party formation under military rule, the *Horário Gratuito* did not affect the number of parties until 1985. Since redemocratization and the liberalization of party registration rules, it now functions as a major incentive for the organization of small parties as a candidate strategy for getting more free time on television.

Politicians who have already achieved a degree of popular recognition may choose to run as candidates of small, recently organized parties rather than large, established parties because, as one of a very few candidates, they can almost

Table 4.
Registration Rules and Number of Parties

Year	Requirements	Law	Number of Parties
1945	10,000 voters in 5 states Minimum of 500 per state	DL-7,568	12
1965	Dissolution of all existing parties Minimum of 120 deputies Minimum of 20 senators	AC-00004	2
1979	5% of vote in national election Minimum of 3% in 9 states, or 10% of House and 10% of Senate	L-6,767	7
1985	3% of vote in national election Minimum of 2% in 5 states Parties in process of registration can run	L-7,454	23
1992	No change		37

Source: H.S. Braga, 1990, *Sistemas Eleitorais do Brasil (1821-1988)* (Brasília: Senado Federal).

monopolize the free time on television rather than having to share it with other candidates. By the same token, some newcomers to politics may decide to form a new party rather than enlist in the existing parties to get greater exposure on television as a means of positioning themselves for future elections.

The free time also interacts with staggered elections to encourage the formation and survival of small parties. Politicians who plan to run for Congress in the future, for example, may run as mayoral candidates of small parties in the municipal elections that precede congressional elections, solely for the purpose of using the free television time to increase their name recognition in the race to come (*O Globo* 1986, 12). In short, free air time gives politicians increased incentives to form and maintain small parties that might otherwise tend to fade away over time.

Observers have always considered the Brazilian party system fragmented, fluid, personalistic, and nonideological (de Souza 1976; McDonald and Ruhl 1989; Mainwaring 1991, 21-44). During the previous democratic period, however, three parties, as shown in Table 2 above, actually dominated national politics.[9] Now more parties are legally registered, and more are represented in the legislature. Party fortunes have risen and fallen rapidly since 1985, and no two or three have established their preeminence in the system. Instead, the representation of the largest party in the Chamber of Deputies, the Party of the Brazilian Democratic Movement (Partido do Movimento Democrático Brasileiro — PMDB), fell from 53 percent in the first legislature under civilian rule to less than 22 percent in subsequent legislatures. The next largest party controls 18 percent of seats, and six others control between 6 and 12 percent each. This distribution makes Brazil one of the most fragmented party systems in the world. It is thus not surprising, given low discipline and the current economic situation, that the politics of exchange have become even more important than they were traditionally.

In addition, party discipline declined from its traditionally low levels during the first governments after democratization. Brazilian parties have never had most of the institutional mechanisms used in other party systems to maintain discipline. Nevertheless, in a fairly stable party system in which presidents came from the largest parties and used their monopoly over state resources and patronage to consolidate party support, party leaders had informal levers with which to ensure some minimal discipline. Moreover, in the stable, less fragmented system of the past, legislators found it more costly to switch parties.

Party discipline, the tendency of party members to vote together as a bloc, has two sources. The first, party leaders' levers, depends on the rewards and punishments party leaders can use to affect legislators' votes. The second grows out of the spontaneous coherence of parties based on similar ideology and political attitudes and out of personal loyalties that develop over time in groups interacting intensely in the struggle to defeat other groups.

The first source of party discipline has been eroded in all but a few parties of the ideological left by the increased fluidity and fragmentation of the party system; the second, by the various manipulations of the parties during military rule. Beginning in 1965, the military carried out a series of manipulations of the party and electoral systems, aimed at shoring up apparent support for the regime (Fleischer

1983), that have had the unintended consequence of reducing party loyalty and programmatic coherence while increasing opportunism.

The military first mandated the formation of two artificial parties in 1965, one to support the military government and one to offer loyal and quiet opposition. Individuals ambitious for political careers joined these two parties, especially ARENA (name later changed to Partido Democrático Social — PDS), the military's party, since no alternative route to office existed. As opposing the regime became less risky in the late 1970s and popular opposition became more widespread in the early 1980s, those ambitious for office during the transition flocked to the military's moderate opposition party, the PMDB. The military's 1979 effort to fragment the opposition by easing the regulations for registering parties had little effect because of the obvious advantages of belonging to the dominant opposition party.

What was a good strategy for securing a peaceful transition to democracy, however, was a bad strategy for building ideologically coherent parties in which deep personal loyalties could develop. Instead, in the interest of ending military rule, committed opponents of the regime with a wide range of political views found themselves uncomfortably yoked together, along with a large number of opportunists who joined the PMDB when it became apparent that the end of the military regime was approaching. In short, the experience of most Brazilian politicians during the last 25 years has been with party organizations in which party discipline based on either ideological coherence or personal loyalty was unlikely to develop.[10]

Another factor contributing to the increase in corruption is the increase in the legislative representation of the backward parts of the country. In these areas, candidates' appeals to voters depend more on particularistic benefits than on programmatic appeals. Deputies from these states tend to be especially concerned about securing such benefits, either from the executive or in deals made within Congress.

Of course, politicians from the northeast have no monopoly on particularism or corruption. Some of the most famous for corruption on a grand scale (for example, Adhemar de Barros, Paulo Maluf, and Orestes Quércia) have come from the developed southeast. Nevertheless, there are some important differences between the south and the rest of the country. The press in the backward areas tends to be linked to reigning political groups: the Magalhães family in Bahia, the Sarneys in Maranhão, the Collor de Mellos in Alagoas. Moreover, the press in these areas depends heavily on government advertising. For these reasons, it has been less aggressive in investigating corruption stories. Furthermore, although some southern politicians rely on the politics of exchange, others represent reformist interests; in the backward areas, exchange-based politics is the only game in town. Consequently, the increase in the representation of the north, northeast, and center-west indicates an increased control of Congress by exchange-based political interests.

Backward states have always been overrepresented in the Brazilian legislature, and that overrepresentation has worsened since 1969, despite substantial population shifts toward the more developed southeast and south (Soares 1973; Braga 1990; Kinzo 1989; de Souza 1976). The 1988 Constitution continued the trend. It mandates minimum representation of eight per state and four per territory, with a maximum representation of 70. In a strictly proportional system, São Paulo,

Table 5.

Percentage of Seats Held by Deputies from the North, Northeast, and Center-West

Year	Percent Seats	Legal Regime
1945	47.2	L-7,586
1947	45.3	1946 Constitution
1969	40.3	EC-1
1977	42.5	EC-8
1982	45.9	EC-22
1988	49.4	1988 Constitution

Source: H.S. Braga, 1990, *Sistemas Eleitorais do Brasil (1821-1988)* (Brasília: Senado Federal).

the largest and most modern state, would have 120 deputies rather than 70, and several smaller and more backward states would have fewer than eight (Coelho and Fleischer 1988).

Table 5 shows the percentage of congressional seats held by states in the north, northeast, and center-west since 1945. Between 1945 and 1969, representation declined as a result of population shifts, but since the backward parts of the country provided the strongest support for the military regime, several reforms of the electoral system initiated by the military increased their representation. As is apparent in the table, this trend was reinforced rather than reversed after redemocratization.

To sum up so far, the political institutions identified as contributing to an increase in party fragmentation and thus to increased reliance on exchange politics include run-off elections, the easing of rules for party registration, and the rules governing free time on radio and television. In addition, rules determining state representation in Congress produced overrepresentation of the more backward areas and thus greater reliance on exchange. The specific institutions identified here as contributing to party fragmentation, and, in turn, to greater reliance on the exchange of pork and privileges for legislative votes, are those relevant in Brazil. These are not the only institutions that increase the president's need to rely on such exchanges. One would expect to see corruption associated with any set of rules that increases the president's dependence on exchange politics and increases the representation of the more backward parts of the country.

The institutional changes contributing to increased reliance on exchange politics were introduced for other purposes, most of them through legitimate democratic processes. The 1988 Constitution, written by a freely elected Congress sitting as a constituent assembly, introduced run-off elections and increased the overrepresentation of backward states. The change in rules for the registration of parties occurred in May 1985, in the immediate aftermath of the transition to civilian rule, as part of an effort to throw off residues of military rule and further democratize the system. The *Horário Eleitoral Gratuito* was introduced by the military government at a time when ARENA controlled most of the seats in Congress and could monopolize the free air time. Its consequences when party registration became easier were unintended and completely unforeseen. The increased party fragmentation and representation of backward areas described above interacted with the devolution of budgetary powers to Congress mandated by the 1988 Constitution to create further opportunities for corruption. This interaction is at the root of the immense congressional corruption scandal involving the budget.

Until 1988, Congress had little say in the details of the budget. It could only vote bills proposed by the executive up or down. The scope of congressional budgetary discretion was limited to the allocation among charitable and social assistance institutions of the amount designated for this purpose by the executive. Within these limits, the investigation begun in late 1993 has turned up evidence of extensive and ingenious corruption. It shows that a large part of such money was allocated to fake institutions headed by associates or family members of congressmen (*Folha de São Paulo* 1993h, A1). According to a study carried out by the Ministry of Social Welfare in 1993, 50,000 different institutions have received resources allocated by senators and deputies during the last 30 years (*Folha de São Paulo* 1993i, A7). The members of Congress involved in the recent scandal have controlled the allocation of these resources since 1985.

With the devolution of budgetary powers to Congress in 1988, the Congressional Budget Committee acquired the power to propose amendments to the federal budget. Since then, a large and sophisticated network of corruption has been established between the politicians who controlled the key positions in the Committee and the country's major contractors. According to press reports, the network reached its peak in terms of size between 1988 and 1991, when the first stories about corruption in the Committee emerged and Deputy João Alves was replaced by Ricardo Fiuza as *relator* (the member who analyzes proposed amendments and delivers a formal opinion about their merits before the vote by committee members) of the Congressional Budget Committee.

Evidence indicates that 18 deputies and senators were directly involved in the elaboration and approval of amendments to the budget designed to allocate public funds to projects proposed by the contractors (*Folha de São Paulo* 1993j, A1). There is also evidence that Fiuza, former Minister of Social Affairs in the Collor administration, and economist José Carlos Alves dos Santos, who worked on the staff of the Committee (and later denounced the scheme), included 600 new amendments to the budget after its approval by Congress, leading to a $640 million increase in expenditures (*Folha de São Paulo* 1994b, A1).

The increase in party fragmentation and the other institutional changes discussed above affected the development of congressional corruption in three ways. First, the high turnover associated with the currently chaotic party system increased the power of the few well-established politicians in Congress who have been repeatedly reelected. They tend to monopolize important positions on critical committees and to face less competition for resources and less monitoring from the ever-changing newcomers than they would if more deputies served long enough to master the rules of the game. As a consequence, it became easier for a relatively small group of politicians to entrench themselves, dominate a committee, and manipulate its decisions to favor their clients, as the so-called "Seven Dwarfs" did.

Second, the overrepresentation in Congress of the more backward areas leads to their overrepresentation on key committees. In addition, deputies from the more backward areas are more likely than others to be reelected repeatedly, so their influence on committees tends to be exaggerated, since they are among the few with long experience. Twelve of the 18 deputies and senators identified for expulsion by the CPI were from the northeast, north, and center-west, as were all three of the governors cited (*Veja* 1994a).

Third, high turnover, the ease with which new parties are created, and the frequency with which members of Congress change parties seriously undermine the ability of party leaders to monitor the behavior of party members. Established party leaders could be expected to have a longer perspective and a concern for the positive image and honest reputation of their parties. In the post-authoritarian Brazilian political system, however, only in a few parties, most notably the ideologically coherent Workers' Party (Partido dos Trabalhadores — PT), do party leaders have the capacity to sanction legislators effectively.

THE EFFECT OF THE ECONOMIC CRISIS

It is the increase in corruption in the strict sense that distinguished the Collor administration from preceding ones. The techniques used by Collor's group had been used before, both in Congress and the executive, but during the Collor government they involved larger amounts of money and enveloped many more activities. In no other postwar Brazilian government were so many government resources — contracts, favors, items of information, and exceptions — sold for personal profit, and in no other were such large "commissions" on transactions with the government collected so assiduously. Collor's personality — headstrong, arrogant, materialistic — exacerbated, some say, by drug use, no doubt accounted for some of the change, as did his experience of familial politics in Alagoas. Accustomed to a political culture in which members of elite families could literally get away with murder, Collor may have failed to anticipate both the likelihood of being caught with his hand in the till and the public's outraged response. Without minimizing the importance of personal characteristics, some situational factors also permitted Collor to express them freely.

When Collor was elected, the yearly inflation rate was above 1700 percent. He faced intense international pressures to liberalize the Brazilian economy, hampered by a constitution that severely limited his fiscal flexibility. To turn the economy around, he had no alternative to radical economic reforms, and he could count on very little support in Congress for those reforms. During the honeymoon period shortly after his election, he was able to use the *medidas provisórias* (provisional measures) feature of the Constitution to cram a set of reforms down the legislature's throat, but the reforms, including the highly publicized freeze on bank accounts, failed to produce promised results, and the honeymoon ended. Collor was left in a situation, partly of his own making, in which the need for public and private goods to cement political coalitions was at its highest in history and in which the Brazilian state had reached a low ebb in terms of its ability to supply such goods.

Decreasing revenues caused by economic decline, inflation, political obstacles to increasing taxes, and the constitutional mandate to turn a large portion of taxes collected over to states and municipalities; the disappearance of foreign loans with which to compensate for budget deficits; and intense pressure from the IMF and World Bank to decrease deficits reduced the size of the pot from which presidents traditionally drew resources. One of the reasons for the unparalleled greed of the Collor administration was the need to supplement state resources with private tribute in order to attend to the demands of potential supporters. Personal greed also played a part, but rulers throughout history have often felt the need to maintain an opulent lifestyle in order to impress potential allies and competitors alike with their power and capacity for generosity.

Corruption during the Collor government was not limited to the network made up of the president and his closest confidants. Many of his appointees simultaneously carried on freelance operations. Many of the appointed members of Collor's original team could expect only a short term in office. This team was made up of obscure individuals, many from Alagoas, and many, as it turned out, of only modest talents. The most important minister of his first cabinet, for example, Economy Minister Zélia Cardoso de Mello, had occupied a third-rate position on the Cruzado Plan team and later worked as a lobbyist who specialized in obtaining federal funds for governors and mayors. Individuals with this sort of background and level of talent could not expect to remain in office for more than five years (the length of the presidential term) at most. If the economy failed to improve, they could expect an even shorter tenure. Few members of the original team could expect to move on to other posts of national prominence.

If the fear of disgrace and dismissal normally deters people from corruption, this deterrence will be less effective when they expect to be dismissed shortly, no matter what, and when disgrace seems, for reasons to be discussed below, unlikely. As the economy failed to improve, the temptation to "take the money and run" increased.

This temptation has lessened in post-Collor administrations. Franco's appointees were mostly career legislators and professionals. Their terms in the cabinet were often short, but most had every reason to expect their careers in public life to continue afterward. Cardoso's appointments to high-ranking positions include many of the best economists in the country, as well as able professionals in other fields. Given their own records of successful performance in the past and the improving economy, such appointees have a longer time horizon. Moreover, even if the economy were to crash tomorrow, internationally recognized professionals such as those Cardoso has appointed would still have more to lose from disgrace in terms of their long-term careers than they might gain through peculation. The stress on the temptations of office implies no lack of confidence in the personal integrity of Cardoso's appointees; its purpose is simply to point out that some situations put a greater strain on commitments to probity than do others.

Yet another circumstance deserves consideration as a contributor to changes in kinds of corruption under Collor: the freeze on bank accounts. The freeze had several perhaps unforeseen effects on the relationship between businesspeople and the government. Most important, it created a near monopoly on liquid assets in the country. Not only did the Collor team control access to state resources, but it also controlled access to most private funds. As would be expected, this monopoly drove the informal price of access to money up. The price of "commissions" rose steeply. Businesspeople were forced to negotiate with government officials not only in the traditional areas of contracts, subsidies, and regulation but for use of their own money to pay salaries, taxes, and other necessary expenses. The dependence of businesspeople on government and the number of business-government interactions increased. Commissions, kickbacks, and the emergence of collusion between businesspeople and officials were the natural consequences of dependence and monopoly.

Collor's influence extended to the corruption operation later unearthed in Congress. He appointed economist José Carlos Alves dos Santos as head of the Federal Budget Department (Departamento do Orçamento da União — DOU). According to investigations by the CPI, dos Santos, possessing both technical expertise and close contacts with the contractors, was the critical member of the corruption ring in the Congressional Budget Committee. At the DOU, dos Santos was directly responsible for allocating, on the basis of "technical" criteria, $1 billion in transfers from the federal government to states and municipalities in 1991 (*Folha de São Paulo* 1993k, A8).

CRIME AND PUNISHMENT

In theory, democracy reduces corruption. A free press informs the public about abuses. Legislatures, police, prosecutors, and the courts are empowered to investigate allegations of misconduct and punish miscreants, and, ultimately, voters can end the political careers of corrupt officials. Why did democracy — at least until September 1992 — apparently not increase accountability in post-authoritarian Brazil?

A series of reasons can be listed, some idiosyncratic and some more systematic. By sheer bad luck, the first two civilian presidents came from backward areas where exchange politics is common and elite families break the law with impunity. Collor himself did not set serious standards, and members of his team did not fear discovery by him. Finally, in the Brazilian political system, the president has sufficient resources at his disposal to buy votes on nearly any issue if he is willing to undermine the economy in order to do it, as Collor and Sarney both seemed willing to do.

These factors all matter. Ultimately, however, accountability depends on something more basic: the public's desire and ability to end the political careers of corrupt officeholders. Most legislators' votes could not be bought at any realistic price if they expected a vote in favor of a president widely believed to be corrupt to result in their rejection at the polls in the next election. Despite the widespread indignation felt in Brazil toward Collor, however, there were some systematic impediments to turning that indignation into effective political action. It was these impediments that made impeachment uncertain.

As legislators decided how to vote on Collor's case, they had to consider, first, whether their constituents would really prefer a vote against Collor to the public and private goods they could extract in return for a vote to support him. They also had to assess how likely their constituents were to make their next voting decision on the basis of this issue. To punish at the polls, voters have to know the names of their representatives, know how they voted, and base their next vote on this issue. Unless these conditions are met, the threat to punish is not credible.

In the United States, only about 25 percent of those who respond to survey questions know the name of their congressional representative. In Brazil, the figure is bound to be lower since average education levels are much lower and the political system much more confusing. In two-party systems, most people can substitute a simple rule — vote against the party responsible for the outcome considered undesirable — for detailed knowledge. With dozens of parties currently in existence, 15 represented in Congress at this writing, and multimember districts with up to 70 seats being contested at a time, the task facing Brazilian voters is infinitely more complex. Moreover, since the vote is mandatory, many people who lack both interest in politics and information about it show up at the polls.

Voters usually find out about the votes of their representatives from three sources: newspapers, communications from the representatives themselves, and campaign speeches by opponents during the next election campaign. Newspapers reach only a very small part of the public in Brazil. Representatives themselves cannot be expected to publicize an unpopular vote. The only thing legislators usually need fear, then, is that their vote will become an issue in the next campaign. This is not a negligible fear, but there were many other disasters in Brazil to take voters' minds off these specific votes.

The huge demonstrations that occurred during the weeks preceding the legislative vote on Collor's impeachment persuaded legislators that citizens cared about the issue and would not forget. The demonstrations, in other words, made the threat to punish at the polls credible.

Two additional circumstances increased the credibility of the threat to punish at the time of the vote to begin impeachment proceedings. First, the Supreme Court refused to allow members of Congress to vote secretly and, further, allowed television to broadcast the roll-call vote. This decision removed the possibility of a dignified obscurity for those who voted for Collor. Second, municipal elections were scheduled for October 3, 1992, only days after the legislative vote. Although deputies might hope that their vote for Collor would have been forgotten by the next scheduled congressional election in 1994, it was unlikely that the public would forget which parties had supported Collor within a few days. In fact, they did not. Most parties and candidates associated with Collor were defeated in the municipal elections. The nearly unanimous vote for impeachment was not sufficient to save them.

CONCLUSION

Collor's innovations — the dramatic increase in the price of "commissions," the increase in the range of services for sale, and the monopolization of profits by a small group of erstwhile outsiders — led to his personal downfall. Police investigation of a murder led, via a sequence of unexpected revelations, to the discovery of a corruption ring in the Congressional Budget Committee. The press and congressional inquiries continue to unearth both large-scale graft and petty peculation. The more general consequences of these episodes, however, remain uncertain.

Although Brazil's economic situation has recently improved, the turnaround remains fragile. The country has fallen behind other developed Latin American countries in adjusting to post-debt crisis economic reality. The costs of adjustment remain to be paid in Brazil, whereas Chile and Argentina have passed through the most painful phase of adjustment and have begun to reap benefits in the form of increased investment, low inflation, and increasing incomes. The corruption scandals diverted attention from inevitable structural and constitutional reforms. The congressional investigation into the activities of the Budget Committee virtually paralyzed attempts to reform the Constitution during 1994, while critics of such reform used Congress's badly damaged reputation as an argument for avoiding it altogether.

These long-postponed reforms now dominate President Cardoso's agenda and must continue to be addressed if the economy is to remain on track. The institutional environment in which he must act is somewhat less hostile than that faced by Collor or Franco. Although Cardoso cannot count on majority programmatic or ideologically based support in the fragmented legislature, unlike Collor and Franco, he comes from a party of respectable size and reasonable coherence. He is supported by a fairly stable coalition. He may have to negotiate continuously for the last few votes he needs in the legislature but not for all of them. Moreover, Cardoso assumed office with very high popularity and prestige as a result of the success of the Real Plan he devised while finance minister. Members of Congress will be inclined to cooperate with the president as long as this popularity lasts, and thus the likelihood of structural and constitutional reforms essential to continued economic success is now higher than it has been at any time since 1985, though by no means certain.

In the political arena, Collor's disgrace and scandal in Congress may produce even more positive effects. Voters rejected many of the politicians whose names were most prominently linked with corruption in the 1994 elections (*Veja* 1994b). Given current levels of public indignation with corruption, it is possible that the Brazilian presidents will continue to feel strong pressure to initiate reforms of the political system, as Italy's and Japan's political leaders are trying to do.

If reforms aimed at reducing the number of parties in Congress, increasing party discipline, and instituting more equitable representation of different parts of the country are not undertaken, however, another window of opportunity will be missed. Brazil is likely to find itself caught once again between the Scylla of corruption on one side and the Charybdis of immobilism on the other. Without changes in the institutions that have made it nearly impossible to form stable executive-legislative coalitions, it is hard to imagine how needed economic reforms can be sustained and long-standing social and economic problems solved.

Notes

1. This study is a much revised and updated version of an article first published in *Third World Quarterly* 13 (1992), 341-361. We would like to thank Antônio Carlos Mendes, Procurador da Justiça Eleitoral de São Paulo, for help in gathering data and Luigi Manzetti, Marcus Melo, William Nylen, Thomas Skidmore, John Zaller, participants in the panel on "Democratic Transition and the Brazilian State" at the Latin American Studies Association meeting, Los Angeles, 1992, and participants in a conference sponsored by the North-South Center, "Whither Brazil after Collor," Miami, 1993, for raising questions that helped us to improve this chapter. Our research was supported by the Conselho Nacional de Desenvolvimento Científico e Tecnológico (CNPq) and UCLA's Latin American Center.

2. Barry Ames shows that the relative weight of public as opposed to private goods in the basket of offerings used by deputies to attract voters varies by region and the distribution of support within the district in Ames (1995, 324-343).

3. Of course, members of the U.S. Congress also help constituents who have difficulties with the Social Security Administration. They help constituents deal with mistakes, lost checks, and so on. In Brazil, in contrast, the intervention of a political patron is routinely necessary in some areas to initiate payments to persons entitled to receive them.

4. At the commercial exchange rate for the middle of July 1992, Cz33 billion was worth about $493,646, while Cz2 billion was worth about $29,917. These figures do not, however, accurately reflect the value of these projects because most of the money was spent earlier when it was worth far more. In January 1992, for example, Cz33 billion was worth $2,514,000 at the commercial exchange rate. Whatever the dollar value of the projects, however, the important point is that the Collor administration spent more than 15 times as much in the districts of supportive members of Congress as it did in the districts of opponents. See Bortot and Silva (1992, 5).

5. Incumbency rates in Brazil, as in most Latin American countries, have never been high compared to those in the United States because Brazilian political careers tend to include posts in several electoral and administrative offices rather than being confined to a single institution as they often are in the United States. We do not believe, however, that this long-standing career pattern explains the sudden drop in incumbency rates in the 1980s and 1990s.

6. See Geddes (1991) for a more extensive discussion of the effects of the open-list system.

7. We focus on Brazilian institutions here, but of course they are not the only ones that increase reliance on clientelism. The multiple-list systems of Colombia and Uruguay have many of the same effects.

8. João Goulart, president of Brazil from 1961 to 1964, is a possible exception to this statement. He also came from a minority party, lacked a stable base in Congress, and faced intense economic difficulties.

9. D'Alva Kinzo (1989). Several authors, most notably dos Santos (1986), have argued that parties were breaking down by the early 1960s. We believe that the disarray apparent

during the Goulart administration was caused by the realignment to be expected as rapid development changed interests and increased the political sophistication of many citizens, along with the economic and political crisis itself. In the absence of military intervention, the Brazilian party system might well have developed into the kind of stable, mildly interest-based system found in other developed Latin American countries.

10. There are, of course, some conspicuous exceptions to the generalization, notably the PT (Partido dos Trabalhadores).

CHAPTER 3

Beyond Collorgate: Prospects for Consolidating Democracy in Brazil Through Political Reform

DAVID FLEISCHER

B razil's tumultuous 1990s have again stimulated debate about a "profound political reform" to rid the Brazilian political system of counterproductive fetishes and political corruption in general. The popular and institutional clamor for impeachment proceedings against President Fernando Collor de Mello in August and September 1992 and the "Budgetgate" Congressional Investigation Committee, also translated as Parliamentary Commission of Inquiry (Comissão Parlamentar de Inquérito — CPI), investigations from October 1993 through January 1994 underscore the critical need for a new set of ethics and morals in the practice of politics in Brazil. Not only did these events make headlines in the First World press and create strong echoes around Latin America, they also had an important impact on the consolidation of democracy in Brazil.

COLLOR'S IMPEACHMENT AND THE
CONSOLIDATION OF DEMOCRACY

D o the events surrounding the investigation and impeachment of Fernando Collor de Mello in 1992 represent a consolidation of democracy in Brazil? The events described by Thomas Skidmore in Chapter One and Barbara Geddes and Artur Ribeiro Neto in Chapter Two of this volume were unprecedented not only for Brazil but for presidential systems everywhere.[1] Brazil became the first presidential system on record to impeach a directly elected president constitutionally and democratically. Until 1992, the only such precedent had been the case of the seventeenth president of the United States, Andrew Johnson, whose impeachment trial was held in the U.S. Senate in 1868 but who was finally acquitted by a margin of one vote. In 1993, however, the Venezuelan Congress impeached President Carlos Andrés Pérez. When one examines whether this represented a victory for the consolidation of democracy in Brazil, a cautious answer must be in some ways "yes" but in other ways "no."

Political Liberalization

Since the mid-1970s, Brazil has been strengthening its system of political representation through decisive elections and increasingly activist political parties. The Movimento Democrático Brasileiro (MDB) congressional delegation doubled in 1974. The military government party Partido Democrático Social (PDS) lost its absolute majority in the Chamber of Deputies in 1982. Also in 1982, the combined opposition of the Partido Movimento Democrático Brasileiro (PMDB) and Partido Democrático Trabalhista (PDT) won direct gubernatorial elections in 10 states containing nearly 70 percent of Brazil's gross domestic product (GDP), tax base, and electorate. In 1984, the nation participated in two mass mobilizations: 1) the *Diretas Já* (Direct Elections Now) movement for approval of the Dante de Oliveira Constitutional Amendment establishing direct presidential elections in November of that year, which was defeated in Congress in April, and 2) the movement in favor of the candidates of the "Democratic Alliance" (Tancredo Neves and José Sarney) in the electoral college in January 1985. This movement generated mass popular rallies in most major cities in the second half of that year.

Finally, during the six-year period from 1985 through 1992, Brazilian voters went to the polls nine times (every year except 1987 and 1991). In 1985, they voted in elections for the mayors of capital and "national security cities"; 1986, governors, state legislatures, and the Congress (that became the Constituent Assembly); 1988, general municipal elections; 1989, two rounds of presidential elections; 1990, Congress, state assemblies, and two rounds of gubernatorial elections; and 1992, general municipal elections with two rounds for mayors of large cities.

This was a more concentrated sequence of elections than in any other country in Latin America. In October 1992, more Brazilian voters went to the polls to elect municipal candidates than U.S. voters in the Clinton-Bush presidential election the following month. The percentage of the Brazilian population registered to vote rose from only 25 percent in 1960 to nearly 60 percent in 1992. Since voting is obligatory, turnouts are very high, on the order of 85 percent of the electorate.

Consolidation?

The next stop on the road to a modern democracy was the Constitution of 1988, which contains a very advanced section on civil and human rights and reestablished most of the prerogatives of the Congress. Organization of groups in civil society in general has flourished since the 1980s, and political action groups representing all sectors of urban and rural society abound and are very active as lobbies and pressure groups at the federal, state, and municipal levels.

Does all this mean that Brazil is a consolidated and stable democracy? Not exactly, but it does mean that Brazil has strengthened its representative political institutions. Figure 1 illustrates this point. Here the consolidation of democracy is seen as a two-dimensional phenomenon: 1) the strengthening of the system of political representation and 2) the deconcentration of society's political and economic "goods" (Dahl 1971; Lamounier 1991).

Figure 1.
The Process of Democratic Consolidation, Socio-Economic
Deconcentration, and Strengthening of Representation System

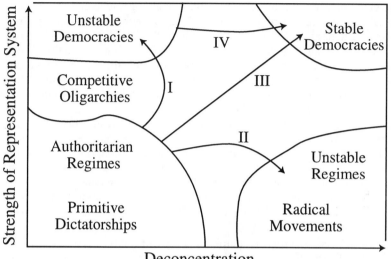

Source: Adapted from Dahl (1971) and Lamounier (1991).

Three basic routes are hypothesized in transitions away from authoritarian, dictatorial regimes:

  I. While not promoting much deconcentration, the representational system is gradually strengthened, and the political system evolves through competitive oligarchies to an unstable democracy.

  II. With rapid "deconcentration," but with little or no strengthening of the system of political representation, a "radical movement" to an unstable regime occurs.

  III. A more direct pathway to a stable democratic regime involves strengthening political representation and promoting deconcentration concurrently.

Brazil appears to have followed the first pathway with rapid strengthening of the system of political representation, both institutionally and through opening of the franchise to a large proportion of the population, allowing illiterate and semi-illiterate citizens the right to vote. On the other hand, a reconcentration of economic and social "goods" has occurred at the same time. With the notable exception of some "islands of political competence," such as the state of Ceará since 1987, most indicators of economic and social inequality have worsened since the 1970s: distribution of income, access to education, housing, health and other social services. From 1989 to 1992, for example, the poorest one-half of the Brazilian population lost 10 percent of its earning power. The "shirtless ones," who were induced to vote for Collor in 1989, by 1992 had lost everything else.

Brazil's large electorate and very high turnouts by no means indicate that a deconcentration of "political autonomy" and "independence of political decision" have been achieved. How can a nation expect to achieve a stable democratic regime with over 7 million children under age 15 out of school? For every 1,000 who begin first grade in primary school, only 45 finish eighth grade in eight years, without repeating grades or dropping out. In 1989, the Superior Election Court (Tribunal Superior Eleitoral — TSE) issued a profile of the Brazilian electorate, based on updates of the total recanvas of voters done in 1986, and concluded that 70 percent of the electorate could be considered illiterate or semi-illiterate, a vast majority of whom are concentrated in the North and Northeast and the less-developed interior of the Central-South states. This leaves a majority of the electorate almost totally vulnerable to political manipulation during election campaigns, either by direct clientelism of vote-buying or favor-giving by corrupt political/economic elites who operate mechanisms perpetuating political dependency. Perhaps even worse, they are also vulnerable to political manipulation by television, through biased news coverage, political subplots in popular telenovelas, and biased content on comedy and interview shows. The latter more subtle political manipulation usually works to reinforce the former more overt manipulation, conforming to the "political agendas" of the owners of national networks and local television stations (Porto 1993; de Lima 1993).

Brazil's lack of progress contrasts sharply with political systems such as those of Chile and Argentina, where political elites had decided as far back as the late 1950s to provide their populations with total access to both primary and secondary public education. Thus, both systems today have generally higher levels of education, broader deconcentrations of political/economic goods, and more articulate and mobilized electorates.

These lamentable conditions lead to the conclusion that Brazil has taken Pathway I in Figure 1. Moving the nation from an "unstable democracy" along Pathway IV to become a "stable democracy" then becomes the most critical issue facing Brazilian democrats. This process must encompass improvements in political, social, and economic equality, that is, promoting deconcentration while, at the same time, carrying out a profound and comprehensive political reform.

POLITICAL REFORM

This drive for political change is not the first (nor probably the last) time that a large-scale political reform was discussed by the Brazilian Congress. In the early 1960s, President João Goulart's agenda of "Basic Reforms" was rebuffed by the Congress elected in 1962, creating a conflict and stalemate that helped precipitate the latter's overthrow by the military in April 1964. During the 1987-1988 Constituent Assembly, a broad agenda of political reforms was introduced, but the Centrão, a middle-of-the-road coalition, defeated most of the more important proposals. In fact, this assembly actually reversed some important political reforms previously adopted; for example, it suspended the anti-nepotism rules for the November 1988 municipal elections.

Even so, the recent political reform movement has made important headway. A series of highly visible investigations, proposals, and political programs have transformed Brazil into a laboratory for modern democracy. From September 1992 to mid-1995, the plebiscite regarding system of government, changes in election and party legislation, the recommendations of the "Budgetgate" CPI, changes proposed for the ill-fated constitutional revision in 1993-1994, and the constitutional reforms championed by President Fernando Henrique Cardoso throughout his term have sustained a continuous and high-stakes political theater.

The Plebiscite

Brazilian voters went to the polls on April 21, 1993, to choose their system of government from among three alternatives: presidential republic, parliamentary republic, or parliamentary monarchy. The timing of the vote raised some doubt, as several constitutional challenges were brought to the Supreme Court, also called the Supreme Federal Tribunal (Supremo Tribunal Federal — STF), prior to the plebiscite, questioning the validity of the Congress's amending the constitution's transitory provision setting the plebiscite for September 7, 1993, and the constitutional revision period to begin on October 5, 1993 — exactly five years after the promulgation of the new Magna Carta. The STF rejected these challenges on April 14, 1993, allowing the date of the plebiscite to be advanced without altering the date to begin the constitutional revision.

The free propaganda time on radio and television allocated for the three alternatives began in mid-March, and on April 21, Brazil's voters decided to maintain the republican presidential system. Because the plebiscite did not alter the system of government and thereby remove the possibility of a "lame duck" Congress conducting the constitutional revision, several challenges against beginning the revision in October 1993 reached the STF. However, all were rejected, and the revision was begun on October 6, 1993. As in 1987-1988, the Congress continued to perform normal legislative functions and thus was not a full-time Constituent Assembly. In addition, there was some controversy over the scope of constitutional reform — whether it should be restricted to implementing the results of the plebiscite or encompass a broader scope of revision. A consensus established a middle ground.

Election Law Modifications

With the Brazilians' preference for a presidential republican form of government firmly established, the Congress began an attempt to reform the election law. On September 30, 1993, Congress passed a new election law (No. 8713), which in many aspects made things worse. It effectively "legalized" massive contributions from businesses and personal fortunes, without transparency of donations. In a feeble attempt at reducing the number of parties in Congress, a "barrier" of 3 percent was introduced — parties not attaining 3 percent of the national valid vote will not be permitted to "operate" in the Congress; those elected by these parties will be allowed to take their seats and choose another party label. The law did, however, impose strict norms for parties to present candidates for president and governor in 1994 — a minimum of 3 percent of the Chamber of Deputies or respective state assembly. This provoked massive party switching and "switch buying" to the tune of tens of thousands of dollars and resulted in the expulsion of three deputies involved in such practices to "inflate" the ranks of the minuscule PSD.

Consequences in 1994

The provisions of Law No. 8713 had little effect on the 1994 elections. The election bonus mechanism for controlling campaign contributions proved useless, as the results were not honored for income tax deductions. The Partido Liberal (PL) presidential candidate resigned when the press (not the Federal Police or the TSE) discovered that his campaign was selling inflated bonuses. Each party duly submitted its financial balance sheet in December 1994, one week before the deadline for certification of those elected, and, hence, the TSE was not able to analyze the latter's veracity. In March 1994, the STF struck down the 3 percent barrier described above for presidential candidates, and three minuscule parties (PSC, PRONA, and PRN) were allowed to field candidates.

THE "BUDGETGATE" CPI OR DEJA VU 1992

One reason for the swift action on the part of the political class to oust Collor in August-September 1992 was the fear that the loss of political control would drown a large proportion of the political elite in the "sea of mud," as explained by Barbara Geddes and Artur Ribeiro Neto in this volume. Thus, its members embarked upon a concerted effort to get rid of Collor as quickly as possible, sweep the mud under the carpet, and then finesse the aftermath to maintain as much of the status quo as possible.

On October 8, 1993, this strategy exploded with the spectacular accusations of José Carlos Alves dos Santos, former director of budget for the Senate, chief of staff for the Congress' Joint Budget Committee (1988-1991), and then-director of the executive branch's Bureau of the Budget (1991-1992). He accused scores of deputies, senators, governors, congressional staff, executive branch staff, and several of Brazil's largest civil construction companies of massive conspiracy and fraud in budget allocations for nearly all federally funded public works and services in Brazil since 1988. José Carlos, in effect, became the Pedro Collor of 1993.

Dos Santos' accusations initially generated a high degree of skepticism. Many considered them to be a smoke screen aimed at diverting attention from his alleged participation in the murder of his estranged wife. The allegations had also been previously superficially analyzed by some newspapers regarding the 1991 and 1992 budgets. The public clamor was such, though, that the Congress was forced to install another CPI, on October 20, 1993, to investigate what became known as "Budgetgate."

This inquiry picked up where the 1992 Collor CPI had left off and soon revealed a lurid maze of corruption and high-stakes influence buying. So massive and bombastic was the evidence uncovered by this CPI that its mandate was extended through January 21, 1994. This slowed down the calendar of constitutional revision by providing more ammunition to the "contras," a group of legislators opposed to constitutional revision, who argued that such a corrupt Congress had even less legitimacy than a lame duck one to be entrusted with such responsibility.

The committee used its powers to unearth a chain of corruption linking Congress, bureaucrats, and government contractors. On November 25, 1993, CPI members and Federal Police obtained a court order to enter the home of Airton Reis, regional director/lobbyist of the Norberto Oderbrecht Construction Company, and seized nearly 100 pounds of documents and scores of diskettes. The CPI's analysis of this new evidence revealed that Oderbrecht was the "CEO" of a "cartel" of construction companies that had manipulated nearly all public works in Brazil since 1988. Apparently, this "Mafia of the construction companies" had total control over the process of planning, budget, bidding, appropriating, and disbursement of government contracts. First, corrupt civil servants within each respective ministry or federal agency would articulate the budget planning stage with the cartel, even before the budget reached the Congress. Then, within the congressional Joint Budget Committee, the president [Deputy João Alves (PPR-BA), later Deputy Ricardo Fiuza (PFL-PE), and finally Senator Renato Aragão (PMDB-RO)], together with the respective reporter and subreporters — nicknamed "the Seven Dwarfs" — made sure that the previously established scheme was maintained or enhanced. Finally, upon approval of the annual budget, the cartel's agents in the respective federal agencies of the executive branch would intervene again to rig the bidding process in favor of the company designated by the scheme, complete with a designated loser to "protest" (Krieger, Rodrigues, and Bonassa 1994; Rodrigues 1994).

A related interview provided insight into pressures created by rampant greed within government circles. In an interview with TV Manchete on January 5, 1994, Justice Minister Maurício Corrêa revealed that in October 1993, President Itamar Franco was pressured by unnamed military and civilian elements in favor of a "Fujimorization" of Brazil, that is, closing Congress and the courts. This discontent had stemmed from frustrations with the massive corruption scandal, high inflation, low military salaries, and the vacillation of the judicial system with regard to prosecution of ex-President Collor and his "gang." According to Corrêa, President Franco resisted these pressures during the worst crisis of his government (*Folha de São Paulo* 1994, 1-9).

Such revelations lifted veils of immunity and protection to an unprecedented degree. After 94 days of investigations, 219 persons and entities had their bank secrecy lifted, and 77 persons were subpoenaed for testimony before the CPI. Of the 43 politicians who were formally investigated, the CPI's 600-page final report recommended that 18 members of Congress be expelled, 14 be subjected to further investigation by the Congress and federal prosecutor's office, and 11 receive a *nil obstat* [no objections] (*Istoé* 1994, 39-54). Of the 18 Brazilian legislators recommended for expulsion, four resigned and only seven were sacked, and the Chamber of Deputies decided not to conduct further investigations of the other 14 deputies.

Even so, this was the first time that a national legislature had proposed to expel such a large number of its members for alleged corruption.

Attempted Constitutional Revision

These actions were bold and highly contentious. They stirred more controversy regarding the timing and convenience of the constitutional revision, given the results of the plebiscite and the fear of many groups that their basic social rights might be aborted. While the Congress finally installed the revision on October 6, one day after the date mandated by the 1988 Constitution, the explosion of the Budgetgate CPI stalled approval of the internal rules until late November. This delayed the opening of voting on the first 16 synthesis reports prepared by the general reporter, Deputy Nelson Jobim (PMDB-RS), until January 26, 1994, before the finalization of the expulsion of those accused of corruption by the Budgetgate CPI (Jobim 1994). Inspired by the swirl of corruption revelations, Deputy Jobim decided to present the political reform measures first, some of which were in line with the recommendations of the CPI final report.

The eventual results of this process were less than inspiring, nevertheless, as all parties were fearful of enacting major constitutional changes in an election year. The only major reform approved was the reduction of the presidential mandate from five to four years and several other minor changes.

PROPOSALS FOR POLITICAL REFORM

The climate of reform was still in the air, and many hoped that popular support for major reforms would prompt lasting changes in Brazil's political systems. In particular, nine areas of the political reform analyzed below involve modifications by constitutional amendment or ordinary legislation and would have led to smoother operation of a moderate, balanced presidential system. Some were embodied in amendments proposed in 1995, and a special "blue-ribbon" study group commissioned by the TSE proposed others.

The Election System

The Congress first adopted proportional representation (PR), as currently known in Brazil, in 1932, but the onset of the *Estado Novo* delayed its implementation until it was incorporated into the Constitution of 1946. Brazil's system is one of a few that adopt the "open list" variant, the worst possible form of PR. Under this variant,[2] potential candidates who are not permanently associated with a party label spend private fortunes to sway the voters. There is no debate among parties for legislative office, and the political parties emerge from the elections torn to pieces by a total lack of cohesion and solidarity among those elected. Instead of fostering political competition and debate among parties, this system encourages competition and conflict among "colleagues" on the same party slate. Other candidates on the same slate become the candidate's worst enemies by employing a variety of disloyal and despicable tricks to win the election and reduce the "colleague" to alternate status.

Any serious political reform should at least contemplate modifying the PR system to use closed and blocked lists, so that the voter is only allowed to vote for the total party list and does not have the option of selecting individual candidates. In this case, parties would have to commit themselves to a preordered list filed with the election court prior to elections. Parties would be free to use any method of choosing and ordering their candidate lists, such as primaries, executive committees, or party conventions. The level of campaigning would be elevated from the sad, 15- to 20-second spectacle of "vote for me" every other night on television to a more responsible debate among parties committed to programs, platforms, ideas, and policy proposals.

Some of these features were present in three alternatives for election system change discussed initially by the Brazilian Congress in 1995 but, as of early 1998, have not been adopted. These would 1) maintain the current PR system, with the adoption of closed lists; 2) adopt a single-member district system; or 3) adopt a "mixed" PR and district system, similar to that used in Germany. The "pure" single-member district system apparently has little chance of passage, so the debate focused on choosing between a "perfected" pure PR system and a "mixed" system. Although a perfected pure PR system would be a definite improvement, a variation on the German system — the mixed system — would tend to maximize the positive points and minimize the negative aspects of both "pure" systems (district and PR).[3]

The mixed system provides results that are strictly proportional and gives voters more power to remove a "nonperforming" deputy, either by the ballot box or through a recall. It would also avoid the "outsider/carpetbagger" who "parachutes" into a region where he/she has no political ties, money bags in hand. No municipality goes without representation under this system, and the relationship between voter and deputy would be strengthened. It also would have accommodated deputies with well-defined pseudo-districts and those with a more dispersed voting pattern. Finally, it would have given small parties a fighting chance, while greatly strengthening the party mechanism itself.

Instead of adopting these changes, the Brazilian Congress has thus far approved only several minor changes to the PR system, including a quota for female candidates for proportional office. Parties were obliged to have at least 20 percent women candidates on their lists for city council in 1996, and this was expanded to 25 percent for state and federal deputy races for 1998. In 1996, there was a slight increase in women elected to city councils, up from 7.6 percent in 1992 to 11.2 percent in 1996. Also, for the first time since proportional representation was introduced in its present form in the mid-1940s, blank votes will no longer be included in the calculations in proportional representational elections, starting with the elections for federal and state deputy in 1998. This leads to the expectation that a smaller total of valid votes will lower the election quotient substantially, perhaps as much as 40 percent lower than the 1994 elections, because traditionally at least 50 percent of the voters cast blank votes for deputy. Small parties expect that they will benefit, as fewer seats will be distributed by the "remainders."

Election Legislation

Another important imperative for Brazil to become an effective representative democracy is to eliminate or severely reduce the great regional inequalities in the Chamber of Deputies by adopting an apportionment system based upon "one-person, one-vote." The current system that underrepresents the more populous, generally more developed, states (mostly in the Center-South) and greatly overrepresents the less populated and underdeveloped states (of the North and Northeast) was first adopted by Congress in 1936 and put into practice in the Constitution of 1946.[4] Fearful of repeating the earlier political dominance of the two most prosperous and populated states (São Paulo and Minas Gerais), the smaller peripheral states took full advantage of their absolute majority within the hegemonic PSD in the 1946 assembly. They imposed their will regarding minimum delegation size (favoring the small states) and progressive representational brackets, resulting in a severe underrepresentation for the larger units. During the military years, the system was further skewed by raising minimum delegation size to eight deputies and placing a limit on São Paulo at 60 deputies. During the Constituent Assembly of 1987-1988, São Paulo achieved an important victory. The peripheral northern region was awarded 16 new deputies and nine senators, and São Paulo's "cap" was increased by 10 to 70. In practice, however, the TSE and STF disavowed this article in the 1988 constitution and, while allowing the increased representation for the North, maintained São Paulo at 60 deputies for the 1990 general elections because of the lack of "enabling legislation." However, in 1994, São Paulo finally was allowed to elect 70 deputies.

Even this increase leaves the São Paulo residents grossly underrepresented. With 23 percent of Brazil's population, São Paulo is represented by only 13.6 percent of the Chamber's 513 deputies. Eleven small states are overrepresented; each has less than the 1.6 percent of population that would entitle them to eight deputies. The worst case is the newly emancipated state of Roraima, which elects eight deputies (1.6 percent of the Chamber), with a mere 0.08 percent of Brazil's population. This system allocates one deputy to São Paulo for every 534,850 residents, while Roraima elects one deputy for every 14,500 residents, making the vote of one citizen in Roraima 36.9 times more powerful than the vote of one *paulista.*

Finally, the system is further distorted by elevating the power of conservative politicians from these underdeveloped, overrepresented states in the North and Northeast, where political and economic manipulation of the mass of poor voters by local elites is strongest. Such opportunities encourage members of economic elites from the more developed South to become northern-bound carpetbaggers, where their political campaign investments pay much higher election dividends. Votes are much cheaper in the North than in the South, campaign expenses are generally less, and one's political clout is greater than elsewhere.

Politicians from São Paulo pressured the Congress to modify this system before the April 21, 1993, plebiscite, arguing that the current misapportionment would make a parliamentary system less viable, if adopted, and would discourage many southern voters from choosing the parliamentary system of government if the election system were not changed. Recently, several southern states have taken this case to the STF, alleging that the current skewed system violates their basic human rights of political equality.

Reforms designed to overcome this malady aim at increasing São Paulo's Chamber delegation to 112 deputies, reducing the small peripheral states to one, and reapportioning the seats allocated to the states falling in between. This mission is not as impossible as it might seem at first glance. Legislators from states that would either gain seats or not lose any constitute over three-fifths of the Chamber and nearly an absolute majority in the Senate. Since constitutional revision was decided by an absolute majority of the Congress in 1993 and 1994, such a change might have been possible (*Jornal do Brasil* 1993, 4). However, as of early 1998, the skewed representational system installed by the 1988 Constitution remained in place.

Reinforcing positive features of current election legislation that have made inroads toward controlling most blatant forms of corruption could complement these reforms. Extending laws of ineligibilities to exclude relatives of office holders from candidacy, preventing tax evaders from becoming candidates, imposing stiffer (two- or three-year) residency requirements for candidates, and reinforcing longer grace periods for prior resignations for potential candidates would curb abuses in the current system. Prohibiting changes in party affiliation within two years prior to election and requiring public access to the "Declaration of Patrimony" upon entering and leaving office would also discourage opportunism.

At the heart of any reform of election legislation is the critical need for stiffer rules and better controls over campaign financing. In the general elections of 1986, 1990, and 1994, huge personal fortunes were expended; many of these fortunes were based on abuse of private and public economic power, with some candidates for federal deputy spending over US$4 million. In 1993, São Paulo's courts and federal income tax service began investigating the Paubrasil Company, used as an intermediary "cash box" for financing several million dollars of campaign expenses for Paulo Maluf's successful mayoral campaign in 1992. These "contributions" had come from dozens of São Paulo businesses that had skimmed funds from their double bookkeeping schemes. Early findings quickly mushroomed to scandalous proportions, creating what became known as the "Paubrasil Scandal" in 1993 and 1994.

Maluf's party, the PPR, then countered by promoting a CPI of the CUT labor federation (Central Unica dos Trabalhadores) that allegedly had served as the Workers' Party's (Partido das Trabalhadores — PT) cash box for Lula's 1989 campaign and the PT's 1990 and 1992 campaigns. In addition to this CPI, two others were called for in 1994: to investigate campaign financing generally and to investigate corruption by the large construction companies. Both of these investigations were direct consequences of the Budgetgate CPI, but only the CPI to investigate the construction companies was installed, presided over by Senator Pedro Simon.

Reforms focusing on campaign financing must endow the TSE and the Regional Electoral Tribunals (Tribunais Regionais Eleitorais — TREs) with legal powers to monitor and control the abuse of private and public economic power in elections. These powers would include the right of election courts to examine bank accounts of candidates, their relatives, campaign treasurers, and associates; authorization for courts to cancel individual candidacies and/or whole party slates during the campaign, rather than waiting for prosecution after the election is over; the creation of pragmatic limits on individual and corporate campaign contributions; requiring a public record of campaign contributions; limitations on the amount of contributions that could be deducted from the donor's income tax; an obligation for election courts to monitor "ostentatious campaign expenditures"; authorization for courts and federal police to inhibit the use of U.S. dollars and gold in campaign finance; and creation of a federally financed party fund that would be allocated based on votes received per party in the previous election. This would discourage "dwarf parties" and "party labels for hire," thus reducing the fractionalization inherent in the current system (Fleischer 1993, 243-259).

Electoral reform had made little progress by the 1998 elections, despite the impression that it might have prospered in the initial stages of the 1994 constitutional revision. Delegates proposed changes to Article 14 — Political Rights — that would have made voting optional rather than obligatory; allowed those holding office in the executive branch, including mayors, governors, and the president of the republic, to continue in office rather than resign to be candidates for elected positions; extended ineligibility for candidacy to public servants involved in corruption scandals; and expanded the period for legal challenges to those elected from 15 to 60 days. Other reforms would have changed Article 55, which sets the conditions for deputies and senators to lose their positions, to strip elected politicians who decide to change party affiliation of their mandate, and to make them ineligible for two years. It also recommended major changes in Article 82, setting the presidential terms of office. One constitutional reform that was approved allowed mayors, governors, and the president of the republic to be reelected to one consecutive term. While this was passed too late to benefit mayors elected in 1992 for the 1996 municipal elections, it did allow the incumbent president and 27 governors elected in 1994 to run for election in 1998. Another change reduced the presidential mandate from five to four years with far-reaching implications, since it made all subsequent presidential, congressional, and state government mandates coincide. Finally, the introduction of voting machines has reduced the opportunity for electoral fraud (a significant factor in the 1994 election in Rio de Janeiro) and accelerated the vote tally. In 1996, the electoral tribunal successfully tried out electronic voting machines in the 51 largest cities. Fewer blank ballots were cast by voters using the machines, thereby possibly decreasing the potential impact of the decision not to count blank votes in the proportional calculation as discussed above.

Political Immunity

Perhaps one of the most difficult political reforms for Congress to pass would eliminate its own members' current total immunity from prosecution in return for immunity from "political crimes" only. This drastic measure would be designed to prevent extraordinary cases of abuse that have proved severely embarrassing to the Congress. An especially prominent case involved a notorious drug trafficker arrested in São Paulo in 1992 using a false staff ID card from the Chamber of Deputies issued by the office of his brother, Deputy Jabes Rabelo (PTB) from Rondônia, one of the more notorious drug trafficking states. Under severe popular pressure, and with great reluctance, the Chamber decided by secret ballot to strip his immunity and mandate, so that he could stand trial for common crimes.[5]

This case and the recent CPI on drug trafficking in Brazil have led many political observers to speculate regarding the connection between campaign financing and the search for immunity from common crimes. In Brazil, criminals trying to remain one step ahead of the law often invest heavily in getting elected to legislative office, thus gaining four or eight years of immunity. A case in point appeared on the Roraima-Brasília-São Paulo axis, involving Wagner Canhedo, a notorious entrepreneur in Brasília who bought a majority holding in the privatization of the VASP airline, allegedly with tainted money from the stockpile accumulated by President Collor and his corrupt associates. In 1990, Canhedo wisely financed a husband-wife duo for governor and senator, respectively, in Roraima, the smallest state in Brazil, where "election investments" pay high dividends. Both husband and wife were elected, and Canhedo was discreetly elected the alternate of the wife-senator.

In the meantime, Canhedo was also indicted under the VASP scandal investigations that stemmed from the revelations of the P.C. Farias/Collor scheme, leading political observers in Brasília to speculate as to when the senator-wife will be called to an "important administrative position" in Roraima. This would vacate the Senate seat for Canhedo to occupy until 1999, with total immunity from prosecution.

In February 1995, the question of parliamentary immunity again plagued the Congress. Freshman Senator Ernandes Amorim (PDT-RO) was selected fourth secretary of the Senate. Newspapers soon revealed that he had several scores of unresolved indictments, including some for drug trafficking that had gained him a citation in the *Encyclopedia Britannica*. The Senate decided to investigate its new colleague, who took temporary leave from his post.

Parliamentary immunity has been recognized as a problem, but little progress has been made toward an effective reform. The general reporter of the constitutional revision, Deputy Nelson Jobim, called for a severe reduction in parliamentary immunity. His report proposed that the STF be able directly to indict, prosecute, and convict members of Congress without prior consent of their respective houses. The Congress would be able to cancel such cases, however. The Budgetgate CPI, meanwhile, recommended that all officials automatically lose their bank account secrecy prerogatives upon assuming elected office.

The lack of success of even these measures has been dismaying. Without effective curbs on immunity, congressional positions will continue to be seen as impenetrable shields for the corrupt and corruptible. Regular federal courts should be granted jurisdiction over members of Congress and their staff who have committed common crimes, and the houses of Congress should not be allowed to interrupt proceedings.

Party Legislation

Events of the last three decades have left Brazil's political parties in legal limbo, much to the despair of many parties and their lawyers. The 1970 Organic Law of Political Parties, a remnant of "authoritarian trash" from the military period, remains in effect. Despite its supposed rigor, it has proved ineffective to curtail abuses. For lack of enabling legislation to operationalize the new concepts regarding political parties in the 1988 Constitution, election court judges opt to use the Organic Law, while other magistrates choose to use the concepts in the new Constitution.

Reforms must deal with a multitude of problems stemming from the historic orientation of Brazilian political parties around a charismatic standard-bearer. New parties often rise upon the ambition of new political figures to compete with the relics of previous successful initiatives. Fractionalization of political power, incoherent party platforms, and the resultant voter confusion weaken the parties' contributions to the stable functioning of the democratic process.

A variety of solutions have been debated, and one — the 3 percent threshold rule — awaits final approval in the constitutional amendment process. Overall, new legislation should permit "responsible freedom" to organize political parties but at the same time inhibit the creation of "party labels for hire." This means removing the attractions favoring the creation of such parties — no attractions, no hire.

Imposition of the threshold barrier, along the German model, has gained favor within Congress. Under this plan, a party must surpass a minimum percentage of the popular vote (5 percent in Germany) to elect anyone and retain free access to television and the party fund. If the German norm had been in force in the Brazilian elections of 1990, eight — not 19 — parties would have been seated, and a very different ideological profile would have resulted in 1991. The Chamber Special Committee, which elaborated this new party legislation, adopted a 3 percent threshold that was approved on September 30, 1993. Insertion of any such barrier into the Constitution, as with any major change in party and electoral legislation, would greatly alter the logic of legislative election strategies in Brazil.

Foreseeing possible elimination of their party status, two very small parties (PST and PTR) fused over the weekend of January 30-31, 1993, to form a new Popular Party (PP). This new label attracted many deputies from other parties and was born with 37 deputies, making it the fourth-largest current party in the Chamber of Deputies. Similarly, three months later, the recently elected mayor of São Paulo, Paulo Maluf, engineered the union of his PDS with the PDC, thus making the new Partido Progressista Renovador (PPR) the third-largest party in the Chamber of Deputies, with 72 deputies. It was thought that the new PPR would receive additional "joiners" and displace the PFL as second-rank party by the September deadline, but the Paubrasil Scandal reduced the PPR's attractiveness.

A remaining dilemma faced by the party law "engineers" was how to separate the wheat from the chaff, that is, how to eliminate the party labels for hire but at the same time permit the survival of the authentic, historic ideological parties, most of which are minuscule. One suggestion was to grandfather them in with a clause exempting the historic parties that existed before a certain date. Another idea was to permit coalitions, or the operation of *lemas* and *sublemas* (primary and secondary party slates), as in the case of Uruguay. This system allows parties to field more than one candidate for the presidency or other elected offices. The candidate who receives the most votes in that party accumulates all the votes that were cast for candidates in his party, thereby allowing a candidate to win with only a small percentage of popular support.

Which parties are better prepared to compete in a closed list system? Table 1 lists the party label vote versus the total vote polled by the major parties in the 1990 election for federal deputy nationwide.

Table 1.
Party Label Vote, as Percentage of Total Party Vote for Federal Deputy, 1990 and 1994

Party	Percent Party Label Vote	
	1990	1994
PT	46 percent	33 percent
PDS/PPR	33 percent	02 percent
PDT	24 percent	05 percent
PCB/PPS	23 percent	03 percent
PMDB	18 percent	04 percent
PC do B	18 percent	02 percent
PSDB	10 percent	11 percent
PFL	07 percent	01 percent
Chamber Average	19.4 percent	8.3 percent

Source: TSE Data.

These data imply that the four major ideological parties — PT, PDS (now PPR), PDT, and PCB (now PPS) — based on the 1990 election results, would have been better prepared to compete in a closed list, PR election in 1994. However, the 1994 data show this not to have been the case. All parties listed, with the exception of the PSDB, received fewer party label votes in 1994 than in 1990, and even the PSDB increased only 1 percent, from 10 percent to 11 percent. The PT, although by far the greatest beneficiary in 1994 (33 percent), was greatly reduced from its 46 percent in 1990. This may have been due, in part, to the influence of the concurrent presidential election.

If a 5 percent barrier had been applied, eight parties (PMDB, PFL, PT, PDT, PSDB, PDS, PRN, and PTB) would have survived. By reducing the barrier to 3 percent, the PL would have been included. By further lowering the barrier to 2 percent, the PDC and the PSB would have survived in 1990. Even with a barrier as low as 2 percent, the PC do B and the PCB (now PPS) would not have survived. In both the 1986 and the 1990 elections, these two parties only elected deputies in coalition with larger parties, such as PT or PMDB.

In addition to the minimum 3 percent of the respective legislative body for a party to field candidates for president and governor and the loss of mandate for switching party labels, no other measures affecting the party system were considered by the 1993-1994 constitutional revision, with the exception of a possible stronger threshold for the PR system for the 1998 elections. A new Organic Party Law was passed by the Chamber of Deputies in 1994 and approved by the Senate in August 1995. The law maintained a weak barrier of 3 percent, which, if not surpassed, would prohibit such parties from "operating in the Congress," even though those so "elected" would be seated. However, the new Organic Party Law did adopt very stiff qualifying criteria for registering new parties. It also cut the quota of the party fund available to parties registering less than a 3 percent vote to less than R$3,000 per year and limited their free television time to only a few minutes per half-year.

Bidding Procedures on Public Contracts

This is one of the most "slippery" areas of governance in Brazil, where P.C. Farias's financial suction pump proved most effective and where oversight by internal control agencies and the Federal Accounting Court (Tribunal de Contas da União — TCU) proved most ineffective.

As with other reforms, recognition of the need for change has not led to rapid action. New legislation with provisions for independent technical studies, rigid criteria for prequalification of bidders, and transparent publication of the calls for bids, as well as the final results, was approved by Congress in 1993. President Itamar Franco then vetoed the bill and later changed the law by provisional measure *(medida provisória* —MP). The Budgetgate CPI then recommended that an independent internal control system be created to exercise strong control over the bidding process on public contracts together with strengthened oversight committees in the Congress. In response to the Budgetgate CPI recommendations, President Franco appointed a Special Executive Branch Investigating Commission (Comissão Especial de Inquérito — CEI), headed by General Romildo Canhim, that produced a substantial preliminary report in December 1994 (Comissão Especial 1994). The commission detected severe corruption problems in the Ministry of Transport, but before its task was completed, President F.H. Cardoso abolished the CEI in January 1995. It remains to be seen whether effective controls will function in practice.

Federal Accounting Office

The lack of independent auditors continues to leave Brazilian government ministries at risk for fraud and political manipulation. The internal auditing agencies within each ministry, autarky, or state enterprise are politically subservient to their respective minister or director; thus, no audits can be concluded that contradict the interests of the minister. Likewise, the TCU apparently cannot conclude any audits that run counter to the political and economic interests of the TCU's own ministers (judges).

A flagrant example of the weakness of self-regulation occurred in the middle of the Collor impeachment proceedings. In mid-December 1992, while the president of the TCU was on a leave of absence, the vice president suspended a colleague for reporting out an audit at the direct request of two other TCU judges whose economic interests in their home states were "maligned" by the report. This unprecedented case became even more unusual when the offended TCU judge threatened to appeal to the Supreme Court, seeking redress to have himself restored to the case and thus be allowed to report his audit's findings. With perfect timing, the TCU president reassumed his duties just in time to negotiate a "diplomatic" solution. In January 1994, despite this seamy episode, the same vice president assumed the presidency of the TCU.

This case prompted the professional association of fiscal auditors to propose that the constitutional revision include a complete reform of the TCU, eliminating TCU judges and establishing a professionalized Federal Accounting Office (Auditoria Geral da União — AGU) along the lines of the Attorney General's Office (Procuradoria Geral da República) staffed by career professionals recruited by a public competitive examination. Such an office would have a director with an independent mandate and a bureaucracy totally independent from intervention by the executive or legislative branches of government (*Folha de São Paulo* 1993, 4).

The new AGU would be empowered with "teeth" and "claws" to conduct investigations of current accounts within the current fiscal year and apply severe penalties, similar to the operations of the General Accounting Office (GAO) in the United States. This would be a sharp contrast to the current TCU, which takes some 18 to 20 months to judge public accounting ex-post-facto. The new AGU could be empowered to investigate the efficacy of expenditures, beyond whether the money was spent properly within the law. It could also have the responsibility to judge whether the program's objectives were met and, if not, why not. The 1993-1994 constitutional revision did not make major changes in this area nor follow the suggestions made by the Budgetgate CPI. Subsequent constitutional amendments did not implement any of the recommendations of the Budgetgate CPI.

BUDGET ELABORATION

The 1988 Constitution achieved some improvement in this area by requiring the executive to propose a Law of Budgetary Targets (Lei de Diretrizes Orcamentárias — LDO) during the first half-year. The Constitution also stipulates that once Congress has debated and approved this law, by June 30, the second half-year — August 1 through early December of each year — is to be devoted to elaborating the detailed federal budget based on the targets contained in the LDO.

Serious problems remain, nevertheless. As in many presidential systems, the Brazilian Congress elaborates the budget in a very irresponsible fashion because it has no responsibility for executing the budget once passed. As in the U.S. Congress, where Senator Robert C. Byrd gave up the all-powerful Senate majority leadership to become chair of the appropriations committee, one of the most sought-after positions in the Brazilian Congress is a seat on the joint budget committee. In Brazil, leadership positions on this committee are rotated each year, so that many get a chance to participate. In 1991, the seven subcommittee leaders, all of whom were short, were dubbed the "Seven Dwarfs" by the press and dutifully produced a "dwarfs' budget."

Members of Congress introduce some 100,000 individual budgetary amendments each year without any monitoring by the parties, leading to some glaring abuses. In 1992, for example, investigative journalists discovered proposals for appropriations to construct sections of highway that had already been completed and were open to traffic. Any political reform of the politicians themselves and their political practices should include a reform of the budgetary process in Congress, especially if a "balanced" presidential system is adopted.

A prime target for reform would be the 120-member joint budget committee, called the "fourth house of Congress" because of its power. In the first half of 1993, the newly elected Chamber President, Deputy Inocêncio de Oliveira (PFL-PE), called for total overhaul of the budget process. In his plan, the regular standing committees of each house would examine the respective parts of the proposed budget in light of their normal monitoring function, substituting for the joint committee and its seven subcommittees. A newly created systematization committee would simply integrate and edit the work of the standing technical committees, leading to a sharp reduction in the number of individual members' manipulations of the annual budget. Unfortunately, by the 1998 elections, this call for reform had not been answered.

This inaction also ignored more stringent recommendations from the Budgetgate CPI, which called for a complete reorganization of the budget process. These suggested changes would eliminate the congressional joint budget committee; empower the relevant standing committee to consider respective sections of the budget; create a simple budget coordination committee to integrate the deliberations of the standing committees; reorganize budget planning and elaboration in the executive branch; prohibit budget amendments by deputies and senators; permit only standing committees, party blocs, or state delegations to submit budget amendments; and eliminate "social subsidies" allotted to members of Congress. Most of these recommendations pertain to the internal rules of the Congress, but some could be incorporated into constitutional amendments.

REORGANIZATION OF THE PUBLIC SERVICE

A nother fountain of opportunities for corruption and cronyism, and a necessary target for any reform movement, is Brazil's chaotic system of public service. As U.S. President Bill Clinton slowly decided on nominees for the 3,000 federal appointments he had to make, President Itamar Franco was even slower in naming the 50,000 plus appointments allowed the Brazilian imperial presidency. This system also stands in stark contrast to Western European parliamentary systems, where a change of party or coalition in government means a change of some 50 to 100 top bureaucrats at most in all ministries. The Brazilian president's discretion in the process is also largely unchecked. He must secure Senate approval for only ambassadorial and Central Bank appointments, whereas in the U.S. presidential system, for example, President Clinton had to submit 290 top appointments to the U.S. Senate for approval.

These nearly unmanageable opportunities for largesse contributed to the immobility of Franco's government. They also led to accusations of permitting holdover Collor appointees to continue their same corrupt practices in a more discreet manner. This large number of "confidence appointments" available to the Brazilian president, ostensibly for building his political coalition, is one of the principal reasons for lack of governability in Brazil.

Reform in this arena benefited from considerable support, especially among governors, for drastically reducing the number of these appointments and gradually filling the positions with professionals recruited by public examinations and promoted by merit through a well-organized, rational public career structure. An administrative reform amendment was finally promulgated on June 4, 1998. It is designed to reduce the government's personnel expense and make the civil service more flexible and efficient through a number of important reforms, such as imposing a salary ceiling, eliminating the constitutional barrier to firing tenured civil servants, and restricting tenure to those who have passed public competitive entrance examinations. Important changes include the elimination of permanent job stability for most civil servants and the imposition of a salary cap of R$12,750 on all combinations of public salaries and pensions. The amendment also divided public employees into two tracks, the "strategic nucleus of the state" (judges, prosecutors, diplomats, federal police, auditors, and tax agents, among others), who retain job stability, while the rest become "auxiliary public employees." It also allows management contracts, requires pensions in excess of R$1,200 to be progressively reduced by up to 30 percent, and sets retirement ages by a combination of minimum age and years of contribution.

System of Government

Reform proposals have not overlooked the larger issue of the nature of the presidency, raised by implication in the plebiscite of April 1993. Even though 66 percent of the voters favored maintaining the republic and only 10.2 percent preferred a monarchy[6] when asked for their preference regarding the form of government, nearly one-quarter of the voters favored a parliamentary system of government. The 55.3 percent vote for the presidential system and 24.8 percent for the parliamentary system, with 14.8 percent invalid and 5.1 percent blank ballots (*Folha de São Paulo* 1993, 1-6), suggest that many Brazilians would be open to a more efficient arrangement of checks and balances among the three powers that would avoid the tendency toward an imperial presidency that has plagued Brazil since the 1930s.

Reform proposals may weaken prerogatives granted the presidency by practice and law. Even under the "more balanced" Constitution of 1988, the Brazilian president still enjoys many more levers of power than his U.S. counterpart. These include the line item veto, the provisional measure, liberty to appoint nearly all executive branch positions without Senate approval, and many more (Brito 1993, 9). In 1994, Deputy Jobim included changes in the MP in his report on constitutional revision. The latter calls for severely limiting the occasion for use of the MP, prohibiting "reissue" of an MP, and extending the validity for consideration by Congress from 30 to 60 days.

Chances for reform were increased by the influence of disappointed adherents of the parliamentary system in the 1993-1994 constitutional revision process. They sought to revise the system of government into a very "mixed," moderate, or "mitigated" system, quite similar to that of France or Portugal, with a prime minister heading a council of ministers. The prime minister would be required to submit a "Plan of Governance" for approval of the lower house, with the possibility of censure of individual ministers by Congress. This would greatly reduce the powers of the presidency, relative to those accumulating to the legislature (Sartori 1993, 3-20). The possibility of a constitutional revision that would create a "mitigated," less imperial presidential system, with increased powers of checks and balances reverting to the Congress, gained strength in early 1994 when the PT candidate, Lula, led the preference polls but came to naught when Fernando Henrique Cardoso pulled ahead in polls prior to the 1994 election.

THE PRESIDENCY OF FERNANDO HENRIQUE CARDOSO

With his victory in the 1994 presidential elections and inauguration on January 1, 1995, President Fernando Henrique Cardoso has imparted a distinctive economic element to the constitutional reform issue. Such an emphasis is natural, given the prominence of Cardoso in the "Plano Real" stabilization elaborated by the economic team he coordinated in early 1994 when serving as finance minister. Cardoso resigned in April to become the PSDB presidential candidate, and "his" plan culminated on July 1 with the introduction of the *real* as Brazil's new currency. In practice, the Real Plan so successfully reduced inflation and prices in real terms in July, August, and September that Cardoso was elected by an absolute majority (54 percent) in the first round election on October 3, 1994 (Dimenstein and de Souza 1994; Saussuna, Novaes, and Novaes 1994).

Building upon the success of the Real Plan, President Cardoso proposed massive constitutional changes to reduce the role of the state in the economy, create conditions more favorable to foreign investment, effect fiscal reforms, reorganize Brazil's federalism, modernize state bureaucracies, and generally reduce the "costs of doing business in Brazil." In the long run, these changes may create enough new jobs to reduce unemployment and increase the rate of savings to the point where the federal government has more resources to invest in programs aimed at reducing said inequalities (Tavares de Almeida 1995, 88-108).

While this stabilization plan produced some deconcentration of income in its first 12 months, it also initially produced some unemployment and a slight economic slowdown. However, with the notable exception of the *Comunidade Solidária* program headed by First Lady Ruth Cardoso, in collaboration with IBASE President Herbert de Souza ("Betinho"), the new government has been slow to enact major social programs that might have an impact on the other social and economic inequalities mentioned above.

CONCLUSIONS

So, whither Brazil after Collor's impeachment, the recent Budgetgate episode, and Cardoso's first-round victory? What are the perspectives for consolidation of democracy over the next few years, by the year 2000, by 2010?

The prospects from a popular viewpoint are not very good. A 1993 survey asked whether a strong, perhaps military government could do a better job than the present civilian government. Over 40 percent responded, "yes" or "perhaps," with similar responses to questions relating to a return of the military to power. By contrast, favorable responses to similar questions in Uruguay and Argentina were generally less than 20 percent.

The plebiscite also revealed an underlying weakness of Brazil's democratic reform movement. Pre-plebiscite survey research indicated a very high level of ignorance about the purposes of the plebiscite and Brazilian politics in general. A full 68 percent could not explain what the plebiscite was about or describe the three systems of government under consideration. Only a very low percentage could adequately identify the basic concepts of a parliamentary system. Surprisingly, even after over 100 years under a presidential system in Brazil, only a slightly higher percentage could correctly identify the components of this system. Only a minuscule percentage could describe how a constitutional monarchy operates.

Even though many Brazilians remained uninformed about their preferred system of government, they would soon learn of the defects of its would-be leaders. The approval of the presidential system in the April 21, 1993, plebiscite prematurely opened the 1994 presidential race, with undeclared candidates Maluf, Brizola, and Lula (the same early starters as in 1989) launching stiff criticism of the incompetence and paralysis of the Franco government. These attacks were so pervasive they initially left Franco in a tenuous position in Congress, although he recovered in 1994.

Politics since the plebiscite has returned to a struggle among weak, competing parties that often seek alliances of convenience. Advocates of the parliamentary system who might have used their majority in Congress to weaken the presidency through the constitutional revision process that began in October 1993 were not successful. The drama of the failed presidency of Fernando Collor de Mello and the intensity of the 1994 campaign sapped their political will. Their inclination to modify the presidential system into a more moderate and balanced system, with enhanced powers for the legislative and judicial branches of government and significant reductions in the powers of Brazil's current imperial presidency, came to naught.

Politics in 1994 became dominated by a conflict between Brazil's Center-Right, better organized than in 1989, and its PSDB/PFL/PTB coalition that easily defeated the Left coalition (PT/PSB/PC do B/PPS/PV) led by Lula. The success of the Real Plan provided a big boost for the Center-Right; the struggle further weakened the party system (Abranches 1988; Garner 1992, 59-79); and party accountability vis-à-vis the electorate remains low or nil.

A broad lesson that can be drawn from the foregoing analysis is that Brazil's political system will become more effective only through a general improvement in Brazil's educational system. Education can also contribute to an increased individual autonomy, higher expectations of politicians and bureaucrats, and an unwillingness to remain economically and politically dependent on clientelistic political elites.

Finally, exactly the political class that puts political survival at the top of its agenda must approve new institutional arrangements described above. Pressures for change increased considerably in the immediate aftermath of the Budgetgate CPI investigations, only to subside thereafter. While sweeping institutional changes can be threatening, many politicians also see their political survival threatened by maintaining the status quo. They may take the risk of approving some parts of this political reform agenda in 1999-2000, when preelection pressures are more distant.

Perhaps the most difficult task in Brazil's slow and tortuous movement along Pathway IV (Figure 1) is the deconcentration of political, economic, and social wealth, with better distribution patterns for all classes and improved access to the outputs from the political and economic systems. Equally challenging is the task of providing less privileged classes with better knowledge and strategies regarding the operation of the input mechanisms. Only through effective inputs into the political system can they ever hope to secure policy decisions in their favor.

However, by 1997 and 1998, the public approval of the Real Plan, as well as of the Cardoso government, had diminished somewhat compared to 1995 because the government proved unable to approve a permanent tax and fiscal reform, except for a small austerity package approved in October 1997 in response to the Asian crisis. Thus, Brazil's public accounts have deteriorated and produced a high-interest, slow-growth, increasing unemployment combination by mid-1998. As a result, the economic components of the pathway toward consolidation of democracy, as depicted in Figure 1, have not improved. The consolidation of Brazil's political institutions and the long-term fate of democracy in Brazil, however, still depend in large part on the outcome of the unfinished constitutional reforms (political reform, tax/fiscal reform, judicial reform, revised federalism, among others) and upon internal rules changes within the Congress (CEBRAP 1994). It is possible that a new national constituent assembly, organized on a unicameral and absolute majority basis, may be convoked via plebiscite in 1999. Such a development would greatly facilitate the passage of these last, most problematic reforms.

Notes

1. However, this was not the first time that the Brazilian Congress had gone to the extreme of impeaching a president. In early November 1955, a political conspiracy supported by the then-Governor of the state of Alagoas, Arnon de Mello (father of Fernando Collor de Mello) threatened to impede the inauguration of Juscelino Kubitschek, elected by a plurality in a direct popular vote on October 3, 1955. The Congress voted for the impeachment of acting President Carlos Luz (PSD-MG), who was the president of the Chamber of Deputies, and the then-Vice President of the republic, Café Filho (PSP-RN), who had taken office following the suicide of Getúlio Vargas in August 1954. All this happened in less than 10 days, under severe pressure (in favor of Kubitschek) from the tanks of the War Minister, Marshall Henrique T. Lott, that had effectively occupied the streets of Rio de Janeiro. The next in line of presidential succession, Senate President Nereu Ramos (PSD-SC), was sworn in and governed under a state of siege until Kubitschek's inauguration on January 31, 1956. This was truly a much different "impeachment process" than that of 1992.

2. Open list proportional representation is a seldom-used variant that allows voters to vote for the party list or an individual name from one of the party lists. Because less than 10 percent of Brazilians vote for the party list and prefer to vote for individual names, this provokes severe intra-list competition and very little campaign dispute among parties. The closed list PR system obliges voters to vote only for competing party lists, which are rank ordered prior to the election when registered by each party. This way the competition is only among party lists, which provokes a real debate among the latter about issues and programs.

3. In 1994, Deputy Nelson Jobim reported in favor of a mixed system similar, but not exactly equal, to the German system. See Fleischer 1992, 186-197.

4. Contrary to common belief, these regional inequalities in Brazil's political representation were not imposed by the military regime (1964-1985).

5. A second deputy from Rondônia, Nobel Moura (PTB), was expelled as a result of the party-switching buyout described above. The Budgetgate CPI proposed two more from Rondônia for expulsion, Deputy Raquel Cândido (PDT) and Senator Ronaldo Aragão (PMDB), for a grand total of four.

6. Of votes cast, 13.3 percent were invalid, and another 10.4 percent of the ballots were blank. Because of a record 25 percent abstention, this means that nearly 50 percent of the electorate did not register a concrete opinion in the plebiscite of April 21, 1993.

CHAPTER 4

The Impeachment Process and the Constitutional Significance of the Collor Affair[1]

FÁBIO KONDER COMPARATO

At the time of the drafting of the Constitution of the United States, the idea that the president could be impeached and eventually removed from office by the legislature aroused more skepticism than enthusiasm. Reading the reports of the Philadelphia Convention, one is easily convinced that the founding fathers accepted impeachment for want of a better solution. They conceived of impeachment more as a deterrent than as an effective remedy against serious abuses of power. Jefferson called it a "mere scarecrow," (Rossiter 1987, 38) and Henry Jones Ford compared it to a "rusted blunderbuss that will probably never be taken in hand again" (Rossiter 1987, 38). Representative Theodore Sedgwick of Massachusetts asked if "the tardy, tedious, desultory road, by way of impeachment" must be traveled "to overtake the man who, barely confining himself within the letter of the law, is employed in drawing off the vital principle of Government" (Labovitz 1978, 24).

Eighty years later, the impeachment of President Andrew Johnson showed that this rusted blunderbuss could be a very dangerous weapon in the hands of a politically vengeful House of Representatives and a biased Senate. Modern times have shown the real power of the impeachment provisions. More than a century after the unsuccessful effort to impeach President Johnson, the Watergate affair demonstrated that this mere "scarecrow" could be truly terrifying for a president caught in flagrant misconduct. President Richard Nixon was forced to resign in order to avoid certain conviction on impeachment charges. In the fall of 1998, in the wake of the report by Independent Counsel Kenneth Starr, detailing President Bill Clinton's sexual misconduct with former White House intern, Monica Lewinsky, the U.S. House of Representatives voted formally to open yet another presidential impeachment inquiry.

Impeachment has had a similar history in Brazil. In 1914, after more than two decades of unpunished presidential misdeeds, Rui Barbosa, the principal drafter of the 1891 Republican Constitution, displayed his disenchantment by stating that impeachment, after all, was not even a museum gun but rather a pagoda monster (Barbosa 1992, 97). At the beginning of the Collor affair, Paulo Brossard, now a Federal Supreme Court Justice, concluded in the revised edition of his well-known treatise on impeachment that after one century of nonapplication since its adoption in Brazilian constitutional law, presidential impeachment was only "an institutional fallacy, pompous and useless" (Brossard 1992, 13). Nevertheless, to the amazement of all the political observers, President Fernando Collor de Mello was impeached by the Chamber of Deputies and convicted by the Senate by an almost unanimous vote, less than four months after inauguration of the proceedings.

This chapter provides a legal perspective on Brazil's impeachment process. It begins with a comparative analysis of Brazilian and U.S. constitutional law concerning impeachment. It next analyzes the significant constitutional and legal issues of the Collor case and concludes with a suggestion of how the existing systems of determining the political responsibility of governmental leaders might be improved.

A COMPARISON OF IMPEACHMENT IN BRAZILIAN AND U.S. CONSTITUTIONAL LAW

In 1889, those who overthrew the Brazilian monarchy declared in the first decree of the new government that they were installing a federative republic called The United States of Brazil. Brazil's first Republican Constitution was modeled upon the U.S. Constitution, especially with respect to the powers and responsibilities of the president. Despite the broad similarities between the U.S. Constitution and the Brazilian Constitution of 1891, Brazilian constitutional law on impeachment differs substantially from the U.S. model.

The principal difference between the two constitutional systems concerns the definition of impeachable offenses. The U.S. Constitution characterizes impeachable offenses as "Treason, Bribery, or other high Crimes and Misdemeanors" (U.S. Constitution, Art. II, Sect. 4). While the meaning of bribery is readily ascertainable, and the Constitution itself defines treason,[2] the meaning of the term "high Crimes and Misdemeanors" has always been controversial.[3] It has often been argued, most notably in the cases of Justice Samuel Chase, President Andrew Johnson, and President Richard Nixon, that an indictable crime is always a prerequisite for impeachment (Labovitz 1978, note 3, 38-40, 65-69, 91-100). During the trial of Chase, Joseph Hopkins contended,

> [T]he power of impeachment is with the House of Representatives — but only for impeachable offenses. They are . . . not to create the offense, and make any act criminal and impeachable at their will and pleasure. What is an offense is a question to be decided by the constitution and the law, not by the opinion of a single branch of the legislature (Labovitz 1978, 39-40).

This contention, however, has been consistently rejected by the U.S. Congress. In its proposal for the impeachment of President Nixon, the House Judiciary Committee bluntly stated that "a showing of criminality is neither necessary nor sufficient for the specification of an impeachable offense" (Tribe 1988, 293- 294). According to Professor Laurence Tribe, a distinguished U.S. constitutionalist, "high crimes and misdemeanors" is a category "closely analogous to the 'great offenses' impeachable in common law England," including "misapplication of funds, abuse of official power, neglect of duty, encroachment on or contempt of legislative prerogatives, and corruption" (Tribe 1988, 291).

The American framers intended impeachment to be a political rather than a criminal proceeding. In Alexander Hamilton's oft-cited words, "[impeachment] can never be tied down by such strict rules, either in the delineation of the offense by the prosecutors or in the construction of it by the judges, as in common cases serve to limit the discretion of courts in favor of personal security" (*The Federalist* 65). The ultimate sanction in impeachment cases is not a criminal but a political penalty, intended "to rid the government of a chief executive whose past misconduct demonstrates his unfitness to continue in office" (Labovitz 1978, note 3, 199). If it were a criminal penalty, the further liability of the convicted president to "indictment, trial, judgment and punishment, according to Law" would constitute double jeopardy.

The drafters of Brazil's 1891 Constitution followed a different path, influenced by a tradition concerning the criminal liability of ministers of state stemming from Brazil's monarchical Constitution of 1824. After indicating specific grounds for presidential impeachment, they provided that "said crimes shall be defined in a special law" [Brazil Constitution (1891), Art. 53, Sect. 10]. This feature was maintained by all subsequent constitutions. Brazil has enacted two successive laws defining impeachable offenses (*crimes de responsabilidade*) and establishing the procedural rules for trials of such offenses. The first was Law 30 of January 8, 1892; the second was Law 1079 of April 10, 1950, which is still in force.

Despite the apparent clarity of these constitutional and legal provisions, Brazilian legal doctrine still does not agree about the real nature of impeachable offenses. According to one view, despite the literal meaning of the constitutional provisions, an impeachment proceeding does not deal with crimes at all but with "political offenses, related to unlawfulness of a political nature, and politically sanctioned" (Brossard 1992, note 5, 74). The other view, adopted by the Supreme Court, especially in cases at the beginning of the century, is that impeachment is a mixture of both criminal and political proceedings (Brossard 1992, 83). The latter view is certainly the better construction. Impeachable offenses in the Brazilian legal system are indeed crimes and, therefore, in contradistinction to the U.S. model, are subject to the fundamental principle of *nullum crimen nulla poena sine lege* (neither crime nor punishment without law). However, these crimes, tried before a political branch and not before the judiciary, also have a political sanction.

The second major difference between the U.S. and the Brazilian constitutional law of presidential impeachment is that in the Brazilian system an impeached president is suspended from duty pending the outcome of his trial. During the Philadelphia Convention, a motion to that effect was rejected on the grounds, expressed by James Madison, that the suspension would put the president "in the power of one branch, which could, in order to make way for the function of another who will be more favorable to their views, vote a temporary removal of the existing magistrate" (Labovitz 1978, note 3, 16).

A third difference between Brazilian and U.S. law on presidential impeachment is the procedure in cases of ordinary criminal offenses. According to Article I, Section 3, of the U.S. Constitution, in cases of impeachment the accused is subject to indictment, trial, and judgment before the judiciary only after conviction by the Senate. It follows that if an accused is acquitted in an impeachment trial, he cannot be submitted to subsequent indictment and trial by a court.[4]

The Brazilian Constitution of 1891 adopted such a provision but exclusively in cases of presidential impeachment. Subsequent constitutions, however, plainly separated the political from the judicial jurisdiction: The former has to do with impeachable offenses (*crimes de responsabilidade*); the latter, with ordinary crimes committed by the president. If both types of crimes arise from the same misdeeds, the president shall be tried concomitantly before the Federal Supreme Court for the common criminal offenses and before the Senate for the impeachable offenses.[5] If he is charged only with an ordinary crime, he can be tried before the Supreme Court but only after due authorization by the Chamber of Deputies [Brazil Constitution (1988), Art. 51(I)].

The 1988 Brazilian Constitution expanded the list of impeachable officials beyond those identified in prior constitutions. In addition to the president, the vice president, the ministers of state, and the judges of the Federal Supreme Court, impeachment now also extends to the attorney general of the republic, the federal general counsel, members of the Superior Courts, members of the Federal Tribunal of Accounts, and the chiefs of permanent diplomatic missions. The president, vice president, members of the Supreme Court, the attorney general, and the federal general counsel are tried before the Senate. Ministers of the state are tried by the Senate only in cases of impeachable offenses related to those committed by the president. The remaining officials are indicted and tried before the Supreme Court. Thus far, however, Law 1079 of 1950 defines impeachable offenses only for the president, vice president, ministers of state, members of the Supreme Court, and the attorney general of the republic. Consequently, only these officials can be impeached under the present state of Brazilian law.

The major alleged difference with respect to presidential impeachment between the 1988 Constitution and all the former ones is a substantial change of procedure. The Federal Supreme Court has held that the Senate now has jurisdiction not only to try the president but also to indict him.[6]

This decision, based on literal understanding of the constitutional provisions, is completely unacceptable. If one were to accept this construction, Brazilian constitutional law would distance itself even further from the U.S. model. This interpretation is based upon Article 52(I) of the Constitution, which provides that the Senate has sole authority to "proceed against and to try the President" [Brazil Constitution (1988), Sec. IV, Art. 52(I)]. This is a very poor argument. Article 86 provides that the president, after having been "formally charged by two-thirds of the Chamber of Deputies," shall be tried before the Senate.[7] How can one deny that this decision formally charging the president is the real impeachment power according to the Anglo-American tradition? Shall the absurdity that the president can be impeached without having the opportunity to present a full defense be accepted?

Moreover, the Constitution of 1891, which was more akin to the U.S. model, contained a very similar provision: "The President of the United States of Brazil shall be submitted to proceeding and trial before the Supreme Court in cases of common criminal offenses, and before the Federal Senate in cases of impeachable offenses, after having been formally charged by the Chamber of Deputies" [Brazil Constitution (1891), Art. 53]. While that Constitution was in force, no one claimed that impeachment proceedings had to start before the Senate rather than before the Chamber of Deputies.

In the Collor affair, the proceeding was regulated concurrently by Law 1079, by the internal rules of the Chamber of Deputies, and by special rules drafted by the chief justice of the Supreme Court pursuant to his authority as president of the Senate during the trial. This led to a legal incongruity. The 1988 Constitution formally provides that the rules under which impeachable offenses are to be tried and judged shall be defined by a special law.[8] According to the Supreme Court, if that special law were partially impaired by the new Constitution, the president could not be impeached due to the lack of the necessary legal rules.

The initial complainants against President Collor before the Chamber of Deputies — the president of the Brazilian Bar Association and the president of the Brazilian Press Association — had to remain as parties even during the trial before the Senate, which was politically untenable. According to the British tradition, in cases of impeachment, the complainants act as representatives of the people. The members of Parliament bringing the charges against the impeached officer before the House of Lords declared themselves to be acting "in the name of the House of Commons, and of all the Commons of the United Kingdom." The U.S. founding fathers surely had this model in mind when they provided that the House of Representatives "shall have the sole Power of Impeachment."[9]

That is why in the Collor affair the complainants' attorneys, in accordance with this political principle, emphasized throughout the trial that they were acting on behalf of the Brazilian people rather than as personally aggrieved plaintiffs.

THE MAIN LEGAL ISSUES OF THE COLLOR AFFAIR

The Chamber of Deputies decided the impeachment of President Collor on two grounds: that he allowed, "expressly or tacitly, the breach of law and order"[Law 1079, Art. 8, (7)] and that he behaved in a way incompatible with the dignity, the honor, and the decency of the office" [Law 1079, Art. 9, (7)]. The president pled not guilty before the Senate. Repeating the customary plea in U.S. impeachment cases, he argued that an indictable common crime was required for impeachment and that he had committed no such crime. He also attacked the vagueness of the legal provisions, stressing that they failed to comply with the constitutional requirement of a previous definition of a criminal offense.[10] Since the major count of impeachment alleged that the president, while in office, had received large amounts of money from the former treasurer of his electoral campaign and that those funds came from acts of racketeering, Collor argued that his accusers first had to prove him guilty of bribery or that he was an accessory to his former treasurer's acts of racketeering.

In response to this plea, the accusers pointed out that the Brazilian constitutional system traditionally has made a clear-cut distinction between common criminal offenses and impeachable offenses. The former are duly defined in the

Criminal Code and are tried and punished by the courts; the latter are defined by a special law and, if committed by the president, are tried and punished by the Senate. Even under U.S. law, which lacks precision on this matter, the decisions recognize that a serious moral misdeed, even if it is not an indictable crime, may constitute an impeachable offense.[11] Furthermore, the accusers pointed out that vague phrases and concepts such as an "honest woman" or a "futile motive" can be found easily in the Brazilian Criminal Code. Such vagueness has never prevented the criminal courts from reaching convictions. Finally, the accusers showed that a federal statute considers receipt of any kind of unofficial benefits by a civil officer an act of improbity, even if the facts do not constitute bribery. In any event, this argument by the president became meaningless as soon as he was formally accused by the attorney general of the republic before the Supreme Court of having accepted bribes and participating in a criminal association.

The second main legal issue during the trial arose from the president's request to disqualify more than one-third of the senators because they were allegedly prejudiced against him. Some were said to be his political enemies; others had served as members of the parliamentary investigatory committee whose final report was the official ground for the impeachment voted by the Chamber.[12] The chief justice, who presided over the trial in the Senate, dismissed this request. Since he had no right to appeal, the president applied for a writ of security in the Supreme Court to overrule the decision. The Supreme Court rejected the president's petition on two grounds. First, the contention that certain senators were allegedly personal enemies did not apply to this kind of trial, because the Senate is not a court of law but a political tribunal, where the distinction between adversaries and enemies is not always feasible.[13] The Court also ruled that under Law 1079, some senators having served as members of the mixed investigatory committee was not grounds for their disqualification.[14]

The president's excessive claim led to a legal absurdity. Since the Senate has the sole power to try a presidential impeachment and cannot pass judgment without the concurrence of two-thirds of its members, disqualification of more than one-third of the senators would have meant that the president would have enjoyed total immunity for political crimes.

The most delicate of all legal issues of the Collor affair arose from the president's decision to resign just before the start of his trial before the Senate. The session was immediately suspended, and the Congress formally requested information about the resignation in order to declare the presidency vacant and to swear in the vice president. At the reopening of the trial's session in the Senate, some senators asserted that the impeachment proceeding was already over because the Senate has constitutional authority to try only the president of the republic, not a former president whose resignation had rendered him a common citizen. They also argued that disqualification from the exercise of public duties for a period of eight years is an accessory punishment, which cannot be applied if the principal punishment, forfeiture of the office, can no longer be imposed.

It is undeniable that the mainstream of Brazilian doctrine supports the position of this group of senators.[15] The position of the authors who wrote when the Constitution of 1891 was still in force is understandable, because Law 30 of 1892 expressly provided that proceedings against the president, either for common criminal offenses or for impeachable offenses, should stop if he left office. However, under Law 1079 of 1950, which has no such provision, the argument is hardly acceptable.

There is no clear solution in U.S. constitutional law to this issue. The proceeding against Nixon in the House of Representatives was abandoned as soon as he resigned his office. Similar abandonments occurred in impeachment proceedings against federal judges. On the other hand, there is the well-known case of William W. Belknap, who resigned as Secretary of War in 1876, just two hours before the House was to consider his impeachment. Nevertheless, the House unanimously impeached him despite his resignation. According to the traditional view of the nineteenth-century writers, it was unlawful to proceed with impeachment after the resignation. Today, however, Professor Tribe supports a different opinion.[16]

The decision of the Brazilian Senate to reopen the trial after the resignation of President Collor and to convict him, thereby disqualifying him from holding any public office for eight years, was proper, regardless of one's view of the nature of impeachable offenses in Brazilian law. If impeachable offenses are considered real crimes, the defendant cannot, on his own initiative, preclude the penalty, unless the law so expressly provides. Yet, neither Law 1079 of 1950 nor the Criminal Code, which is the supplementary law in this matter, contains such a provision. The usual argument about the accessory character of disqualification to hold public offices is specious because Brazilian criminal law no longer distinguishes between principal and accessory penalties. Disqualification to exercise rights and duties is an autonomous penalty under the Criminal Code (Art. 44).

The argument that the Senate has no authority to judge an ex-president is illogical and proves too much. President Collor was indicted before the Federal Supreme Court on charges of accepting bribes. This is a crime that can be committed only by a public officer, and Collor was no longer a public officer after his resignation. Consistent with this argument, neither could the former president have been submitted to judicial trial because he was no longer a public officer.

If, on the contrary, the grounds for impeachment are deemed to be political or constitutional violations rather than criminal offenses, allowing the violator to continue to perform public duties is indefensible. Impeachment cases, as Hamilton pointed out, involve "those offenses which proceed from the misconduct of public men, or, in other words, from the abuse or violation of some public trust" (*The Federalist* 65). In a democratic government, how can a person indicted on such a charge by the legitimate representatives of the people once more be permitted to seek the votes of his abused countrymen immediately after resignation, to enjoy all the benefits attached to his condition of ex-president, or to be appointed to another public office?[17]

According to Hamilton, political responsibility "is of two kinds — to censure and to punish. The first," he said, "is the more important of the two, especially in an elective office. Men in public trust will much oftener act in such a manner as to render them unworthy of being any longer trusted, than in such a manner as to make them obnoxious to legal punishment" (*The Federalist* 70). That is why, in the impeachment system, the disqualification to exercise public duties is as important as the removal from office.

Furthermore, one of the fundamental principles of republican government is the accountability of all officeholders for their deeds. The idea that a public officer, particularly the head of the executive, could secure personal immunity for his wrongdoing by resigning from office when faced with imminent conviction on impeachment charges sounds preposterous.

TOWARD REVISION OF THE WHOLE SYSTEM OF POLITICAL RESPONSIBILITY

The Collor affair suggests that now is the time to revisit the delicate question of the liability of political rulers throughout the world. As in many other domains, England was the pioneer, elaborating the remedy of impeachment in place of the old bill of attainder, which was a "legislative act, directed against a designated person, pronouncing him guilty of an alleged crime, (usually treason), without trial or conviction according to the recognized rules of procedure, and passing sentence of death and attainder upon him" (*Black's Law Dictionary* 1951, 162). In comparison with the arbitrariness of a bill of attainder, impeachment is a very reasonable remedy, preserving the rights of defense and a fair trial.

During the Philadelphia Convention, Colonel Mason observed that "as bills of attainder which have saved the British Constitution are forbidden, it is the more necessary to extend the power of impeachment" (Labovitz 1978, note 3, 14-15). When these words were uttered, however, the impeachment procedure in England was already declining, due to the firm establishment of the parliamentary regime. In 1782, Lord North and all the other ministers left the government, simply because he had been censured by the House of Commons. The last attempt to impeach a minister in England took place in 1848 against Lord Palmerston. As Bagehot said, the case concerned "trifles."[18] Robert Peel proclaimed in the Commons, "The days of impeachment are gone" (Brossard 1992, note 5, 29). Since then, ministers are no longer prosecuted on criminal charges but are dismissed by a no-confidence vote.

For the French revolutionaries of 1789, the question of criminal liability of political rulers was high on the agenda. In Saint-Just's opinion, holding political rulers responsible was necessary for the public welfare, as "there are few men without a secret inclination towards wealth . . . [and] few men pursue the general good for its own sake" (Hampson 1991, 108). Restoration sharply diminished enthusiasm for the issue. Writing in 1815 on the monarchical constitution of the prior year, Benjamin Constant praised the wisdom of its provisions concerning the responsibilities of royal ministers, who "will be often denounced, sometimes charged, seldom convicted, and almost never punished" (*Oeuvres* 1957, 173). Actually, since the end of the eighteenth century, no French chief of state has ever been charged, and no minister on duty has ever been convicted.[19]

Introduction of parliamentary government replaced criminal liability of political rulers with dismissal through a no-confidence vote. Some contemporary parliamentary constitutions, such as the German Basic Law (*Grundgesetz*) of 1949, do not even provide for criminal liability of government members. According to the Italian Constitution of 1947, the president of the republic is not liable for acts within the scope of his duties, except in cases of treason or breach of the Constitution.[20] Italian ministers may be indicted on criminal charges by the Chamber of Deputies and tried before the Constitutional Court [Italy Constitution (1947), Art. 96]. Thus far, however, no president of the republic has been accused. Despite the recent wave of judicial investigations against dozens of politicians, no minister on duty has ever been indicted.

The French Constitution of 1958 makes the president of the republic liable for acts within the scope of his duties only in cases of "high treason" [France Constitution (1958), Art. 68]. Some authors suggest that high treason might signify a serious breach of the Constitution, but they also point out that because the phrase lends itself to diverse constructions, it may degenerate into political responsibility, as was once the case with impeachment in England (Burdeau, Hamon, and Trope 1991, 729).

In Brazil, the monarchical Constitution of 1824 provided for criminal liability of government ministers, without acknowledging their submission to a vote of confidence by the Parliament. The formal structure of the parliamentary system was elaborated in practice.[21] Article 38 of the Constitution gave the Chamber of Deputies sole power to indict the ministers on criminal charges. Actually, the Chamber has never had to use this power, since the mere threat of indicting a minister produces his resignation from office.

Yet, it would be a mistake to believe that such a transformation of the criminal liability of government officers into parliamentary domination of the executive branch never occurs in presidential systems. For example, in Chile from 1970 to 1973, many of Allende's ministers were ousted by Congress through impeachment, utilized as a kind of no-confidence vote (Moulin 1978, 303-305).

Should one yield, therefore, either to this actual suppression of political control, prompting the impunity of the rulers, or to the continuous abuse of power by the legislature? Certainly not. The power to control all office holders, which entails both checking and censuring, is essential for the survival of democracy. As one distinguished author pointed out, this control power presently represents the best criterion of the political efficacy of all constitutions (Loewenstein 1957, chap. V).

At the dawn of the democratic regime in Athens, political control was held directly by the people, who had the equal right to question the rulers in the *ekklesi*[22] or to judge them in the *dikasteria*. This was, according to Aristotle, the very essence of citizenship.[23] Besides, public actions (*demosiai dikai*), civil or criminal, could be brought against an office holder before a *dikasterion* by any citizen acting in the name of the *polis*.[24]

The modern constitutional state was instituted on a very different basis. The people are not the government, as was the case in Athenian democracy, where the *ekklesia* was the official meeting of the people itself (*demos*), not of their representatives. In modern constitutional systems, the people elect persons to represent them in the government. That is why horizontal control within the government — the separation of powers — has become almost the only effective political control in the modern state. In the presidential system of government, which achieves the most rigid form of separation of powers, impeachment represents a good test of the effective control by the legislature on the other branches of government.

Today constitutes a third historical stage — the constitutional organization of the state. This third stage recalls the *Aufhebung* of the Hegelian dialectics, combining the good elements of the two precedent phases after the original direct democracy and the representative government of classical constitutionalism. In this third stage, the direct decision of the people acts as a corrective factor in the functioning of all branches of government, especially as to the liability of elected leaders.[25]

One of the major lessons to be drawn from the impeachment process of President Collor, the first presidential impeachment ever to result in a regular removal from office, is the decisive role played throughout by the people, particularly Brazil's youth. This group held center stage for three months, acting as a powerful pressure group, whose force was intensified by the mass media.

In accordance with this historical trend toward participatory democracy, one should consider ways of improving the system of accountability of political rulers, especially the chief officers of the executive. First, in order to avoid the abuse of power by the legislature, a clear distinction must be drawn between criminal and noncriminal liability. To avoid perennial arguments spawned by the loose U.S. definition of impeachable offenses, it is essential to distinguish ordinary from political crimes. The latter should be accurately described, in conformity with the constitutional principle of a previous legal definition of all crimes. With respect to ordinary crimes, one should dispense with the requirement of previous authorization by the legislature to proceed, whether the accused is a representative or a member of the executive. The requirement of prior authorization to proceed is an unjustifiable privilege. Moreover, any citizen should be able to bring a criminal action if the official prosecutor fails to start one within a given period of time.[26]

A certain number of issues concerning political crimes of chief members of the executive need to be reexamined. These include the capacity to be both prosecutor and judge, the rules of procedure, and the kind of punishment. There is no reason for withdrawing from the representatives of the people the prior capacity to prosecute the accused for political crimes. The rationale expressed by the framers of the U.S. Constitution is still irrefutable. The offenses in question, as Hamilton put it, "are of a nature which may with peculiar propriety be denominated POLITICAL, as they relate chiefly to injuries done immediately to the society itself" (*The Federalist* 65). The power to prosecute, therefore, should be "lodged in those who represent the great body of the people, because the occasion for its exercise will arise from acts of great injury to the community" (*The Federalist* 65). Yet the decision of the legislature to prosecute ought not to be hindered by a requirement of a two-thirds majority, as set out in the present Brazilian Constitution. Any citizen should be able to file a substitute complaint within a reasonably short time period following a legislative decision not to impeach, provided at least one-third of the representatives voted to impeach.

The U.S. solution of allowing the impeached president to continue with his duties during the trial seems dangerous, for the president has too many powers at his disposal, notably the powers to disburse public funds and to secure free access to broadcast and television networks. He can thus exert considerable pressure on public opinion, as well as on the people who will judge him.

The authority to try impeachments should be maintained in the upper house of the parliament in bicameral governments; otherwise, it should be lodged in a special high court.[27] Hamilton's arguments against giving the power to try political offenses to the judiciary are still powerful.

The Collor affair showed how important it is to simplify impeachment procedure, without undermining the right to a full defense. Strict application of the procedural rules contained in Law 1079 could easily have dragged out the preliminary process for six months, which would have been politically and economically disastrous for Brazil. The great majority of Congress was relieved by the ruling of the Supreme Court that several provisions of that law had been repealed by the new Constitution.

The last question to be reexamined regarding political crimes is the penalty. The constitutional text should be clear that the disqualification to perform public duties is not ancillary to actual removal from office. Impeachment should proceed even if the accused no longer holds the office, in order to disqualify him from holding public office in the future. Furthermore, disqualification to discharge public duties should be permanent, as it is in the United States, rather than temporary, as it is in Brazil.

Finally, with respect to purely political liability of public officers, one must go beyond the formal distinction between presidential and parliamentary systems of government and introduce an element of administrative rationality, which is normally required for business enterprises. In both systems of government, the top executive officers — ministers of state or cabinet officers — should be liable before the legislature not according to a no-confidence vote but rather for breach of a law on public responsibility, previously approved by the representatives of the people.

Notes

1. I am indebted to Professor Keith S. Rosenn, who carefully revised the original text and made important comments about the meaning of Article I, Section 3 of the U.S. Constitution concerning the possibility of indictment of the president before being impeached.

2. Article III, Section 3 of the U.S. Constitution states: "Treason against the United States shall consist only in levying War against them, or in adhering to their Enemies, giving them Aid and Comfort."

3. George Mason proposed this phrasing during the meeting of the Constitutional Convention of September 8, 1787, in response to Madison's criticism that "maladministration," the term originally employed, was too vague and would be equivalent to tenure at the pleasure of the Senate. Farrand 1937, 550.

4. Nevertheless, this interpretation of the U.S. Constitution has been rejected by several U.S. Courts of Appeal with respect to federal judges. See *Michigan Law Review* 1987, 420-463. For the argument that the U.S. president may be indicted prior to impeachment, see Freedman 1992, 7-68.

5. This was not properly understood during the impeachment proceeding of President Collor. The Mixed Congressional Committee's final report pointed out some ordinary crimes, besides the impeachable offenses indicated by the complainants. Nevertheless, when the attorney general of the republic charged the president, who was already impeached, before the Supreme Court with commission of ordinary crimes, it was deemed necessary to ask for the Chamber's authorization to proceed.

6. Mandado de Segurança 20941 of February 9, 1990.

7. Since the Constitution of 1967, elaborated under the influence of the military who had seized power in the coup d'état of 1964, the necessary majority for impeachment of the president, which according to the U.S. model had been one-half of the deputies plus one, was changed to a two-thirds majority.

8. Article 86 (sole paragraph) of the Brazilian Constitution (1988). This is a well-known principle of statute law reserve, stressed by German jurisprudence of the late nineteenth century (*Vorbehalt des Gesetzes*).

9. Hamilton acknowledged that the English system of impeachment was "the model from which the idea of this institution has been borrowed" (*The Federalist* 65). Addressing the North Carolina ratifying convention of the Federal Constitution, James Iredell asserted that the power to impeach "is lodged in those who represent the great body of the people, because the occasion for its exercise will arise from acts of great injury to the community, and the objects of it may be such as cannot be easily reached by an ordinary tribunal." Consequently, he concluded, "there are no persons so proper to complain of the public officers as the representatives of the people at large" (Labovitz 1978, note 3, 20).

10. Article 5 (XXXIX) of the Brazilian Constitution provides that "Unless defined in prior law, there are no crimes, nor are there any penalties unless previously imposed by law."

11. According to Professor Black, an example of a nonindictable impeachable offense would be a U.S. president moving to Saudi Arabia so that he could have four wives and proposing to conduct the office of the presidency by mail and wireless from there. Black 1974, 33.

12. This was another unfortunate consequence of the decision that the official proceeding had to begin before the Senate and not before the Chamber of Deputies. According to Law 1079, the investigatory committee should be composed only of deputies, who would not have to judge the president. When Congress decided to investigate the corruption charges against the president and his former treasurer made by the president's brother, the Congress decided to create a mixed committee, composed of both deputies and senators.

13. The accusers' attorneys refuted this contention by citing the opinion of U.S. writers, such as Charles L. Black, Jr.: "It must almost always be the case that many senators find themselves either definitely friendly or definitely inimical to the president. In an ordinary judicial trial, persons in such a position would of course be disqualified to act, whether as judges or as jurors. It cannot have been the intention of the Framers that this rule apply in impeachments, for its application would be absurd; a great many senators would inevitably be disqualified by it, and it might easily happen that trial would be by a quite small remnant of the Senate" (Black 1974, note 31, 11).

14. The Supreme Court chose which provisions of Law 1079 were to be enforced, but the rationale for this choice was not always evident.

15. See Barbosa 1933, 451-453; Cavalcanti 1924, 135-136; Brossard 1992, note 5, 99. The sole author with a contrary opinion under the 1891 Constitution was da Fonseca 1916, 86-87.

16. Professor Tribe wrote, "Although of course private citizens are not subject to impeachment, the resignation of a 'civil officer' does not give immunity from impeachment for acts committed while in office. Congress might wish to continue an impeachment proceeding after its target has resigned from office in order to deprive the resigned officer of any retirement benefits affected by the fact of impeachment or conviction; to solidify the lesson of the officer's misconduct in the form of clear precedent; or simply to make plain to the public and for the future that the resigned officer's withdrawal from office was the result not of unjust persecution but rather of the way in which the officer had abused an official position" (Tribe 1988, note 11, 290).

17. The resistance of U.S. legal doctrine to this political argument stems from two facts. One is the precedent of President Andrew Johnson's impeachment, which stressed the danger of miscarriage of justice when the House, after a period of serious political crisis, was largely dominated by one party. The other is that the U.S. Constitution imposes on the convicted a permanent disqualification for holding public office, rather than a temporary prohibition, as imposed by Brazilian Constitutions since 1934.

18. "Lord Palmerston was for once in his life over-buoyant; he gave rude answers to stupid inquiries; he brought into the Cabinet a nobleman concerned in an ugly trial about a woman; he, or his Foreign Secretary, did not answer a French despatch by a despatch, but told our ambassador to reply orally. And because of these trifles, or at any rate these isolated *un*-administrative mistakes, all our administration had fresh heads" (Bagehot 1872, 176-177).

CHAPTER 5

Collor's Impeachment and Institutional Reform in Brazil

AMAURY DE SOUZA

INTRODUCTION

The impeachment of President Fernando Collor de Mello on charges of having accepted millions of dollars in illegal payments is a reminder that presidential abuse can produce extreme counterclaims of congressional power. Collorgate was a political affair of extraordinary proportions. Collor was the first Brazilian president to be elected by popular vote in nearly three decades. Moreover, he was elected pursuant to a new double-ballot system designed to grant office holders undisputed legitimacy. Yet, the dashing 42-year-old president did not even complete the first half of his term. Mounting evidence connecting him to graft, tax fraud, and influence-peddling by his campaign fund-raiser, Paulo César Farias, crippled the effectiveness of a president elected on promises of throwing out the rascals. It also aroused the indignation of millions of citizens who flooded the streets in the largest demonstrations since the 1984 Diretas Já civic movement. Brazil's Congress set in motion for the first time in more than 100 years of presidential rule what James Madison called the "decisive engine of impeachment." When Collor resigned on the eve of his trial, Congress also stripped him of his political rights for eight years, almost as an act of revenge.

What has been the impact of the impeachment process on domestic political institutions and processes? Did it produce lasting changes in the actual distribution of power between Congress and the president? Did it attest to the capability of the political system to deal effectively with its own transgressions? Did it at least serve notice on future presidents that they must adhere to the rule of law? Or was Collor's impeachment the product of an unpredictable and highly unlikely configuration of events that left untouched or even aggravated the underlying causes of Brazilian ungovernability?

Collorgate, it will be argued here, resulted from unsettled institutional rivalries between Congress and the presidency that crystallized in the transition to civilian rule. After 1974, Congress was the driving force behind the redemocratization process, channeling intense plebiscitarian pressures from below to score spectacular victories against military governments in elections for the Senate and the Chamber of Deputies. In 1982, however, direct gubernatorial elections created an odd dyarchy in which the military executive and opposition governors began vying for power. This latent struggle culminated in the massive popular mobilization for direct presidential elections, the Diretas Já movement. Popular pressure for direct election of all executive offices seemed to indicate the public's preference for presidential government, leaving Congress to play a supportive role.

On the surface, the executive branch had apparently gained the upper hand in the political transition. In reality, congressional resistance to military rule and the public's desire to elect a president with sufficient authority to change the course of public policy led to a serious ambiguity. At the same time, people were demanding direct presidential elections and increasing their support of parliamentarism.[1] Sensing the undertow of public opinion, Congress and the executive branch have since clashed repeatedly over issues of the separation and balance of powers. The 1998 Constitution did not settle the controversy. On the contrary, it failed to separate clearly the powers of the legislature and the executive, thus rendering the latter unable to govern effectively. This, as Collor painfully learned, was the crux of the matter.

This chapter first describes how the 1988 Constitution greatly increased the vulnerability of Brazil's political institutions. Second, it discusses how the newly introduced constitutional provisions affected the 1989 presidential elections and the performance of the Collor government. Third, it highlights the exceptional character of Collor's impeachment process. Finally, it stresses the need to reform Brazil's institutional framework and speculates about the long-term impact of Collor's impeachment on the overall political system.

Institutional reform has gained new urgency since 1994, when Fernando Henrique Cardoso, a preeminent advocate of parliamentarism and of electoral and party reform, was elected president. More than any president in memory, Cardoso is uniquely poised to promote institutional change and to halt the drift of the political system toward institutional polarization and crisis. The real test of whether he can accomplish these formidable tasks is still to come.

INSTITUTIONAL STRUCTURES AND THE 1988 CONSTITUTION

In the past 10 years, generalized concern with Brazil's governability in the face of extremely adverse economic conditions has led many observers to question whether the institutional framework built since the 1930s is still adequate to tackle the challenges posed by modernization. That framework combines strong consociational elements in electoral procedures, the party structure, the legislature, and federalism with a popularly elected presidency that is supposed to make the whole system cohesive. This constitutional component is characterized, on one hand, by extremely permissive arrangements designed to provide easy access to party and congressional power and, on the other, by the concession of a virtual veto power to minorities "with the explicit intent of preventing majority groupings from dominating through sheer numbers."[2]

A key consociational element is the proportional representation system designed to secure the participation of small parties in the political process. Originally instituted by the 1932 Electoral Code, the Brazilian mix of proportional representation with elections contested in extremely large districts and with open party lists has traditionally led to party proliferation and rampant party disloyalty. Renegades constantly break away to form new splinter parties. Party cohesion has also been weakened by the possibility of entering electoral alliances with little regard for programmatic affinity. In addition, the absence of a rule excluding representatives from parties with little electoral weight undermines the building of stable majorities in Congress. Finally, smaller and less populous states are overrepresented in Congress as a means of attenuating the electoral strength of the larger states. This allows the executive to intervene in congressional politics, for representatives of the smaller and poorer states find it hard to resist the exchange of favors for support of the government.[3]

Superimposed on a highly fractionalized multiparty system, presidentialism bred a plebiscitary presidency claiming superior legitimacy over a fragmented legislature. This combination constantly weakened the fabric of politics. Between 1964 and 1984, the military government further strengthened the trends toward centralization and exclusion. In reality, the unprecedented concentration of executive power under the military made an equally radical shift of power to Congress a central tenet of the process of redemocratization.

Parliamentarism emerged in the mid-1980s as a pivotal element of institutional reform. In late 1985, President José Sarney appointed a commission headed by jurist Affonso Arinos to prepare a draft constitution. The draft delineated the broad contours of a full institutional reform, including specific recommendations for the extension of political rights, the overhauling of the electoral and party systems, and the adoption of a parliamentary system of government. Predictably, the Arinos commission's recommendations sought to strengthen Congress and the party system. It proposed a French-style dual executive model of parliamentarism, with a prime minister approved by Congress and a president elected by popular vote. The electoral system was to be reorganized along German lines: representation based on small electoral districts with a majority-*cum*-proportional electoral rule. To discourage party proliferation, it also recommended a threshold of 3 percent of the national vote for party representation in Congress. The constitutional draft of the Arinos commission so displeased President Sarney that he refused to submit it to the Constituent Congress.

Nevertheless, a strikingly similar proposal was brought to a vote in the Constituent Congress (1987-1988). Unfortunately, the issue of parliamentarism became inextricably tangled with an attempt to shorten President Sarney's term of office. On March 22, 1988, the parliamentary proposal was defeated by 344 to 212 votes. However, dissident members of the Constituent Congress succeeded in postponing a final decision on the matter by securing adoption of a transitory article in the 1988 Constitution requiring voters to choose between presidentialism or parliamentarism in a plebiscite scheduled for September 1993.

A piecemeal approach to institutional reform prevailed thereafter, with predictably disastrous consequences. Presidentialism was superimposed on a Constitution granting Congress a set of prerogatives that revealed the drafters' original intent to adopt a parliamentary system of government. To cite but one instance, the Constitution justifiably restored congressional power to approve and to oversee the budget but also empowered Congress to meddle in the organization of the executive branch.

Perhaps more important, the new Constitution established not only a stronger Congress but also a stronger presidential office. Presidential authority was strengthened in two major ways. First, the new Constitution required that presidents be elected by an absolute majority of the popular vote, with a run-off election if necessary to assure an absolute majority, thereby endowing the office with a commensurately greater measure of legitimacy. Second, to prevent the president from being harried into paralysis, the Constitution granted him the right to enact "provisional measures" to deal with "matters of a serious and urgent nature." The provisional measure is an executive decree that has the force of law. The chief advantage is that such decrees go into effect immediately. The main drawback is that they are automatically canceled if not approved by Congress within 30 days. Both Congress and the Supreme Court, however, have recognized the president's power to reenact a provisional measure after the 30-day deadline, unless the provisional measure has actually been rejected by Congress. Thus, the 1994 provisional measure creating the new currency, the *real,* was reissued 12 times before final congressional approval. In practice, therefore, presidents have been granted the prerogative to legislate by decree, hence weakening the role of Congress and blurring the separation of powers.[4]

Finally, as if to counterbalance the plebiscitary authority of the presidential office, the 1988 Constitution stretched to the hilt the consociational character of the system of political representation. First, the Constitution maintained the traditional principle of proportional representation in the Chamber of Deputies. Second, it exacerbated overrepresentation of smaller states in the Chamber of Deputies.[5] Third, it imposed virtually no restrictions on formation of new political parties, which increased from six to nearly 30 between 1985 and 1990.[6] Fourth, it greatly increased the power of state and local government by a dramatic redistribution of tax revenues from the federal government to the states and municipalities.

One year after the Constitution was promulgated, the belief that a plebiscitary presidency could act as a unifying force in the face of a powerful but internally divided Congress and a fractionalized party system was put to the acid test. The crisis that tested the presidency, as well as the other powers, was Collorgate.

THE MAKING OF COLLORGATE

M uch of the concern surrounding the outcome of the 1989 presidential elections stemmed from the gravity of Brazil's economic and political situation. The country teetered on the brink of hyperinflation. Throughout the year, polls registered dramatic shifts in voter preferences, as the public searched for a candidate who could bring the economy under control. Economic ills, however, were not the only factor behind the ebb and flow of public allegiances. Political volatility was also greatly intensified by the crumbling of the political party system because of overly permissive electoral laws. Party loyalties had never been as weak and fluid as they were in 1989, turning the presidential race into an almost exclusively personality-centered contest.

Such a scenario permitted Collor, running as the candidate of the National Reconstruction Party (PRN), a makeshift organization facing its first election, to emerge as the front-runner. A total of 22 candidates ran for office in the first round of the presidential election, backed by a disparate array of more than 30 political parties that had formed over the past three years.

The discredit into which the more established parties had fallen was reflected in electoral returns. As shown in Figure 1, Collor and Luiz Inácio Lula da Silva, who between them accounted for practically one-half the valid votes cast in the first round, were supported by parties that held only 5 percent of the congressional seats. In contrast, the presidential candidates of the parties that held 61 percent of the seats (the PMDB and the PFL) were unable to muster more than 5 percent of the presidential vote.

Figure 1.
Popular and Congressional Support for Candidates in the
First Round of the 1989 Presidential Elections
(Percent)

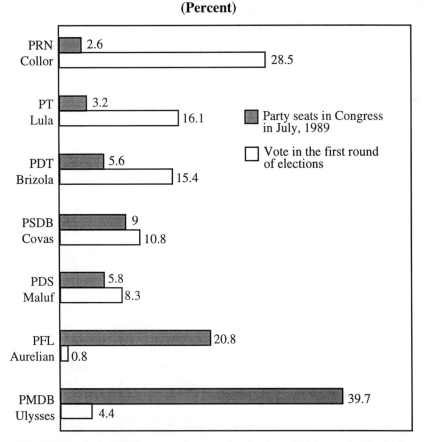

Note: Other parties held 13.3 percent of congressional seats, and 15.6 percent of the total votes were null or blank votes.

The run-off election led to a polarization of left and right, pitting the winner against an opponent of almost equal electoral weight. Vowing to rid government of the "maharajahs," overpaid and underworked public employees, and to implement bold free market economic policies, Collor generated intense and often unrealistic expectations.

From the start, ample popular support for a president with an extraordinarily precarious congressional backing raised serious concerns of an executive-legislative showdown. The first shock came the day after inauguration, when the government froze all bank accounts with balances exceeding the equivalent of about US$1,200 for 18 months in a draconian effort to halt the hyperinflationary spiral. Next, the regime embarked on an extremely ambitious program of economic deregulation and public sector reform.

Congressional reaction to the Collor government actually went through two distinctive phases. During 1990, the president's assertiveness raised fears of an overly powerful plebiscitary presidency. To accomplish much of his program, President Collor promulgated nearly 100 provisional measures, provoking concern that he intended to govern by dictatorial means. In early 1990, Congress was cowed by Collor's electoral victory and by the threat of hyperinflation. By mid-1990,

Figure 2.
Collor's Popularity Plunge, 1990-1992
(Percent)

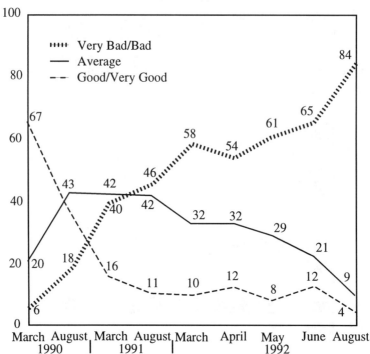

Source: Instituto DataFolha, surveys taken in the city of São Paulo.

however, resistance to Collor began to rise not only in Congress but also in the judiciary. In October 1990, the Supreme Court ruled that three of Collor's provisional measures were unconstitutional. Congress, exercising its power, refused to take another into consideration. By 1991, however, Congress had entered a second phase in which its main concern was the president's increasing political isolation and the rising threat of ungovernability (Lamounier 1991).

By early 1991, Collor had slipped badly in the polls. The return of high inflation, the decline in real wages caused by austere economic policies, and a string of scandals involving cabinet members caused his popularity to plunge.

Collor's popularity ratings, as shown in Figure 2, went from a towering 67 percent on inauguration day down to about 11 percent by mid-1991, setting a low mark that lasted to the day he was impeached. "Initial support," remarked Bolívar Lamounier, "was transformed into rancor in direct proportion to the expectations raised by the economic shocks" (Lamounier 1991, 194).

Collor's personal style and his loss of popularity during the first two years of the mandate clearly affected his credibility in Congress. A poll taken by the Institute of Economic, Social and Political Studies of São Paulo (Instituto de Estudos Econômicos, Sociais e Políticos de São Paulo — IDESP) between September and November 1991 found that only 6 percent of the 406 respondents (357 federal deputies and 49 senators) rated the Collor regime as "very good" or "good" (Lamounier and de Souza 1991). As shown in Table 1, the PRN tried to stand up for Collor but could muster the approval of only 48 percent of its legislators.

Table 1.
Congress's Evaluation of the Collor Administration,
November 1991*
(Percent)

Ratings	All	PFL	PDS	PRN	PTB	PMDB	PSDB	PDT	PT	Other*
Very good	1	-	-	10	-	-	-	-	-	-
Good	5	3	4	38	14	-	-	3	-	3
Regular	35	66	68	48	36	17	21	11	3	46
Poor	34	18	25	5	39	51	45	43	23	33
Very poor	24	10	4	-	11	30	33	40	73	16
No opinion	2	3	-	-	-	1	-	3	-	1

Source: IDESP survey of 406 members of Congress on September 25-November 11, 1991. The question was: "Generally speaking, and taking everything into consideration, how do you rate the performance of the Collor government in the first year and half of his term?"
(*) Includes unaffiliated members of Congress and members of small parties.

Unsurprisingly, disapproval was considerably higher among Collor's congressional opponents. The percentage describing overall government performance as "poor" or "very poor" ranged from 78 percent in the PSDB to 96 percent in the

PT. Even supporters were critical of his administration. Poor ratings were reported by nearly one-third of the PFL and the PDS and a full one-half of the PTB.

The IDESP poll also asked members of Congress to evaluate the performance of the Collor government in specific areas. Its inability to fight corruption drew the highest disapproval ratings (79 percent), followed by its failure to reactivate the economy (74 percent), reduce inflation (72 percent), increase wages (69 percent), and improve social conditions (68 percent). Disaffection also stemmed from the quality of Collor's relationship with Congress (69 percent), as well as from his flamboyant to abrasive personal style as president (52 percent).

The issue of corruption in government came to the public's attention as early as October 1990, when the Chief Executive Officer of Petrobrás, Luiz Octávio da Motta Veiga, was dismissed after accusing Paulo César Farias of influence-peddling. A series of scandals came to light in the subsequent year. In April 1991, the Minister of Labor, Antonio Rogério Magri, was accused of accepting kickbacks from public contractors. In August 1991, the scandal reached closer to home when the president's wife, Rosane Collor, was forced to leave the Legião Brasileira de Assistência, a public social assistance institution, under a heavy cloud of suspicion. In January 1992, the Minister of Health, Alceni Guerra, resigned under charges of approving shady government contracts.[7]

In an effort to halt the rising tide of accusations, Collor accepted the collective resignation of his cabinet on March 30, 1992. He then surrounded himself with respected members of Congress, the judiciary, and the professions, hoping to lend strength and credibility to his regime and to get off to a new start. Earlier, in a speech delivered on the anniversary of his second year in office, Collor presented an "agenda for consensus" centered around four main goals: strengthening democracy, investing in health and education, promoting economic modernization, and fostering public morality. "We are ending," he announced, "the cycle of impunity in the public sector." Both initiatives were greeted with cautious optimism in Congress.

Public reaction was mixed at best. A DataFolha survey taken in São Paulo in early April found that the cabinet changes had failed to improve the regime's image. Asked why Collor had changed ministers, respondents indicated that the main reasons were "accusations of corruption"(47 percent) and "the need to gain political support in Congress" (32 percent). Respondents also believed that there was now more corruption than under the José Sarney administration (51 percent) and that President Collor knew about corruption in government but did nothing (49 percent). Surprisingly, only 31 percent of respondents believed that Collor was personally involved in the corruption (*Folha de São Paulo* 1992a).

There were good reasons to believe that corruption charges might soon dissipate. The overhauling of the cabinet met with general approval in Congress. Confirmation of Marcílio Marques Moreira, a respected diplomat and banking executive, as finance minister signaled a commitment to more stable macroeconomic policies. Although the monthly inflation rate hovered above 20 percent, Minister Moreira was able to renegotiate Brazil's foreign debt and to restore the inflow of foreign capital. Collor was careful to stress on every possible occasion his desire to collaborate with Congress and to point out that his new cabinet included many distinguished members of Congress.

In light of these developments, Collor's impeachment was far from a foreordained retribution for past failures and missteps. Indeed, it came as a surprise to all. In Lamounier's words, it was the unexpected result of "a virtually impossible combination of five extremely rare circumstances" (Lamounier 1992b).

The first and the most fateful of these circumstances was that the president's own brother, Pedro Collor de Mello, was the first to accuse him. Indeed, a serious blow to the president was delivered on May 27 when Pedro Collor told *Veja* magazine that his brother was a hidden partner of P.C. Farias in illicit business dealings. Despite the seismic impact of these accusations, the odds still favored the president. Allegedly at the urging of his mother, a few days later Pedro Collor backed away from his charges against Fernando, focused his attacks primarily on P.C. Farias, and said that he had no proof of the president's personal involvement in shady deals. Moving swiftly to hush the scandal, President Collor sued Pedro for libel and announced that his administration would undertake a broad investigation of corruption.

The public uproar, however, forced Congress to set up a commission to investigate the charges. Even though many of Collor's opponents viewed the congressional investigation as a golden opportunity to weaken him or force him out of office, the ostensible target was P.C. Farias, not the president. Congress as a whole seemed to be unwilling to enter a direct confrontation with Collor. The scandal was expected to dissipate in a couple of months as public opinion grew once again complacent toward corruption. After all, argued his supporters, Collor's alleged campaign practices did not differ from those of other politicians. In addition, Vice President Itamar Franco was generally regarded as an unattractive alternative to Collor. Many viewed him as a backwater politician and feared that his well-known nationalist and statist inclinations might derail the government's economic modernization drive. Collor's Chief of Staff, Jorge Bornhausen, felt secure enough to boast that "the congressional commission will get nowhere."

The second circumstance was the extraordinary ineptitude of Collor and P.C. Farias in hiding their alleged corrupt activities. What Lamounier aptly described as "an exceptionally clumsy bunch of crooks" left behind an incredible amount of evidence of their scheme, such as canceled checks, computer programs, and witnesses, all of which came unexpectedly to light. When the commission met for the first time on June 1, its members took full advantage of the 1988 constitutional provision endowing congressional commissions with judicial powers to summon witnesses as well as to have unrestricted access to bank accounts and telephone bills. As the investigation unfolded, new witnesses kept coming forward with more specific allegations, citing names and dates. Congressional testimony and press reports gradually unveiled an elaborate scheme to amass hundreds of millions of dollars in bribes and kickbacks. The appearance of the president's ex-aides before the commission undermined his claim to innocence. His former campaign fund-raiser, P.C. Farias, startled commission members by stating, "We are all being hypocrites here. Nobody complies with the campaign financing law."

A third highly unlikely and equally unfavorable circumstance was the fragility and political ineptitude of the president's support in Congress. By early July, Collor seemed to be again in control. Many cried for his resignation, but he vowed to remain in office until his term expired. There had been prior scandals in the presidential office. Moreover, it was hard to find a congressional inquiry commission with a successful track record. The commission set up to investigate charges of corruption in the Sarney administration had quietly shelved its conclusions. Cynicism about corruption also permeated public opinion. A DataFolha poll taken in São Paulo on June 24 found that even though 65 percent thought that the president was involved in corruption, a majority (71 percent) also felt that the commission was a sham and would get nowhere (*Folha de São Paulo* 1992b).

When Collor's supporters in Congress failed to obstruct the investigation, as had been so often done in the past, the avalanche of accusations began to weaken his position seriously. Many feared that he would no longer be able to govern the country until the end of his term. Yet, he might still have avoided impeachment had he changed his way of dealing with Congress. The congressional inquiry commission was almost evenly divided among 12 opponents and 10 supporters. While the commission wanted its work to be viewed as an unassailable investigation, few of its members were willing to recommend that the president be impeached. Even opposition leader Leonel Brizola declared that it would best serve the country to keep Collor in office. Collor, however, chose to keep on a collision course with Congress, denying all charges, even in the face of irrefutable evidence, and then offering federal largesse in exchange for support against impeachment. In the end, the president's congressional support was reduced to the three senators who voted against his impeachment.[8]

The fourth critical circumstance was that there were no attempts to censor the press or to cut short the political process. Brazil's democracy was put under tremendous strain as the Collorgate affair unfolded. Even though many feared that the flood of damaging allegations might aggravate the economic slump and endanger political stability, "[a] healthy climate of trust in democracy," remarked Lamounier, "allowed extremely grave accusations to be brought against the President for months in a row without fear of extraconstitutional intervention." From the beginning, the military dispelled any notion that they might interfere. When retired Army General Euclydes Figueiredo issued a call for Collor's resignation in mid-June, he was careful to stress that he spoke only for himself and that the time for military coups was long past. Also, key actors in the investigation and impeachment processes displayed uncommon zeal for due process of law. An unexpected consequence was that people in lowly positions volunteered to testify before the congressional inquiry commission. In what is generally regarded as a strongly deferential culture, some of the most damaging evidence, showing that thousands of dollars had been transferred from an account controlled by P.C. Farias to one controlled by Collor's private secretary, was presented by the secretary's private chauffeur, Eriberto França.

The unobstructed media played a decisive role in changing public attitudes. Media attention was immediately galvanized by Pedro Collor's sensational charges. Television followed the press as they investigated Pedro Collor's allegations against the president. As the salience of the political scandal grew in the news media, so did public concern.[9]

Figure 3.
Changing Public Perceptions of Collor's
Involvement with Corruption
(Percent)

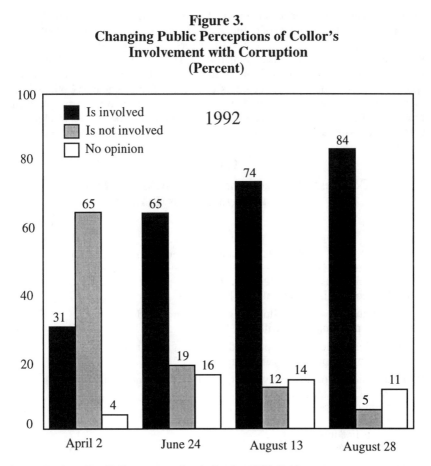

Source: Instituto DataFolha surveys taken in the city of São Paulo.

The fifth unforeseen but fateful circumstance was Collor's obstinate resolve to cling to power until the last moment. This gave the public sufficient time to gain ample knowledge of the facts. In four separate polls taken between April and August 1992, the DataFolha Institute monitored the changes in popular sentiment toward President Collor. The results are shown in Figure 3.

In the April survey, only 31 percent felt that the president was personally involved in wrongdoing. By late August, when the congressional commission's report was made public, an overwhelming majority of 84 percent was certain of it.

At the height of the Collor affair, one single act brought the public to a clear and conclusive verdict about his government. As questions raised in the course of the inquiry went unanswered, the congressional inquiry commission prepared to release an allegedly damaging corruption report. Fighting for his political life, Collor made a catastrophic mistake. Already a highly unpopular figure, blamed for mounting economic hardship and charged with corruption, Collor suddenly challenged his detractors to a duel of public support. On August 13, the president called for Brazilians to don green and yellow, the colors of the flag, and to demonstrate in the streets their support for his administration. The following Sunday, August 16, became known as the "national day of mourning." Thousands of demonstrators spontaneously paraded in the streets dressed in black. Protests against Collor spread rapidly across the country. Crowds in excess of a quarter million people were reported in Rio de Janeiro and São Paulo. Collorgate became an overwhelmingly personalized issue, and support for the president evaporated in Congress and among the public.

Table 2.
Congress Members' and Voters' Attitudes Toward the Impeachment Process (Percent)

Opinions	Voters[1]	Congress Members[2]
(Percents indicate agreement with statements.)		
President Collor has not adequately responded to allegations of involvement with P.C. Farias.	67	60
Convinced that President Collor is involved in graft and influence-peddling along with P.C. Farias.	65[3]	41
President Collor should be impeached if the congressional commission's report implicates him.	70[4]	59
While accusations of his involvement with P.C. Farias are being investigated, President Collor should		
remain in office.	43	62
resign.	36	17
leave office temporarily.	17	14
No opinion.	5	6
If President Collor resigns or is impeached, Vice President Itamar Franco should		
assume office to finish his term.	19	77
Congress should advance the date of the plebiscite on the system of government.	7	14
A new president should be elected by popular vote.	54	8
No opinion.	13	8
President Collor should be impeached and deprived of his political rights.	83[5]	—

Sources: DataFolha surveys of [1] 5,484 voters in 10 capital cities on July 1-2, 1992; [2] 439 members of Congress on June 6-10, 1992; [3] 1,080 voters in São Paulo on June 24, 1992; [4] 5,497 voters in 11 capital cities on August 7-13, 1992; [5] 630 voters in São Paulo on December 28, 1992.

A series of DataFolha polls taken between early June and December 1992 provided valuable information on the changes in public opinion as the impeachment process moved to its conclusion. As shown in Table 2, public and congressional opinions evolved in a double and partly contradictory movement. They converged in disbelieving President Collor's denial of involvement with his former campaign fund-raiser. It was widely held, both inside and outside of Congress, that Collor would be impeached if the congressional commission's report implicated him.

Disagreement, however, surfaced on several matters of procedure. Possibly out of fear that he might again abuse the power of his office, the people were more anxious than Congress to oust Collor. As early as July 1992, 36 percent of a national sample thought he should resign while accusations of his involvement with P.C. Farias were being investigated. Another 17 percent felt that he should at least temporarily step aside. In contrast, 62 percent of Congress felt that he should remain in office until the commission's investigation was completed. The possibility that Collor might be able to block the impeachment process seemed within reach to many of his followers. The fear that he might stage a successful comeback after resigning without being proved guilty haunted an equally large number of his opponents.

A more consequential parting of opinion between Congress and the public had to do with respect for the rule of law. The DataFolha survey asked which among three alternatives should be chosen if President Collor resigned or was impeached. Mass respondents opted as follows: elect a new president by popular vote (54 percent); have Vice President Itamar Franco serve out the presidential term (19 percent); and advance the date of the plebiscite on parliamentarism or presidentialism (14 percent). Congress, in turn, radically opposed all courses except for following the constitutional line of succession (77 percent). In retrospect, Congress made a wise choice. By forcefully rejecting alternatives that eventually might be construed as extraconstitutional measures, such as calling new elections or an earlier plebiscite on the system of government, Congress gained the support of key opinion makers and elite groups.

On September 29, the Chamber of Deputies voted 441 in favor and 38 against to approve the impeachment charges and to suspend the president's powers. Nearly everyone now agreed that, if impeached, President Collor should be deprived of his political rights. On the eve of the December 30 Senate trial, an overwhelming majority of São Paulo voters (83 percent) had already made up their minds that Collor should be ousted. The next day an even more impressive majority — 76 out of 81 senators — voted to convict President Collor on the impeachment charges. The general acceptance of the verdict of the Senate trial ruled out whatever divisive impact the affair might have in the future and effectively buried the political career of Fernando Collor de Mello.

The ultimate political lesson had been taught. However, did it leave behind a suitable mechanism to prevent institutional rivalries from maturing into political impasse and confrontation in the future?

USING THE WEAPON OF LAST RESORT

Impeachment, in Arthur Schlesinger's fitting words, was conceived of as a "weapon of last resort" (Schlesinger 1973, 415-418). To be set in motion, impeachment proceedings should not only be intentionally cumbersome and exacting but also should demand irrefutable evidence of high crimes. Making impeachment easy amounts to granting Congress the means to dominate the executive, reducing it to a state of subservience through intimidation. In retrospect, the distinctive characteristic of Collor's impeachment was precisely the bizarre intent to turn the presidential system into a quasi-parliamentary regime in which impeachment would serve as the equivalent of a vote of confidence.

Presidential and congressional desire to override the separation of powers was at the core of the Collorgate affair. Political conflict and bickering and even stalemate are to be expected in any presidential system because of the constitutional arrangement in which separate institutions share power, but being independently elected can lay competing claims to legitimacy. What makes Brazilian presidentialism unique in this respect is the odd conjunction of factors that exacerbate rivalry between presidents and legislatures while simultaneously weakening the decision-making capacity of each. Even under normal conditions, presidentialism and a highly fragmented party system make it exceedingly difficult to muster a stable congressional majority.[10] The potential for an executive-legislative showdown, however, is dramatically increased in the event of an economic crisis. A serious economic crisis almost invariably produces political pressures for strong presidential leadership to bring the economy under control. Under such circumstances, the temptation to claim a superior plebiscitarian legitimacy and to bypass Congress can become irresistible for any president, as was the case during Collor's first year in office. Congressional reaction can be equally divisive. As the president's popular support withers, Congress begins to veto his policy initiatives or to demand prohibitively high payoffs in exchange for providing a temporary majority. This happened to former President Sarney. Collor did not fare much better in this regard during his second year in office. Defensive collusion, however, may be required as power imbalance becomes dangerously high. That was the case when it became apparent that Collor would have to resign or be removed from office.

In a warped way, Congress and the president's cabinet negotiated a truce. The political system made a sudden turn toward what came to be known as "informal parliamentarism." On August 25, 1992, Collor's ministers issued a statement serving notice of their intention to remain in office and to assume responsibility for the conduct of government until the political crisis involving the president was resolved. Presidentialism had been turned on its head.[11]

"Informal parliamentarism" created a *sui generis* form of "congressional government" in which the legislative branch supported the cabinet but assumed no responsibility for the affairs of the executive branch. The pretense of parliamentary rule demanded dramatic change within Congress, substituting "consensual politics" for the politics of a congressional majority in support of the regime. Consensual politics, in turn, required the creation of a maximum-sized coalition to accommodate the full spectrum of political parties and factions, blurring the division of forces in Congress. The new line of cleavage cut across institutional boundaries, pitting Congress and the cabinet against the presidential office, isolating Collor and assuring the continuity of regime. "Informal parliamentarism" made it possible to turn impeachment into a practical recourse.

Signs that the impeachment had been turned into the equivalent of a vote of no confidence surfaced time and again during the congressional investigation and trial. To achieve the degree of cohesion necessary for unseating the president but not the regime, Congress pushed the politics of consensus to the limit by seeking pressure from without to ward off reluctance within. On July 26, the Speaker of the Chamber of Deputies, Ibsen Pinheiro, predicted that it would be far easier to approve the impeachment "by unanimity rather than by a two-thirds majority," lest the president succeed in blocking it through the mobilization of the remaining one-third of the congressional vote (*Folha de São Paulo* 1992c). The real battle, he added, "will not take place in Congress but in society. If there is a national sentiment that it is impossible to keep in power a regime which has so compromised itself, then it is obvious that external unanimity will create an internal unanimity as well."

The congressional commission's report did not shy away from the notion that the president's failure to live up to the expectations that he himself had created should be considered improper conduct in office: "Hopes for a renewal were largely thwarted by the facts. It was expected that Brazil would escape its political, economic, and social chaos toward the path of an orderly development process." Collor's use of the provisional measures that Congress had voted into the constitution four years before was deemed a high crime. "Under a surge of shock measures from March 15, 1990, onwards, the country was metamorphosed into an immense laboratory where a deluge of provisional measures — 141 in 1990 alone — forced society and the economy to suffer a veritable conceptual and operational earthquake." More ominously, poor macroeconomic management was equated with corruption as grounds for impeachment: "What were the expected results after the turmoil? Redirection and development. What was achieved? Stagnation, recession, and decay not only in economic but unfortunately also in moral terms."

The intention to behave in a parliamentary-like manner also transpired in the Chamber of Deputies' high-handed interpretation of the law. The 1988 Constitution consigned to Congress the task of defining through ordinary legislation the proper procedures for impeachment. Rather than making a law, the legislators chose to define the process of impeachment by means of a collage of constitutional provisions and bits and pieces of an old impeachment law (Law 1079 of 1950), as well as its own internal rules. Something similar occurred when Collor resigned on the eve of the Senate trial. Even though the senators acknowledged that the resignation had eliminated the motive for the impeachment, they voted to impeach Collor and to strip him of his political rights for eight years. Similar to Watergate, the real issue was the need to roll back the expansion of presidential power and to do it in such a way that it did not leave any appreciable basis for a future revival of the Collor affair.[12]

The former president was later brought to trial on charges of corruption. His acquittal by the Supreme Court in mid-December 1994, on grounds that the charges were based on flimsy evidence, failed to breathe life into his career. The political persona of Fernando Collor de Mello had already been buried under opprobrium.

A brush with disaster should prompt a sober assessment of political risks. In retrospect, one realizes how easily the outcome of the impeachment process might have taken a turn for the worse. Senator Marco Maciel's assertion that "the recourse to impeachment in an extreme case which threatened Brazil with ungovernability and civil disobedience showed that the presidential system possesses consistent and efficacious remedies to solve crises involving the highest levels of power" hardly finds support in the observed facts of Collor's impeachment (Maciel 1993).

First, had the congressional inquiry commission proved that President Collor was not only involved in corruption but also had committed electoral crimes, the vice president would have been automatically implicated. In that case, the 1988 Constitution determines that the speaker of the Chamber of Deputies takes over temporarily and must call a new election within 90 days. It is not difficult to imagine the impact of an election requiring an absolute majority after the agonizing process of investigating corruption charges against a president elected fewer than three years earlier. Worse still, the way in which such an election would be carried out would have hinged crucially on the date of the double impeachment. The Constitution mandates that if impeachment occurs before a president serves the third year of his term, a new president must be elected by popular vote. However, if it takes place in the last two years of a presidential mandate, Congress is transformed into an electoral college that selects the new president. An indirect presidential election after an impeachment trial can hardly be considered a "consistent and efficacious remedy."

Second, there was always the possibility that Collor might block the impeachment process. "What can be obtained in a parliamentary regime in a matter of hours, leaving no traumas or scars," wrote Supreme Court Justice Paulo Brossard:

> took us three months of anxiety and uncertainty. After the indictment of the president was approved in the Chamber of Deputies by 441 votes, the impeachment conviction required the vote of 54 out of 81 senators. The votes of 28 senators could have prevailed over the votes of 441 deputies and 53 senators. Suppose now that the 28 dissidents represented the ten smallest states, with a combined population of less than 10 percent of the nation. It might have been as illogical as that (Brossard 1993).

Despite considerable evidence indicating that recourse to impeachment carried the seeds of a potentially disastrous institutional crisis, many insisted that impeachment should be used as the equivalent of a no-confidence vote. More disturbing still was the notion that executive-legislative conflicts should be routinely settled by a plebiscitarian tug-of-war.[13] Yet, mimicking a parliamentary system and prodding one branch of government to cow the other one into subservience are not remedies for the real vulnerability of the system of government. Overblown presidential claims to legitimacy in the face of a Congress too fragmented to provide stable support — but strong enough to foster gridlock — remain the core problem of Brazil's presidentialism.

BEYOND COLLORGATE

The controversy over the impact of an impeachment process on the overall political process is far from settled in Brazil and elsewhere. In his monumental study of the U.S. presidency, Schlesinger argues that impeachment has had a cleansing effect on politics that can be expected to last about 50 years, serving notice to future presidents to exert their powers within the rule of law (Schlesinger 1973, 417-418). Other analysts of presidentialism, however, hold considerably more skeptical views. Even though an impeachment trial has an impact of seismic proportions, its effects are short-lived and tend to dissipate as political institutions resume their routine performance. Theodore J. Lowi, for one, suggests that Watergate-like behavior is part and parcel of the institutional makeup of the modern presidency, compelling presidents to resort to unconventional if not illegal means in pursuit of their goals.[14]

Watergate may be the prime example of an issue that exerted great impact in the short-term but failed to leave a permanent imprint on the political system.[15] Collorgate is seemingly no different. There is no denying that the memory of street demonstrations and the congressional hearings will clearly affect the strategic calculations of future incumbents. What remains to be seen, however, is whether these lessons will constrain presidents to govern within the limits of their powers. Public scrutiny can hardly be counted upon as a long-term deterrent of improper behavior in high places. As the events that led to the impeachment fade in public memory, the issues of corruption and mismanagement are bound to lose their ability to shape public opinion. Indeed, it will be argued here that the impact of impeachment is likely to be short-lived unless the undercurrents of public indignation stirred by it result in a major realignment of political forces or unless institutional reform alters the power imbalance that made impeachment inevitable.[16]

The anticorruption drive was not quelled by Collor's downfall. The "cleansing effect" Schlesinger referred to was clearly at work in the aftermath of Collorgate. Of all the ironies that followed Collor's impeachment, none was more startling than the fall of Deputy Ibsen Pinheiro, the shining speaker of the Chamber of Deputies, a casualty of the next major governmental scandal, popularly known as "Budgetgate." One of the main changes introduced by the 1988 Constitution was to give to Congress the prerogatives, suspended under military rule, to amend, approve, and oversee the budget. Rather than fostering democratic control, however, the immediate result of change was increased corruption. The Congressional Budget Committee rapidly became the focal point for the exchange of kickbacks from major private contractors for budgetary allocations to public works of their choosing. On May 11, 1992, Congress voted down a request for the creation of a congressional inquiry committee to investigate allegations of corruption and influence-peddling in the budget committee. Three months later, many of the involved legislators saw in Collorgate a chance to save their own hides. It was only in late 1993 that a fortuitous event brought to light another major corruption scandal. The police, investigating the disappearance of a congressional aide's wife, found hundreds of thousands of dollar bills stashed in his home. The aide revealed that a group of congressmen were involved in the misappropriation of vast amounts of public funds. A congressional inquiry commission was set up to look into what became known as the "budget committee scandal." On January 21, 1994, the commission recommended that 18 legislators, Deputy Ibsen Pinheiro included, be stripped of mandates and ousted from Congress to face trial.[17]

Corruption remained a warhorse of political rhetoric during most of the 1994 presidential race. Early in that year, Congress approved Law 8713 in the hope that it would cleanse electoral practices, making corporate donors accountable and reducing corruption in campaign financing. In retrospect, the impact of the new law was substantially less impressive than expected. Massive fraud in the state of Rio de Janeiro indicated that much more remains to be done if Brazil is to have a tamper-proof electoral system. A major concern is to bring in computer automation to pave the way for clean elections. Although voter registration was made digital years ago, only in 1996 was an automated counting system set up to replace paper ballots. The new law also failed to cope with the issue of campaign financing. It sought to discipline campaign donations through the purchase of vouchers that permitted disclosure of the donors' identity. In practice, corporations continued to evade control through unreported donations to candidates and political parties.

Accusations of illegal campaign financing and improper conduct in office created new victims before 1994 was over. Deputy Flávio Rocha, a presidential candidate backed by the small PL liberal party, went first. He withdrew from the race after the news media reported his involvement in a shoddy deal to launder campaign donations. Senator Guilherme Palmeira, who had just been chosen to run as Fernando Henrique Cardoso's vice presidential mate, was next. Charged with having received illegal corporate donations for his senatorial campaign, he was replaced by then Senator Marco Maciel.

No reversal of fortune was as startling as Senator José Paulo Bisol's, the vice presidential candidate on Lula's slate. The PT had been one of the very few parties untainted by charges of corruption. In mid-June, however, the press disclosed that Senator Bisol had submitted an amendment to the 1994 federal budget to fund the construction of roads and a bridge in a small municipality where he owned a farm. The press also unearthed evidence that he had obtained several loans at negative interest rates from official banks. A retired judge and a former television talk show host, Senator Bisol was renowned for his severity and zeal as a member of the congressional inquiry commission that investigated the budget committee scandal in late 1993. He was implacable with fellow legislators, dubbed the "budget midgets," who stood accused of fraud and embezzlement. Protesting that he had been deceived into signing the budget amendment without reading the fine print, Senator Bisol resigned and was replaced on Lula's slate by Deputy Aloizio Mercadante.

As the presidential race unfolded, the saliency of corruption as an issue of popular mobilization withered away. In late August, a slip of the tongue by Finance Minister Rubens Ricupero showed that off-the-record remarks can occasionally turn out to be cataclysmic. While waiting to be interviewed on national television, the seasoned career diplomat boasted that he had no scruples in hiding unfavorable cost-of-living data if it helped to elect Cardoso. Domestic dish antennas intercepted the broadcast, and the next day video recordings of the chat were delivered to the news media. Although Ricupero was swiftly replaced by Ciro Gomes, a former governor affiliated with the PSDB social democratic party, the opposition talked of massive fraud. Yet, the flood of accusations that the federal government had been altering economic data to favor Cardoso produced but a ripple in voter preferences. A DataFolha poll conducted on September 5, 1994, showed that support for Cardoso had dropped only one percentage point nationwide.

Significant events in the aftermath of Cardoso's landslide victory in the polls further muddled the post-Collorgate issues of political morality and decorum. The disclosure by the news media of a list of corporate donations in 1994 brought campaign financing to center stage again. This time the PT appeared in an unfavorable light. Party activists were chagrined at the news that Odebrecht, the huge public works contractor, charged by PT legislators in 1993 as being the main culprit in the Congressional Budget Committee's corruption ring, had contributed a sizable amount to the party's campaign. Even though the PT could not credibly be accused of being in the pocket of special interests, the party's reputation as a paragon of morality was shaken.

The final blow was the acquittal of Collor by the Supreme Court in mid-December 1994. Straining to maintain impartiality, the judges ruled that the charges of corruption were not substantiated by sufficient evidence. The people were outraged by the news. In their responses to a poll conducted by the newspaper *O Estado de São Paulo* in late December, a cross-section of São Paulo dwellers disagreed with the court's decision: 88 percent said that justice had not been done. Only 9 percent believed that Collor had been acquitted because he was innocent. As facts changed, emotions were exhausted. The popular impulse that had helped unseat Collor ebbed, and new policy concerns pushed the issue of ethics in politics to the back burner.

Collorgate fell short of redeeming Brazilian politics. Even though the temper of public opinion changed, no institution or political party was able to capitalize fully on the public's outrage to shape new and more effective mechanisms of political accountability. What Collorgate did accomplish, however, was to engender the illusion of impeachment as panacea for the ills of presidentialism.

PERILS OF UNREFORMED PRESIDENTIALISM

It did not take long for the new administration to face many of the difficulties that dogged past presidents. Never having sought the presidency, Vice President Itamar Franco and the nation seemed equally baffled when he unexpectedly succeeded Collor as president of Brazil, not that anyone could muster much personal animosity against the introverted, self-effacing Franco. Almost from Collor's inauguration day, Franco had distanced himself from the ex-president, at times conveying the impression of being in opposition to the administration he served. Even though the differences between them were striking, both Collor and Franco were political loners. Franco did not even belong to a political party when he became Brazil's new president.

If the ghost of an overbearing executive had been partly laid to rest, another now stalked the corridors. Many feared that Franco lacked the aptitude to govern the nation. In an instinctive act of political survival, key political actors rushed to accommodate the new administration. President Franco sought to avoid any policy initiatives that might threaten support for the regime. Congress and the public at large tacitly agreed to gloss over the president's shortcomings. Again, the design was for government by consensus.

President Franco's extraordinarily high popularity ratings reflected more the nation's resolve to prop up his government than confidence in it. That disposition was put to hard tests. During the 1994 Carnival parade, for instance, President Franco allowed himself to be photographed holding hands with a nearly naked young model. Charges of indecorous behavior were rapidly raised by opponents, but the polls showed that even though the public also deplored the president's recklessness, an overwhelming majority of respondents briskly dismissed the incident as cause for impeachment.

The Franco administration had debilitating consequences for Congress. Consensus politics — now renamed "condominium" for a government operating under the joint rule of the executive and legislative branches — dissolved into a chaotic hodgepodge of blocking coalitions. Consensus was often reached in Congress by rubbing off rough edges and substituting new issues for issues that could not be resolved. "Hyperactive paralysis" was the term coined by Lamounier to describe these frantic attempts to reverse declining legitimacy by greatly increasing the number of issues on the political agenda while actually accomplishing little or nothing (Lamounier 1994a, 73). Inaction hiked the already corrosive public cynicism about Congress.

Perhaps more important, Collor's impeachment effectively halted the drive toward institutional reform. To its credit, the 1988 Constituent Congress anticipated the need for change and accordingly scheduled two major political windows to update the Constitution. One such occasion was the 1993 plebiscite on parliamentarism or presidentialism. The other was a full-fledged constitutional revision mandated by the Constitution to take place five years after its promulgation. During that revision period, the exacting procedure for approving constitutional amendments — a three-fifths majority in two separate votes in each house of Congress — was replaced by an absolute majority rule of both chambers in unicameral session.[18]

The 1993 plebiscite dashed the hopes of the advocates of a parliamentary system of government. For a second time this century, the plebiscite chose presidentialism over parliamentarism by a two-to-one margin.[19] Overall, 57.2 percent of nearly 67 million voters voted for presidentialism, 25.4 percent opted for parliamentarism, and 17.2 percent cast blank or void ballots. The 17 million voters who leaned toward a parliamentary system were disproportionately concentrated in the large cities of southeastern Brazil, notably São Paulo. This result dovetails with available survey evidence on the prevailing distribution of preferences for each system of government.

To gauge the preferences of Brazilians for presidentialism or parliamentarism, two interlocked samples of Congress and the mass public were interviewed in 1991 by IDESP. Responses are shown in Table 3 along with the results of a previous survey conducted with the Brazilian elite between December 1989 and June 1990.[20]

Even a cursory reading of the data shows the glaring discrepancy between congressional and popular opinion. Support for parliamentarism grew in Congress and among elite groupings from 1989 as the economic and political crises deepened.[21] In contrast, the 1991 opinion poll found no clear majority for either alternative among the public at large. The results indicate that voters were almost evenly divided in their preferences. One-third supported parliamentarism; one-third, presidentialism; and one-third had no opinion to report. However, more politicized, middle-class respondents were disproportionately more likely to choose parliamentarism over presidentialism.

Table 3.
Elites', Congress Members' and Voters' Preferences for a Presidential or Parliamentary Government (Percent)

System of government	Elite 1989-1990[1]	Congress Members			Voters July-Aug 1991[5]
		June 1991[2]	November 1991[3]	June 1992[4]	
Presidentialism	30	26	24	31	36
Parliamentarism	69	67	74	67	32
No opinion	1	7	1	2	32

Sources:
1. IDESP survey of 450 national elites interviewed between December 1989 and June 1990.
2. IDESP survey of 469 Congress members, June 4-6, 1991.
3. IDESP survey of 406 Congress members, September 25-November 11, 1991.
4. Instituto DataFolha, survey of 439 Congress members, June 6-10, 1992.
5. IDESP survey of 1,030 voters in Rio de Janeiro and São Paulo interviewed between July 27 and August 10, 1991.

Why Congress and the elite failed to steer public opinion toward their preferred alternative is likely to remain a matter of controversy for decades to come. The impeachment process itself had a noticeable impact on the drift of public opinion, as shown in Figure 4.

Popular support for parliamentarism reached its highest point on the eve of Collor's trial and declined gradually afterward. Two related factors are important for understanding the popular verdict. First, loss of faith in Congress reinforced the trend toward presidentialism.[22] Second, the congressional majority in favor of parliamentarism was the manifestation of a "low intensity consensus" among politicians who were unwilling to shoulder the costs of turning words into deeds (Lamounier 1996). Undeterred by the majority's qualms about defending Congress, the presidentialist camp put on the speaker's dais an unlikely but vociferous assortment of leaders ranging from Lula to former governors Leonel Brizola and Orestes Quércia.

Figure 4.
Popular Preference for Parliamentarism or Presidentialism
Dec. 1992 - April 1993 (Percent)

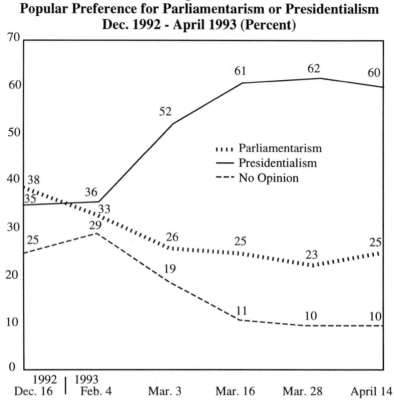

Source: Instituto DataFolha surveys.

The defeat of parliamentarism was not followed by the reform of presidentialism. Congress appeared to be keen to flex its muscles in the revision period. Stirred by the possibility of amending the Constitution by only an absolute majority of Congress, over 17,000 proposed amendments were presented by the end of 1993. Yet, only six constitutional amendments were ever approved. What went awry is still cause for debate. Obstruction by the "contras" (as oppositionist parties were dubbed), the upcoming presidential elections, and the corruption scandals in Congress are among the most frequently mentioned causes. It has also been argued that the revision rapporteur's piecemeal promulgation of amendments, dubbed the "salami" method, caused legislators to lose interest in the revision once their amendment proposals had been brought to a vote.[23] The major cause of the failure of the constitutional recision process, however, was probably the Franco administration itself, because the determination to bring inflation under control prior to the October 1994 presidential elections superseded all other considerations. By mid-1993, the fear that the country was badly adrift led President Franco to appoint Senator Fernando Henrique Cardoso as finance minister and to grant him free rein to carry out a new stabilization program, the Real Plan. The Plan's success relied heavily on the ingredient of power, and the government fully resorted to it to assure the approval of a crucial amendment creating the Social Emergency Fund. The regime's subsequent lack of motivation to strive for other reforms sealed the fate of the revision process. Congress approved only a single political reform amendment, which reduced the presidential term of office to four years without permitting incumbents to run for a second consecutive term, as was originally proposed.

On the bright side, Collorgate induced an extraordinary convergence of liberal and social democratic forces that had been at loggerheads in the 1989 runoff race between Lula and Collor. Since the early 1980s, as the economy stagnated and inflation soared, opinion leaders and policymakers began to reevaluate the role of the public sector and the need for structural reforms. The failure of economic stabilization and the opening of Brazil's domestic market to international competition under the Collor administration added a new urgency to the debate about public sector reform. Gradually, it shaped a process of ideological convergence in which part of the left accepted the need for public sector and market-oriented reforms and part of the right agreed to support a serious effort to reduce poverty and to redistribute income more equally (Lamounier 1996).

The 1994 presidential election provided a unique opportunity to transform the ideological convergence into a viable political coalition. Well before Finance Minister Fernando Henrique Cardoso's success in reducing inflation turned him into a nearly invincible candidate, an alliance was woven among his social democratic PSDB party, the right-of-center PFL liberal party, and the PTB labor party. Although they made strange bedfellows, the coalition provided Cardoso and the PSDB with badly needed grassroots support nationwide, as well as with a sizable block of votes in Congress to approve constitutional reforms and thus assure the Real Plan's success.

Lula was again the PT workers' party candidate. Until August 1994, he was the indisputable frontrunner. The party relied strongly on his charisma as a unifying force for electoral victory. Charisma, however, in this case carried the danger of political isolation. Hoping to win in the first round of elections, the PT stood virtually alone except for its alliance with the small PSB socialist party and the unreformed communists of the PC do B party. As inflation ebbed under the Real Plan, the presidential race underwent a remarkable turnabout. Support for Lula plummeted. Fernando Henrique Cardoso gradually widened his lead so far that he received a majority in the first round of elections. To a great extent, he framed the debate over inflation to ensure that he was perceived as a candidate who had already accomplished something palpable. Overall, Cardoso personified continuity versus upheaval.

Even before the news of the social democratic PSDB party's ascendancy swept across the networks, it became clear that President-elect Fernando Henrique Cardoso had won Brazil's most striking postwar victory at the polls, winning with 54.3 percent of the vote. Lula trailed in a distant second place with 27.0 percent of the vote. Other parties and candidates were also caught unaware. Perhaps the most telling verdict was Enéas Carneiro's extraordinary third place in the polls. Charismatic and staunchly conservative, Carneiro was running a second time for the presidency. In 1989, the renowned cardiologist and head of the minuscule Party for the Reconstruction of the National Order (PRONA) used his allotted 15 seconds of free television campaign time to announce in a rasping voice what has since become his rallying cry: "My name is Enéas!" In 1994, with one minute and 17 seconds of free time to broadcast his undisguisedly authoritarian views, this improbable candidate received 7.4 percent of the vote, out-ranking political pros such as the PMDB's Orestes Quércia (4.4 percent), PDT's Leonel Brizola (3.2 percent), and PPB's Esperidião Amin (2.7 percent).

More than the size of Cardoso's popular mandate was at stake. The logic behind the president's calculation was to build a winning political coalition to end congressional gridlock. To move Brazil toward a sustained period of low inflation and steady growth, the president must muster sufficient political support in Congress to carry out structural reforms. The composition of the newly elected Congress has been favorable to Cardoso. His party coalition has held nearly one-half of all congressional seats. Support from other parties, notably the PMDB, has provided Cardoso with the two-thirds majorities required to pass constitutional amendments.

Cardoso's victory carried with it an ominous implication. Since 1946, only two popularly elected Brazilian presidents have completed their terms of office.[24] At the bottom of this chronic instability lies Brazil's odd combination of presidentialism and a highly fragmented party system that enables all parties, no matter how small or insignificant, to gain seats in Congress. As of 1998, 17 different parties are represented in Brazil's Chamber of Deputies. In practice, this means that no one party can gain a majority. It condemns the country to a government by coalition, which means endless negotiating before any decision is made.

In the best of times, Brazilian law-making is extraordinarily complex. Under normal circumstances, the administration drafts bills to be submitted to Congress. However, when a government must engineer a majority each time it needs a favorable decision, parliamentary sabotage rather than cooperation becomes irresistible. To avoid decisional paralysis, all administrations since 1989 have resorted to provisional measures to govern. The frequent use of these executive decrees is a sign of institutional fragility rather than vitality.

Both as finance minister and as president, Cardoso has made ample use of provisional measures. Moreover, the Franco and Cardoso administrations began to use provisional measures not only to govern but to legislate effectively by successively reissuing executive decrees that had not been passed by Congress.

Between 1988 and 1996, 1,506 provisional measures were issued by the government. Of these, only 316 were voted by Congress into law, and another 60 are currently on the congressional agenda. The remaining 1,106 provisional measures have been reissued by the government because they lost validity before being brought to a vote. It ought to come as no surprise that a negative reaction to the use of provisional measures has been building up in Congress. Many legislators argue that there is a very thin line separating a government by executive decree from a dictatorial government. However, simply depriving the president of the prerogative to issue executive decrees will accomplish little beyond making him hostage to Congress. What is needed is major institutional reform.

TOWARD INSTITUTIONAL REFORM?

Institutional rivalry has been the hallmark of post-1930 relations between Congress and the presidency. This conflictive relationship has often spurred Congress to override presidential initiatives or, conversely, stimulated presidential intimidation and attempts to expand the legislative powers of the executive branch.[25] Understanding Collor's pained bewilderment over what happened in Congress begins with the recognition that such rivalry fosters impasse and confrontation.

Less than a political morality renaissance, Collor's impeachment brought about a critical awareness of the need to change Brazil's political institutions. The memory of street demonstrations and congressional assertion of power over a

Figure 5.
Governing by Decree
(Number of executive decrees issued by presidents since 1988)

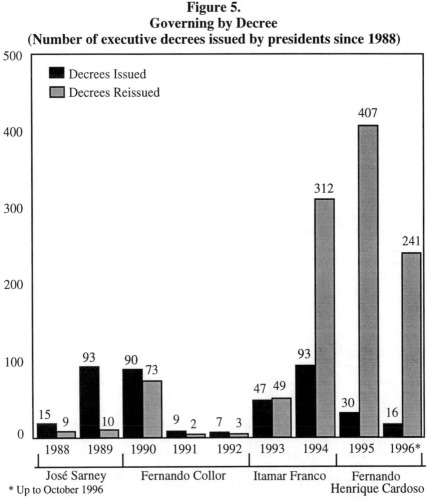

* Up to October 1996

Source: Secretaria Assuntos Legislativos do Ministério da Justiça e Departamento Intersindical de Assessoria Parlamentar (DIAP).

wayward president will probably loom large in the calculations of future incumbents. However, the lessons of Collorgate will have little lasting value if the institutional imbalances that caused his downfall are not resolved.

Since the triumph of presidentialism in the 1993 plebiscite, efforts at institutional reform have been largely abandoned. Not that the ills that led Brazil to undertake two plebiscites on presidentialism or parliamentarism in this century have evaporated. On the contrary, presidential-congressional conflicts have been exacerbated by a perverse combination of factors. One is that the 1988 Constitution blurred the separation of powers, granting to Congress and the president the prerogatives to meddle in areas that had hitherto been the exclusive province of the executive or the legislative. Another is the intrinsically unstable combination of presidentialism and a fragmented multiparty system. Although the opportunity to change constitutional provisions was missed during the 1993 constitutional revision, at least the boundaries of policy prescriptions are now relatively well defined.

Proposals for the reform of presidentialism should aim at increasing the governing capacity of the presidential office. In particular, the Constitution should be amended to grant the president the exclusive power to structure and reorganize the ministries and public administration agencies; to create, change, and eliminate job positions in civil service; and to decide about national, regional, and sectoral development programs and plans. Curiously, a diametrically opposite reform proposal was defended by the presidentialist camp in 1993. The driving force of "mitigated presidentialism" was to weaken rather than to enlarge the power of the presidential office by making the appointment of cabinet members conditional on prior approval by the Senate, granting the Chamber of Deputies the power to issue a no-confidence vote against the cabinet and establishing a recourse to the Supreme Court to overrule a presidential veto (Maciel 1993b, 141-149).

Hand-in-hand with the devolution of power to the presidential office goes the decision to grant sitting presidents the right to run for a second consecutive term. Though reelection runs counter to Brazilian political tradition, the possibility of winning a second term of office not only allows the president to pursue long-term strategic goals but also strengthens his bargaining power vis-à-vis the Congress. Surveys conducted by IDESP with representative samples of federal deputies and senators from two different legislatures, elected in 1990 and in 1994, respectively, show that support for a reelection clause increased from 42 percent in June 1991 to about 71 percent in October 1996.[26] On June 4, 1997, a constitutional amendment was adopted, permitting an incumbent president, governor, or prefect to run for reelection for a single subsequent term.

Reform of presidentialism should create incentives to force legislative-executive agreements and to provide devices to break the stalemate when there is no explicit agreement between Congress and the president. Specifically, the regime must have the power to act or to compel Congress to decide when a lingering policy deadlock entails dangerous economic or political risk. Provisional measures are the primary impasse-breaking device available to the executive, but the controversy stirred by excessive usage threatens to impair its efficacy. As depicted in Table 4, since 1991 over 80 percent of members of Congress have called for the abolition or drastic limitation of the president's power to issue provisional measures. A bill presently before Congress purports to limit the use of provisional measures without depriving the president of efficacious means to avoid policy deadlocks.[27]

More important than all other considerations, however, is the need to provide presidents with enduring majorities in Congress. The set of reforms advocated to bridge the gap between the president and Congress typically entails sweeping changes in the electoral and party systems. Some significant changes have already been introduced, notably the decision to make election years for federal and state executive and legislative offices coincide. Thanks to this provision, President Cardoso was able to lead a multiparty coalition, which, for the first time in half a century, succeeded in electing the president and winning a majority in Congress at the same time.

Table 4.
Congressional Preferences Regarding Institutional Reform,
1991-1995 (Percent in favor)

Issue preference	June 1991[1]	Nov. 1991[2]	Sept. 1993[3]	Mar. 1995[4]	Oct. 1996[5]
Presidential government					
Right to reelection	42	-	-	62	71
Abolish or drastically limit the president's power to issue provisional measures.	85	-	-	88	83
State representation in the Chamber of Deputies					
Seats should be apportioned in strict proportionality to the states' respective populations.	58	-	55	59	69
Legislative elections					
Keep the existing proportional representation system.	24	32	35	30	-
Adopt a "first-past-the-post" system.	8	7	3	7	-
Adopt the German proportional-*cum*-single member district system.	67	61	57	60	65
Party representation in Congress					
Require a 5 percent share of the national vote for party representation in Congress.	78	-	64	68	61
Party switchers should be stripped of mandate.	-	28	-	47	76

Sources: [1] IDESP survey of 1,030 voters in Rio de Janeiro and São Paulo interviewed between July 27 and August 10, 1991; [2] IDESP survey of 469 Congress members, June 4-6, 1991; [3] IDESP survey of 278 Congress members, September 1-30, 1993; [4] IDESP survey of 484 Congress members, February 15-March 31, 1995; and [5] IDESP survey of 311 Congress members, October 1- 31, 1996.

Other reforms, however, are required to strengthen political representation in Congress, as well as to inhibit party proliferation. Changing the rules of membership in the political system is probably the foremost strategy for institutional reform. Brazilian federalism is characterized by profound imbalances in political representation, principally in the allocation of seats in the Chamber of Deputies. To dilute the power of the larger and more populous states, constitutional provisions have allotted seats in excess of population to smaller and thinly settled states. This matters because deputies from such states are a majority in the Chamber, often substituting regional allegiances for party loyalty. Requiring strict proportionality in the states' share of seats is a means of devolving legislative power to the electorally strongest political forces in the country. The results in Table 4 indicate that although reapportionment remains a highly controversial issue, congressional support for reform has been rising gradually over the years.

The composition of Congress is also affected by the existing proportional representation electoral system. The introduction of a mixed proportional representation-*cum*-single-member district system along the lines of the German model has been advocated as a means for creating a less-fragmented, less faction-ridden Congress. As shown in Table 4, only about one-third of Congress wishes to keep the existing proportional representation system. Although there is some controversy as to what kind of electoral rules should be adopted if the existing system is scrapped, about 60 percent of the legislators lean toward a German-style district system.

Limiting party representation is another useful reform strategy for producing a Congress with majority parties. Adoption of a German-style requirement of receipt of at least a 5 percent share of the national vote in order to be represented in Congress would bar smaller parties from cluttering up Congress and encourage them to merge into larger, more politically viable organizations. Support for this reform is dropping, probably because current statutes that restrict party alliances in legislative elections are likely to have a similar effect. Moreover, party mergers are already occurring. The outstanding example is the right-of-center PPB party. Under the leadership of former governor Paulo Maluf, three smaller parties complementary to one another at the regional level — the PST, the PTR, and later, the PDC — merged with the older PDS to form the fourth-largest party in Congress. Symptomatically, party infidelity is now rampant in Congress, with renegades breaking ranks to join parties in the coalitional majority. This is perhaps the reason why support for party discipline measures, such as stripping party switchers of their mandate, has risen dramatically in the past year.

Unreformed presidentialism can neither hold presidents accountable nor make the Congress act responsibly. The task ahead is to revitalize the separation of powers model by clearly defining the prerogatives and competencies of the executive and legislative branches and overhauling the electoral and party systems in order to provide presidents with a clear majority in Congress. Otherwise, presidents may succumb to the old temptation to resort to the concept of a strong presidency, accountable to no one but the mass of voters and governing by subordinating Congress to massive outpourings of popular will.

Institutional reform is necessary to prevent presidentialism from regressing into what Fernando Henrique Cardoso described as the crux of populism: "the messianic belief in a grand salvation plan that would lead the nation toward its manifest destiny under the leadership of a president acting in unison with the mass of the population over the head of elites" (Cardoso 1993). Indeed, of all the consequences of Collorgate, none would be so ironic as the possibility that the plebiscitary presidency that caused Collor's dramatic fall should be energized by his impeachment.

Notes

1. See Lamounier and de Souza 1993, 295-326. An overview of the relationships between the executive branch and Congress up to 1988 is found in Baaklini 1993.

2. On the evolution of institutional structures in Brazil since 1930 and the reevaluation of institutional premises in the context of the Constituent Congress from 1987 to 1988, see Lamounier 1992a, 117-137, and Lamounier 1995a, 2-112. See also de Souza and Lamounier 1990, 81-104.

3. The evolution of Brazil's party system up to Collor's election is discussed in de Souza 1992, 157-198.

4. In Argentina, the adoption of the ballotage and the executive decree ("decreto de necesidad y urgencia") also contributed to strengthen the presidential office and to concentrate power in the hands of the executive branch. See Rubio and Goretti 1995, 69-89.

5. It raised to eight the minimum number of federal deputies per state and created three new states in the federation, all of which had hitherto been federal territories at the edge of the agricultural frontier, hence thinly settled. More ominously, the Constitution set for the first time a ceiling on state representation in Congress, establishing a maximum number of 70 federal deputies per state.

6. In 1998, 17 political parties are represented in the federal Chamber.

7. Mr. Guerra was later acquitted on all charges of wrongdoing, but his downfall was a serious blow to the Collor administration.

8. "It may sound strange," warned the December 29, 1992, editorial of the newspaper *O Estado de São Paulo*, "but it is necessary to recognize the fact that what made it possible to bring the President to trial was that he lacked both strong political support in Congress and an organization able to counter in the streets those who, in the name of public morality, mobilized the 'caras-pintadas' and part of society to demand his deposition."

9. The news media played a similar role in raising public awareness about Watergate. See Weaver, McCombs, and Spellman 1975, 458-472. The news media also affected the evaluation of presidential performance, further eroding Collor's support. For a careful analysis of how reports of policy outcomes in the news media shape public opinion about the president, see Brody 1991.

10. Barry Ames (1995, 406-433) aptly demonstrated that the present proportional representation system induces representatives to weaken representational linkages with constituents, foster pork-barrel politics, and reduce party discipline and cohesion.

11. In an interview granted to *Jornal do Brasil* on July 26, 1992, federal Deputy Nelson Jobim denied that the impeachment process might bring the country to a halt: "The crisis has to do with the President, not with his cabinet. All the facts under investigation happened before the change of ministers. After that, everything changed." In the same vein, the *O Estado de São Paulo*'s editorial of August 27, 1992, acknowledged with surprise that "the ministers are the ones who prop up the President of the Republic. It is a *sui generis* parliamentary regime."

12. Arthur M. Schlesinger, Jr. (1975, 133) correctly noted that "the expansion and abuse of presidential power constitute the underlying issue that Watergate has raised to the surface, dramatized, and made politically accessible."

13. "Under a parliamentary system," noted PT federal Deputy Sandra Starling, "the problem would have been settled by political elites through a vote of no confidence in government. People would not have taken to the streets, citizens would not have been convoked to act. . . . Presidentialism compels legitimately empowered executive and legislative political forces to negotiate disagreements and, should an impasse arise, vie for a hegemonic position in the society at large." See *Jornal do Brasil* 1992.

14. It is worth quoting Lowi's argument (1985, 177-178) at length: "No substantial direct lesson can be learned from Watergate," he writes, "except not to engage in illegal activities or be caught doing so. Except for the violation of a few criminal provisions, the Watergate case is confirmation of and consistent with the nature of the modern presidency, not an aberrant episode. In every aspect other than the extent of illegal activities, there is a Watergate of some kind every day in the life of a president. The scale of presidential power and of mass expectation about presidential power is so great that presidents must, as in Watergate, attempt to control their environment to the maximum, especially those aspects of it that might tend to be barriers in the way of meeting presidential responsibilities."

15. Even the short-run effect of such issues may be dismal. Most analyses of the 1974 mid-term elections in the United States failed to find significant effects for Watergate, despite the prominence of this issue in the campaign. See, however, Fiorina 1981, 164-167, and Uslaner and Conway 1985, 788-803.

16. In his otherwise admirable account of the rise and fall of Collor, Kurt Weyland (1993, 1-38) minimizes the importance of institutional reform to enhance the quality of Brazilian democracy. Narrowly equating institutional reform with changes in the system of government, he fears that "the structural preconditions for patronage, favoritism, clientelism, and even corruption, may very well persist" even if parliamentarism were to be adopted. The major flaw in Weyland's argument is that institutional reform proposals have deemed indispensable an overhauling of the electoral and party systems along the lines originally laid down by the Arinos Commission. In this light, it can be argued that clientelism and pork-barrel politics are more likely to persist under unreformed presidentialism.

17. For details, see Krieger, Rodrigues, and Bonassa 1994.

18. The plebiscite on a parliamentary or presidential system and the 1993 constitutional revision were mandated respectively by Articles 2 and 3 of the Transitory Constitutional Provisions.

19. In November 1963, President João Goulart convoked a plebiscite to decide whether the parliamentary system introduced in 1961 to permit his inauguration as president should be maintained or replaced by presidentialism.

20. The study interviewed a sample of 450 elite respondents, as follows: 76 business-men, 34 labor leaders, 26 associational leaders, 34 journalists, 78 intellectuals, 26 public-sector managers, 108 politicians, and 68 high military officers (Navy and Air Force). For details, see Lamounier and de Souza 1990. The interlocked samples of members of Congress and voters are described in Lamounier and de Souza 1991 and Lamounier and de Souza 1992.

21. Overall, congressional and elite opinion tended to coalesce around one basic model of parliamentarism in which the president was to be elected by direct popular vote and, should an impasse arise, have the power to dissolve the Chamber of Deputies and convoke new

elections. Moreover, if adopted, parliamentarism was to be extended to state governments. On this matter, see de Souza 1992, 9-23.

22. The relevant survey data are found in *Opinião Pública* 1, 1993. In the same issue, see articles by Rubens Figueiredo (13-18) and Gustavo Venturi (50-54).

23. The revision rapporteur was Federal Deputy (Representative) Nelson Jobim. His job was to receive proposed amendments, sort them by subject matter, and eliminate redundancies in order to prepare them to be brought to a vote. The "salami" method refers to the rapporteur's decision to bring selected amendments to a vote one at a time in lieu of presenting Congress a more integrated package.

24. The elected presidents who succeeded in completing their terms of office were Eurico Gaspar Dutra (1946-1951), Juscelino Kubitschek (1956-1961), and Fernando Henrique Cardoso (1994-1998).

25. Federal Deputy Sandra Starling half-facetiously defined Congress under Cardoso as the "Ministry of Legislative Matters." See her interview in *Folha de São Paulo,* March 15, 1996.

26. These figures include legislators who support the right to reelection but only for future presidents as well as those who wish to see it granted to the incumbent president.

CHAPTER 6

The Conflict Between Civil and Political Society in Post-authoritarian Brazil: An Analysis of the Impeachment of Fernando Collor de Mello

LEONARDO AVRITZER

INTRODUCTION

Modernization and societal organization have been in opposition in Brazil throughout the twentieth century. Economic modernization has been the guiding principle of the most important political projects in the country, starting with the presidency of Getúlio Vargas, who first came to power by military coup in 1930. Vargas was committed to economic modernization, which he viewed as a fundamental change in the country's economic structure in order ". . . to exploit the land and to treat industrially mineral resources . . . coal, iron, and oil — as well as to create an advanced metal industry. . ." (Vargas 1938, 331-335). His economic modernization program had to reconcile the forces of political control stemming from the persistence of patrimonial political relations with the need to insulate from political control the techno-bureaucracy directing state intervention in the economy.

Vargas' regime inherited an oligarchic and patrimonial political system from the Old Republic. Patrimonialism is a traditional political system in which the ruler determines all political and administrative decisions. Since he cannot guarantee the allegiance of his dependents, the patrimonial ruler relinquishes some of this absolute power by ceding special rights or privileges to officials or private citizens in exchange for goods, services, or allegiance. All administration becomes negotiation, bargaining, and contracting about privileges, whose content must then be fixed. In patrimonial systems, the "legal order is rigorously formal but thoroughly concrete and in this sense irrational. Only an 'empirical' type of interpretation can develop" (Weber 1967, 263). There is "one pattern of political rule of universalistic and legal institutions at the center of the power structure and traditional elements at the periphery. . ." (Weber 1946, 299-300). Patrimonialism, which Brazil inherited from Portugal, was the solution found to accommodate the two main elements of the

Brazilian process of state building: privatism (Leal 1949; Duarte 1939) and statism (Faoro 1975). At least since the mid-nineteenth century, when a national state was consolidated, a centralized government with a rational bureaucracy has coexisted with private sources of power at the local level (Uricochea 1980).

Vargas was confronted with a political system dominated by local oligarchies, which was one of his justifications for closing Congress and dissolving local governments (Gomes 1977). Vargas' electoral reform of 1932 was not enough to diminish the power of such oligarchies in the political system. Subsequently, Vargas resorted to two solutions to permit his economic development projects, which needed a modern, state-run economic sector, to coexist with a backward political system. The first solution that Vargas adopted in the period between 1937 and 1945 was closing Congress and governing Brazil by executive decree. The second solution, adopted during his tenure as the constitutionally elected president (1951-1954), was restricting the ambit of patrimonialism or clientelism[1] so that the bureaucratic agencies responsible for economic development were effectively insulated from the system of exchange of benefits for political support (Nunes 1984). While the areas of social policies and public works were subject to the influence of clientelist politics, the state-run economic sector was not.

Vargas' solution to harmonize economic modernization and political backwardness in the late 1930s was facilitated by the weakness of societal institutions. He rejected societal autonomy and directed the government to interfere with every attempt by social actors to establish autonomous forms of organization. After being defeated on this matter in the Constituent Assembly of 1933-1934 (Barbosa 1980), Vargas reintroduced restrictions on free organization of labor unions and on the existence of civic associations in the Constitution of 1937. This has led to a long-term dissociation between economic modernization actors and democratic social actors. In the brief democratic moments in twentieth-century Brazilian history, economic modernization has coexisted with a system of cooptation by clientelist politicians, often by use of unlawful means. Even though strongly disapproved of by society, this clientelist system survived until the 1980s because of the weakness of organized society, controls on the press, and the small degree of political influence held by the middle-class. With the return of democracy in 1985, however, the clientelist system began to face serious societal opposition, in large part because a more organized civil society resulted from the process of reaction against the long period of authoritarian rule.

This chapter analyzes the impeachment of ex-President Fernando Collor de Mello as part of the contradiction between civil and political societies in recently democratized Brazil. The chapter has six parts. The first briefly presents the Brazilian bureaucratic authoritarian regime as a modernization movement that insulated itself against patrimonialism and at the same time strengthened certain features of patrimonialism in order to compete electorally. The second and third parts follow the process of democratization of Brazil from the perspectives of civil society renewal and political society negotiations. The fourth, fifth, and sixth parts explain why the conflict between civil and political society that emerged after democratization led to the impeachment of former President Collor de Mello.

AUTHORITARIANISM AS MODERNIZATION AGAINST SOCIETY

Authoritarianism in Brazil was part of a project of systemic modernization that coordinated societal activity through impersonal means and refused to allow the emergence of forms of citizenship that could have offset the interference with traditional types of organization of everyday life. The first of the systemic measures introduced by the Brazilian authoritarian regime was an administrative reform designed to make the state more efficient in achieving speedy economic development. This reform attempted to make the bureaucracy more rational, to improve its insulation from patrimonial pressures, and to establish administrative criteria for career bureaucrats (Martins 1975). The authoritarian regime consolidated in power an economic technocracy that had emerged in the early 1950s within the National Economic Developmental Bank (Banco Nacional de Desenvolvimento Econômico — BNDE). This group of technocrats, who had been in charge of the planning and implementation of developmental projects in the late 1950s, concluded that the stalemates of modernization were linked to the inability to insulate state economic intervention from the political process. Their presence among the 1964 conspirators expressed their belief that the economy should be insulated from political demands, although it should not necessarily be an autonomous subsystem. Therefore, they defended seizure of economic control by a techno-bureaucracy with ties to the military regime.

From the very beginning, the military regime faced the same problem that had confronted Getúlio Vargas: how to reconcile its modernization efforts with the operation of a backward political system. The military did not want to permit the political process to disturb the process of economic development. Yet, the military did not want to close down the political process entirely, for it regarded the military takeover as merely a provisional break that should not be transformed into a permanent nondemocratic solution (Martins 1975). Therefore, the military decided to allow the political system to function in a limited fashion. After initially purging the undesirable representatives, the military permitted Congress to operate normally. It also permitted the courts to function normally. Permitting normal operation of political and juridical institutions was intended to limit the powers of the authoritarian regime and to legitimize it by consensus building of a democratic order. The operations of law and free elections were integrated into a process of authoritarian power building.[2]

The authoritarian regime allowed partial functioning of political society, conditioned on its submission to the basic goals of the regime. The military utilized two devices to ensure that political society adhered to its imperatives: selection of the president by a process in which only top military officers had the right to vote and the search for its own political base outside the large cities. The latter choice eventually led to a rupture with the new actors, created by the regime through economic modernization. The authoritarian regime assumed that its electoral success would make it legitimate, not because its policies happened to coincide with the will of a majority of the electorate but because it could manipulate the electoral process enough to guarantee long-term control of the state apparatus. The problem with such a strategy was that it created a political process that led not to legitimacy but to authoritarianism. This strategy became even more problematic once the initial purge of the political system and the imposition of a new authoritarian constitution proved insufficient to guarantee the military regime's electoral success. At that point, the need to resort to patrimonial politics reemerged.

The military regime initially rejected patrimonial practices because the desire to eliminate corruption was one of the reasons for the coup. Once the military regime perceived that the opposition to its policies was concentrated in the large cities, however, it realized that a convenient way to maintain power under the political system it had created was to rely on patrimonial politicians and their largely rural constituencies. This meant that the regime would have to exchange administrative favors for political support, which implied making concessions compromising the efficiency of state enterprises. Reliance on the support of patrimonialist politicians increased both the antidemocratic and the antimodern tendencies within the political system.

To avoid compromising the efficiency of its modernization projects, the military regime exchanged administrative benefits for political support in much the same manner as Vargas had done during his second tenure (Camargo 1989). The regime radically separated the areas of public administration responsible for the formulation and implementation of economic policies from the areas responsible for the implementation of social policies. Two types of measures deepened this separation. One was a provision inserted into the 1967 Constitution granting the president the power to enact decrees with the force of law on matters of national security and public finance. This power was expanded in the 1969 Constitution to include the creation of government positions and determination of salaries.[3] The second was the maintenance of autonomy of state-run enterprises from actions aimed at gaining the political support of patrimonialist politicians.

The authoritarian regime's choices had one consequence to political society: the dissociation of morality and legitimacy from the process of power accumulation. The instruments of legitimation and communication that the military substituted for traditional ways of building political support were utilized in a way that were perceived as unfair. By purging the opposition and establishing an all or nothing dynamic at the political level, the authoritarian regime excluded power-sharing and negotiation. By strengthening patrimonialism at the political level and moderniza-tion at the economic level, the military regime produced the anomaly of generating political support for authoritarian modernization from nonmodern constituencies. This strategy was viable only as long as parts of the state apparatus were both insulated and protected from the political system. Insulation also led to the absence of communication between the actors who favored modernization and the new actors who were created through this process. As the political system passed through a process of democratization, the techno-bureaucracy became politically isolated from modern social actors.

Two important consequences of the model of state organization established by the authoritarian regime were the diminution of societal autonomy and the augmentation of social inequality. In choosing a model of radical interference with traditional economic activities, the authoritarian regime assumed that introduction of new economic activities would automatically generate modern social forms of life. The authoritarian state had two strategies to pursue societal modernization: 1) making resources extremely scarce to economic actors whose activities it did not consider modern, such as small agricultural producers, and 2) transferring resources to the sectors it wished to sponsor. The overall result of such policies was the creation of an extremely unequal society rather than a modern and developed society. Resources that could be spent to offset the detrimental side effects of economic modernization were instead used to sponsor a development process that increased social inequalities (Cardoso 1989). The authoritarian regime fomented economic and administrative modernization designed to produce rapid changes in social structure to make Brazil into a "modern" nation. Introduction of structures of efficiency and instrumental action, however, was not offset by the creation of modern and democratic forms of control of social relations. On the contrary, efficiency and instrumental reason were transformed immediately into instruments of social control. Thus, power and knowledge were utilized throughout a process in which state and market actors attempted to create a modern society without acknowledging the identities of social actors as members of economic, civil, and political society.

THE EMERGENCE OF CIVIL SOCIETY IN BRAZIL

The Brazilian authoritarian regime tried to create a modern, urban, and industrialized country with a large internal market. It intended to change social actors' everyday lives in order to integrate them into the modern society that was being created. The meaning of modern, however, was somewhat blurred. The identity of the worker as a producer was certainly part of the modernization effort, but the instruments to furnish such an identity were missing because free social organization was forbidden by the state (Weffort 1978). The narrow arena of autonomy not regulated by the state was left to the market and to the factory, considered private spaces where domination could be exercised to some extent.[4] The rights that could have furnished the identity of the modern urban dweller as a citizen were either lacking or attenuated. While the functional aspects of the institutions that constituted Brazilian citizenship existed, the societal aspects did not. Institutions that might have protected individuals against the destructive aspects of the modernization process and facilitated their adaptation to a new economic environment did not exist. Modernization in Brazil was authoritarian because it lacked the structures of societal autonomy complementary to the forms of systemic change.[5] Yet, emergence of modern social actors did not evolve as a complement to the process of economic modernization, which was what the military regime had expected. On the contrary, social actors emerged as social movements disputing the articulation of modernity by the military regime in modern as well as traditional economic and social spaces.

Contrary to the authoritarian regime's intentions, the modernization process led to the emergence of new democratic actors. In the late 1970s, three strong social movements emerged that challenged the authoritarian form of Brazilian modernization. Each was associated with a specific modernization proposal of the authoritarian regime. Each demanded a new and democratic relationship with market and state actors.

The New Unionism

The first of these movements was the "new unionism." This movement began in the industrial belt around the city of São Paulo known as the ABC region, where most of Brazil's auto and electronic industries are concentrated. The number of workers in the movement's most important city, São Bernardo, jumped from 4,030 in 1950 to 20,039 by 1960. By 1970, São Bernardo had 75,118 workers, and its industrial complex encompassed another city in which another 50,372 workers were employed (Humphrey 1982, 128-129). Those workers constituted the best case for the success of economic modernization. Most came from the countryside or smaller cities, were young, had no previous political experience, and enjoyed above-average levels of education and income. Moreover, they were employed in the most productive enterprises in the country. Modernity was part of their employers' discourse, which stressed that these workers played a role in the world economy (Sader 1988, 72). The workers understood they were making an important contribution to Brazilian economic modernization and development.

The internal organization of the factories and the relationship between employers and trade unions, however, signified a different meaning of the idea of being modern. Internally, the factories were organized according to a method called "routinization" (Sader 1988), an adaptation of Taylorism to Brazilian reality. Corporatist labor laws forbade free trade union organization and restricted the right to strike. Trade unions that failed to abide by the complex rules of the Consolidated Labor Laws (Consolidação das Leis do Trabalho — CLT) were subjected to state intervention. The policies of employers and government gave auto workers a feeling of ambiguity about their modern identity. "The professional pride of working in the country's most modern enterprises was intertwined with a feeling of deep unfairness" (Abramo 1988). Underlying such a feeling lay the perception that to be modern one had to give up complete control over decisions about one's daily life.

For a long period, the state and employers successfully convinced workers that being modern implied having no control over one's social and political life. That political and economic limitations to workers' autonomy were built into the labor laws, however, played a dual role. On one hand, it led to compliance due to the fear of sanctions. On the other, that social action was not outlawed but only severely restricted gave workers the chance to act and to learn from their actions. By the mid-1970s, the new leadership elected to run the metal workers' trade union in São Bernardo began taking small steps to demonstrate that the labor laws were not simply a mechanism of social organization but were also a mechanism of social exclusion. The auto workers' leaders demanded freedom to act and to negotiate by presenting different proposals to both employers and the state. The continuing denial of their claims for greater freedom of action helped constitute a new workers' identity. This identity involved learning about the ineffectiveness of existing institutions for improving the conditions of their lives and about the incapacity of union leadership to fight alone against the state and employers. This learning process resulted in an attempt to build more horizontal relations at the workplace that eventually became the basis for a struggle for autonomy.

The first stage in this process was self-valorization of the workers' role as producers. The second stage in the construction of this new identity was the identification of movements with the capacity to perform social action at the grassroots level. Labor's new identity was based on the valorization of the worker as a producer of both wealth and social action. It implied questioning authoritarian modernization as a whole both by breaking state control over the trade union movement and by struggling for rights at the workplace.

The struggle began in May 1978, when the metal workers went on strike, the first group in more than 10 years to do so. Defying a wage settlement imposed by the Labor Courts, the metal workers staged a sit-down strike in a plant in São Bernardo's industrial belt. No one voiced demands, and the trade union leadership did not claim any leading role in the strike, which spread to other plants. The sit-down strike demonstrated not only the extreme form of social exclusion implemented by the process of "authoritarian modernization" but also the spaces left for social action. Since it claimed no leadership over the movement, the union could not be held responsible for it. Indeed, the first metal workers' strike was a movement with only one discourse, the grassroots discourse in which workers assumed responsibility for their actions.[6] The importance of the first metal workers' strike was that it showed Brazilians that workers were social actors who claimed rights. As Luiz Inácio Lula da Silva explained:

> We cannot consider what happened to have been abnormal. The strike was perfectly normal. It was a manifestation of the working class, who only wanted to show that it does in fact exist and is a living part of the nation. As such it must be respected and considered. The strike was legitimate . . . it was only the use of the bargaining weapon of a class. The fact that it was judged illegal has no validity, for the workers made strikes legal from the moment that so many practiced their real human right (Alves 1985, 195).

The first metal workers' strike challenged two assumptions of authoritarian modernization. First, it challenged the notion that social actors are a dependent variable within the modernization process. Second, it challenged the notion that the workplace is a private area that does not allow negotiations over everyday practices. When workers challenged both features of authoritarian modernization, they did so to establish the principle that they had enforceable rights. In 1979 and 1980, two additional confrontations among metal workers, employers, and the state took place. By this time it had become clear that this was a movement for citizenship. As a Volkswagen worker expressed it, "The strike was not for a wage increase, it was for honor. It was either them or us." The sponsors of authoritarian modernization had to make their power so visible that it did not work. In the nine weeks after São Bernardo's 1978 strike, 245,000 Brazilian workers had gone on strike. In 1980, the number of striking workers nearly tripled to 664,700, including 240,000 rural workers (Alves 1985, 208). Many of those strikes were simply a request for acknowledgment. Throughout the period between 1978 and 1981, almost every Brazilian worker decided to show that he or she was a social actor eager to defy the state veto on working class autonomy and to propose creation of free arenas of negotiation among different social actors.

Organizations of the Urban Poor

Parallel to the rise of the "new unionism," authoritarian modernization was challenged on a second front. Poor urban dwellers challenged the regime's urban policies. Repression of urban social movements was an important aspect of authoritarian modernization. Millions of people migrated from the countryside to the cities through the operation of impersonal economic processes, and determination of how they would settle and organize themselves became a relevant aspect of modernization. Economic planners had to determine the kind and quality of services that would be provided to these urban migrants. Because its priorities were investment of scarce resources in industrialization, the regime decided to allocate only minimal resources to urbanization. In the democratic period between 1946 and 1964, there were attempts to meet the needs of the urban population through populist policies (Gohn 1982; Afonso 1987).

After the overthrow of the populist order in 1964, the military instituted a policy of slum relocation. Slums were removed from the central areas of the major Brazilian cities and replaced by middle-class neighborhoods. The justification for slum clearance (desfavelização) was the protection of property rights — these settlements illegally occupied property belonging to others. Political repression was obviously a complementary feature of the relocation policies. Robert Gay (1988) and Marcelo de Azevedo (1987) found fear as the main cause for disarticulation of neighborhood associations in post-1964 Brazil.

After slum dwellers had been removed from urban central areas and resettled in the periphery, they faced another feature of the regime's urban policies — lack of social services to the periphery. Resettlement signified poor education for their children, several hours each day on public transportation, flooding, lack of access to public sanitation, and lack of police protection. The reality of urban living was initially experienced by a poor group of migrants who lacked knowledge of rights that might have avoided their dispossession and relocation. Failure to own a plot of urban land was associated with the experience of being excluded from most of the rights and services provided by the administrative state.

In the beginning of the 1970s, the Catholic Church withdrew from its prior alliance with the military regime. This withdrawal was a decisive factor in the emergence of urban social movements to challenge the regime's policies toward the urban poor. It is beyond the scope of this work to discuss why the Church broke its alliance with the state.[7] What is important is that once it left this coalition, the Church immediately criticized the model of development in course in Brazil, asking for ". . . reconsideration along the lines of integral development in which the human being is given a value" (Bruneau 1974, 222). The critique of authoritarian modernization was part of a broader reconsideration by the Church of its role within Brazilian society. The Church moved away from the role of justifying in symbolic terms the misfortunes affecting the everyday lives of Brazilians and started to understand the poor population as a base deprived of power and knowledge. The Church also attributed a second meaning to the idea of a "base," a meaning related to its willingness to sponsor ". . . a local environment . . . for personal, fraternal contact among its members" (Azevedo 1987, 75).

The Church simultaneously challenged authoritarian modernization. It proposed, for the first time in Brazil, a third principle for the organization of society, the principle of social interaction. Between the early and mid-1970s, the Church hierarchy sponsored organization of the urban poor in the periphery of the major Brazilian cities in Christian (or ecclesial) base communities (comunidades eclesiais de base — CEBs). The CEB became a major source of reflection on the condition to which the urban poor had been reduced in Brazil. It also became a major source for the poor's rearticulation in the struggle for improvement of their lives as well as for acknowledgment as a societal group.

By the late 1970s, urban associations emerged throughout Brazil. They were the result of the slow process of learning taking place at mothers' clubs, CEBs, and secular associations linked to the traditional left. In Rio de Janeiro, 166 neighborhood associations were created between 1979 and 1981, more than the 124 associations created during the entire previous democratic period (Boschi 1987, 68). Within the state of Rio de Janeiro, one neighborhood association was created every week in 1980. In São Paulo, more than 1,300 Societies of Neighborhood Friends (Sociedades Amigos de Bairros — SABs) were created in 1978 (Alves 1985, 174). Although SABs had played an important role in the city since the 1950s (Gohn 1982), they had been inactive for a long period. After the early 1970s, the orientation of their activities changed dramatically. In Belo Horizonte in 1980, there were 202 neighborhood associations, 65 percent of which emerged after 1974 (Somarriba 1987, 89). Most associations organized democratically at the grassroots level, disputed the state's capacity to determine social policies, and organized around specific demands. Most were suspicious of traditional political channels and preferred public and open forums for negotiation with local administrators. In sum, they presented a challenge to authoritarian modernization by producing the knowledge necessary to challenge state policies and by making power visible.

Urban social movements that emerged in Brazil by the late 1970s challenged a second foundation of authoritarian modernization: the capacity of state and market actors to determine the everyday life of the poor population. To defend themselves from authoritarian modernization, the poor created associations, convincing large constituencies of the utility of social action. The consolidation of modern forms of social action led to the challenging of state and market actors on their own grounds. Throughout this process, learning about the use of the legal system, which had never constituted a strategy for action among the poor population, was crucial. Brought to the social movements by external agents, the legal system was incorporated into the strategy of social action, transforming urban social movements into an enormous effort for citizenship.

Middle-Class Associations

A third form of associations emerged in Brazil in the same period: middle-class neighborhood and professional associations. The middle-class was the model of depoliticized citizens who exchanged political participation for well-paid jobs. The authoritarian regime viewed this class as logical supporters of the modernization process. For a long time, the highly educated individuals who worked as administrators and technicians in the most modern economic enterprises and administrative offices were among the principal beneficiaries of economic modernization. If they were submitted to the same process of disempowerment, they were also well rewarded for narrowing their identity as citizens. The systemic structure of determination of everyday life would, however, prove to be as intolerable to them as it was to the new working class and poor urban dwellers.

Middle-class movements and associations blossomed in Brazil during the late 1970s and early 1980s. They had one major difference and one major similarity in comparison with the two movements explained in the previous sections. The difference was that middle-class social movements did not have to reappropriate knowledge in order to construct an identity of their own. The similarity was their need to transform power into a societal resource. The first middle-class movements to emerge in Brazil were urban movements. Middle-class neighborhood associations were created in larger Brazilian cities at a fast pace. In Rio de Janeiro between 1979 and 1980, 30 middle-class associations were created, a number equal to the total number of such associations created in the previous 33 years (Boschi 1987). The second important middle-class movement was the movement for the renewal of professional associations. New associations of lawyers, doctors, and university professors were constituted in this period. In the city of Rio de Janeiro, the 94 professional associations formed between 1978 and 1983 represented almost one-half of the 228 associations then extant in the city (Boschi 1987). Moreover, an important political phenomenon was taking place, involving demands for the renewal of the forms of political action in existing associations. New lawyers' associations demanded more support from their national bar association for the cause of democratization. New medical associations demanded more public health centers. New university professors' associations demanded more public schools. In this sense, they not only organized themselves to lobby for specific issues but also established structures of solidarity with non-middle-class associations.

The transformation of middle-class social actors' patterns of action dealt the final blow to the project of authoritarian modernization. Middle-class associations pointed in the same direction as the new unionism and the movements of poor urban dwellers. The willingness of the middle-class to resume open political action for pursuit of its own interests was additional evidence that the cost of economic, technical, and administrative modernization had become unbearable for all societal groups. It showed that the identities formed throughout the process of authoritarian modernization encompassed not just the pursuit of individual interests but also the formation of solidarity. These associations sought the democratization of everyday life through the constitution of public political spaces to substitute for the impersonal authoritarian arenas that imposed decisions on social actors. The joining of associations by the middle classes led to the generalization of economic and civil society as differentiated, interactive spaces for negotiation and decisions about labor conditions and urban policies. Those spaces of negotiation were based on the preference for legal rights and universalistic application of the law rather than clientelistic concessions. All these movements operated within the framework of a future democratic order and institutionalized their demands in legal terms, making them part of the ongoing democratization process in Brazil. They were not, however, integrated into the concerns of the members of political society who negotiated the new democratic order that was going to be enforced in Brazil. The radical dissociation between the democratization of everyday life, the political conception brought about by social movements, and the conception of democracy institutionalized through the negotiations of the democratic transition in Brazil are the subjects of the chapter's next section.

THE TRANSITION TO DEMOCRACY IN BRAZIL

In its first 10 years of existence, the Brazilian authoritarian regime was highly successful in setting an agenda for political society. The opposition's attempts to defeat the regime consistently failed in the political arena, in large part because the regime constantly changed the rules of the political game. Every institutional defeat of the authoritarian regime led to changes in the rules, indicating that political overthrow of the regime would not be possible. Therefore, the opposition had to negotiate with the authoritarian regime. Democratization involved building reciprocal confidence.

The first political opening, which took place in 1974, signified the authoritarian regime's willingness to write rules of exception into the legal system in order to institutionalize a semi-democratic system. The authoritarian regime's proposal of restricted redemocratization led to the restructuring of the political system in 1977. Political reform, in turn, led to an increase in patrimonialism, which was strengthened by a constitutional amendment that increased the representation of the northern and northeastern states at the expense of southern states, especially São Paulo.[8] The aim of this reform was to strengthen further traditional and patrimonial constituencies at the expense of modern political forces and social movements. The authoritarian regime tried to shape the political process and the opposition party to make both less sensitive to societal changes. In the first four years of the *abertura* (opening), the authoritarian regime pursued a strategy that combined survival with shaping the opposition party, the Brazilian Democratic Movement (Movimento Democrático Brasileiro — MDB). The nature of the MDB became an even more important issue after the MDB won the elections of 1974 and 1978 and faced, with as much surprise as members of the authoritarian regime, the rise of noninstitutional social movements. The reaction of the MDB to the policies of the authoritarian regime and to the challenges it received from the social movements would determine the regressive nature of political society in the moment of Brazil's transition.

The Makeup of the MDB

By the end of the 1970s, the MDB, after being the only opposition party for 15 years, constructed its identity as the opposition struggling for congressional majority. As the authoritarian regime directed its policies for political society to guarantee a congressional majority, the MDB revolved around its ability to block the authoritarian regime's initiatives in Congress. The most important moments of the MDB were those in which a united opposition defeated authoritarianism in Congress. The MDB did not try to include politicians with patrimonialistic constituencies, and there was little incentive for such politicians to join the MDB. After 1974, however, it began to make increasingly greater sense for local oligarchies to join the MDB or to have at least one foot there, because the strategy of plebiscitary elections could help them gather the urban support that they lacked. It also made sense because the type of legislation they were interested in seeing passed was still partially decided in Congress. Therefore, the conciliation of plebiscitary opposition against authoritarianism with daily patrimonialistic practices was not difficult to accomplish. The strengthening of the MDB was not going to lead to the strengthening of societal opposition.

A second important aspect of the MDB's self-understanding was its relation with the social movements, such as the new unionism and the grassroots urban movements. No party was better located by the end of the 1970s to attempt to incorporate the social movements. The incapacity of the MDB to incorporate social movements stemmed from its links with the project of authoritarian modernization. The role of institutional opposition played by the MDB did not include a radical challenge to the authoritarian regime's policies at the level of labor constituencies. The demand for workers' autonomy was never part of the MDB's program. The links of MDB politicians to the populist past, a past rejected by the social movements, also did not help their relations with the opposition party.[9] On the other hand, the MDB, despite its initial positive reaction to social movements, did not take seriously the social movements' claim for a new form of politics. The MDB rejected this claim because it conflicted with the strict competitive logic that was part of its self-understanding. To incorporate the discourse for changing political practices would have led to the alienation of patrimonial constituencies, weakening the MDB in the states where patrimonialism prevailed.[10] Social movements and the MDB followed separate paths between the late 1970s and the early 1980s, creating a dissociation between the logic of the social actors generated by modernization and the politics of opposing authoritarianism at the institutional level.[11] This dissociation became sharper in the final episodes of the transition to democracy in Brazil.

The Direct Elections Movement

Although restoration of direct presidential elections had been a demand of the opposition as a whole, the extreme institutional form of opposition pursued by the Brazilian Democratic Movement Party (Partido do Movimento Democrático Brasileiro — PMDB), the successor to the MDB after the party reform of 1979, had never led to any public campaign for the restoration of presidential elections. Instead, toward the end of 1983, sectors of civil society began a public campaign for direct elections called *Diretas Já*. The PMDB joined the *Diretas Já* campaign in January 1984, helping to make it a massive movement. In a few weeks, *Diretas Já* had become the largest campaign in Brazil's history. Millions of people gathered in large, mid-size, and small cities. By the beginning of March, a constitutional amendment for direct presidential elections started to gain support among the authoritarian regime's members of Congress. Even though opposition parties controlled only 244 congressional seats, the amendment received 298 votes (Mainwaring 1986). Although the *Diretas Já* amendment fell 22 votes short of the necessary two-thirds majority, it guaranteed disintegration of the regime's party, tolling the death knell for authoritarianism in Brazil. The precise path for restoration of democracy would be a matter of the moves of the regime, the opposition, and the social movements.

The defeat of the *Diretas Já* amendment opened up several possible strategies at the level of political society. As it became clear that continuation of the military regime was unacceptable to civil society, to the social movements, and even to the opposition, the probability of another authoritarian president became less likely. The authoritarian regime opened channels of negotiation with the opposition even before the vote on the *Diretas Já* amendment. However, it was clear that the condition for any serious negotiation was ending political mobilization. To the dismay of the social movements, the Church, the Bar Association, and the small Workers' Party, PMDB withdrew from the opposition coalition following the *Diretas Já* vote in order to pursue a negotiated path of transition to democracy centered around the electoral college, the forum created by the authoritarian regime to elect the president. That the PMDB's strategy concentrated on the electoral college shows the overall success of the authoritarian regime's strategy for political society.[12]

The transition to democracy in Brazil was negotiated in a forum shaped by the authoritarian regime, by a political society formed according to the rules enforced by authoritarianism. The electoral college did not fairly represent the electorate because nonmodern regions of the country were overrepresented. Moreover, the division of political society between acceptable and unacceptable members played a fundamental role in the negotiation of the transition. The negotiation of the transition led to the consolidation of the dissociation between political society and the process of emergence of new social actors at the level of economic and civil society. In this sense, the negotiation of the democratic transition in Brazil meant the provisional success of the project of the authoritarian regime for political society.

DEMOCRATIZATION AND THE ACCENTUATION OF THE POLITICAL CRISIS

The itinerary of democratization in Brazil poses a problem of primary importance because the social movements and civil society operated on a contradictory trajectory from political society. The dissociation between the two trajectories is directly linked to pursuit of economic and administrative modernization along with the disempowerment of social actors. The last authoritarian period in Brazil was characterized by the rise of social movements in economic and civil society that challenged authoritarianism at the everyday level. Those movements challenged an authoritarian legal order in which their very existence constituted a problem.

The conquest of basic rights at the economic and urban levels made Brazilian democratization a movement initiated at the societal level. This movement faced a clear limit: the nature of political society, which did not follow the pace of modernization or adaptation to the existence of new social actors. On the contrary, the Brazilian democratization movement incorporated the reaction of the authoritarian regime into the organization of society. The dynamics of Brazilian politics between the mid-1970s and mid-1980s reacted to the rise of modern social actors by strengthening traditional constituencies, which were supposed to be abolished by the process of modernization. While this process was triggered by an authoritarian regime, the major opposition party under authoritarianism, the PMDB, was certainly incorporated.

Negotiation of the transition to democracy was the decisive moment for transformation of the relationship between tradition and innovation. The *Diretas Já* campaign could have connected civil and political society. Their radical dissociation after the *Diretas Já* defeat consolidated the split between social and political actors and between civil and political society. Democratization in Brazil was sponsored by semidemocratic actors reacting to the plea for democratization by social actors. The sponsors of democratization did not incorporate into the political system any of the enormous changes that had taken place in the country's political culture. They did not break with patrimonialism. Instead, patrimonialist features were strengthened after democratization.

The Return to Traditional Politics

Several indicators point toward strengthening of traditional politics throughout 1985, the year of return to civilian rule. First, there was a sharp movement of former supporters of the authoritarian government to the PMDB. The Social Democratic Party (Partido Democrático Social — PDS), the authoritarian regime's party, lost more than one-half of its congressional seats in less than two years. Part of the loss has to be attributed to the formation of a party of authoritarianism's dissidents. The other part, however, was a movement of patrimonial politicians looking for electoral viability. They knew that they could keep traditional clienteles, but they also forecast the likelihood of a strong anti-PDS vote in the coming elections. To increase their electoral viability, they decided to move to the PMDB, which, somewhat surprisingly, accepted them without restrictions. A second important and correlated phenomenon taking place inside the PMDB was the strengthening of traditional politicians who, although influential before the transition, had played a secondary role until then. They took advantage of the PMDB's dominant position in the federal government to construct political machines, based either on the exchange of central government resources or on the offer of local administration jobs. By the end of 1986, after the astonishing PMDB victory, in which it elected a majority of the constituent assembly and an absolute majority of state governors, its leadership perceived that it had partially lost control of the party. Its patrimonial wing, which included a substantial portion of its congressional members, was willing to compromise with the party's program only to a very limited extent. At this point, José Sarney, the first civilian president, decided to distance himself from the platform on which he had been elected vice president and to build a patrimonial network of support. Sarney decided to rebuild a conservative alliance between the former supporters of the authoritarian regime in Congress and the recently elected PMDB governors. This new alliance presupposed that patronage had become the common currency of Brazilian politics.

Growth of Patrimonialism

The Sarney government built its patrimonial structure at three levels. The first level was the Ministry of Planning, the central institution of the developmental state. Sarney transformed the Ministry of Planning into a mechanism for organizing patrimonial exchanges. He chose his new planning minister for his experience as a negotiator of government concessions (Dimenstein 1988). Throughout 1987, Sarney's new minister of planning transformed the ministry into an agency designed to support the president in the constituent assembly. He did this by setting up a system for distribution of resources on political grounds. The quality of projects approved was far less important than the willingness of the politicians sponsoring them to support the president. At this point, corruption became a significant problem. Resources were being distributed on a political basis, and liberation of public funds became more important than control over how they were employed. Government funds were granted to nonexistent institutions linked to congressional members. A considerable part of the resources received by these institutions went to finance electoral campaigns or to build patrimonial networks of support (Dimenstein 1988).

The Sarney government transformed planning agencies and welfare institutions linked to the federal government into institutions whose resources were allocated according to political criteria. The relationship between citizenship and application of federal government resources was abolished. In a survey of the resources distributed by the Ministry of Housing in 1987, the state of São Paulo, with almost one-fourth of the population of Brazil, received no funding, and Rio de Janeiro received only 8 million *cruzados*. In contrast, the state of Amazonas, with 1 percent of the population of Brazil, received 520 million *cruzados* (Mainwaring 1991).

Two criteria became crucial in the distribution of central government resources: the construction of political support at the local level and the fulfillment of clientelist demands. The construction of political support was built from the middle to the bottom through the establishment of a system of reward and punishment of mayors of small and mid-size cities. Their loyalty to governors or, in the case of governors hostile to the Sarney government, their direct loyalty to the president, became a *sine qua non* for receipt of resources from the federal government. Funds received from the federal government were used by local or state governments to provide jobs for their constituencies or allocated to their wealthy clients. In some states of the Northeast, as much as 35 percent of the workforce was employed in public administration (Mainwaring 1991). This system of patronage became so pervasive that it eliminated any efficiency those agencies had acquired in previous periods. At the state and local levels, the overemployment of underqualified personnel increased the weight of payrolls on the total budget generally without providing better services to the population.

Efficiency was even more compromised by the new relationship the state established with wealthy clienteles. Wealthy clients became the financiers of very expensive electoral campaigns, thereby making themselves favorite bidders for public works. The bids were overpriced, and a generalized system of kickbacks was established. Political campaigns became more expensive as the practice became more generalized. The only limits on such practices were the protest of public opinion and the opposition of the press, which began to investigate suspicious deals involving the government and its clients.

Sarney's strategy of pervasive patrimonial concessions proved to be useful in winning elections and building majorities in Congress. However, pervasive patrimonialism had two pernicious consequences: 1) the destruction of the efficiency of government agencies and bureaucracy and 2) the creation of a huge crisis of legitimacy due to the reaction of organized sectors of society to particularistic political practices. The use of patrimonialism led to an extensive number of suspicious deals between government and congressional members, centered in the Ministry of Planning. Publication of a list of members of Congress who lobbied for special resources and the amount involved in each case was the first big scandal involving a president in post-authoritarian Brazil. A Parliamentary Inquiry Commission (Comissão Parlamentar de Inquérito — CPI) was set up to investigate the acts of the Minister of Planning. After a few weeks of investigation, the CPI came very close to holding the president responsible. His own state had received 16.5 percent of the total resources liberated by the Ministry of Planning. Most of the resources were misused and involved generalized corruption. Sarney survived the condemnations that would have led to his impeachment by negotiating votes in Congress. He did not, however, survive the judgment of public opinion. His rate of approval sank below the 20 percent level, and in the last two years of his government, he could no longer make public appearances.

Limits on Patrimonialism

Patrimonial practices have political limits in contemporary Brazil. They are based upon a political system dominated by extreme particularism. Brazil has become, however, a society in which a considerable part of the population already has an abstract relation with the political system. Those who pay taxes feel cheated when they learn that public funds are misused. Qualified civil servants become discontented when their compensation declines because of growth in the number of unqualified people placed on the state payroll. Patrimonialism also entails legal problems that would cost the next president his mandate. In a country where public administration is at least formally rationalized, patrimonialism faces internal and external opposition. The internal opposition comes from those who have internalized a bureaucratic ethos. Private deals between a government agency and its clients are leaked to the press, nullified by the judicial system, and opposed by the nonpatrimonial sector of political society. The government loses legitimacy, and the unlawfulness of its practices makes it vulnerable to public opinion. Once private deals become public, a government's possibility of survival within the democratic order is jeopardized. This was what led to the impeachment of former President Collor de Mello.

Collor de Mello's Ties to Patrimonial Politics

Collor de Mello belonged to a traditional oligarchy in Alagoas, a very poor state in Brazil's northeast. Members of his family and his wife's family together held 75 political jobs in Alagoas, including the governor, three federal Congressmen, two state assembly members, and dozens of people in first echelon jobs (*Veja* 1991). Collor campaigned against traditional political oligarchies by portraying himself as independent from them and their practices. Collor's capacity to distance himself from his political origins was crucial for the success of his political program, which required that the poor and the middle-classes bear enormous sacrifices. Paradoxically, Collor counted on the relative alienation of the poor from politics and on his independence from the organized sectors of society, which had rejected his candidacy. By deciding to remain aloof from organized sectors of society, Collor was forced to search for patrimonial support. In the process, he disregarded legal and bureaucratic traditions on the limitation of state power.

Collor inherited from the Sarney regime the federal mechanisms for patrimonial politics. He not only kept most of these mechanisms intact, but he also personalized their use. Collor generalized the system of kickbacks that was already widespread and monopolized it in the hands of his former campaign treasurer, P.C. Farias. By doing this, he further particularized the state and contributed to the reduction of his capacity to compensate the poor clients that voted for him. The state lost not only the capacity to perform any administrative role but also the capacity to generate minimal standards of social cohesion. Due to its incapacity to generate a universal political relation with its constituencies, the Collor government had to appeal to the particularistic forms available. This contradicted Collor's goals of reducing the size of the government and modernizing it.

Collor underestimated societal reaction to the system he was setting up. The influence of social and political movements that had emerged in authoritarian Brazil had increased since the return of democracy. The influence of nonpatrimonial politicians accountable to the press and to social movements had grown enormously. The press, freed from military censorship, joined the antipatrimonial political movement, increasing public opinion's rejection of patrimonialism. The heart of the antipatrimonial constituency was the urban middle-class and the modern working class. Their votes elected a group of congressional members who were not dependent upon the resources of patrimonialism. The consolidation of this group represented a definite renewal of the composition of political society.

The influence-peddling system set up by Collor collapsed when his brother Pedro gave an interview to the popular weekly magazine *Veja*, revealing that the president was the chief organizer of the influence-peddling system (*Veja* 1992). The initial response of the Collor government was denial. Collor expected that the CPI, formed in the same way as the one that had whitewashed the previous government, would reach a similar result. The president's chief of staff stated clearly, "This commission will lead nowhere." Contrary to the president's expectations, the CPI acquired real power because it expressed a new relation among the modern actors who had emerged because of the modernization process and the restoration of democracy. Throughout the CPI investigation, the Collor government behaved as if no legal and bureaucratic mechanisms for control of abuse of power were in place in Brazil. Much to the president's surprise, those in charge of the investigation were only waiting for evidence. After receiving a tip that most of the president's personal expenses were paid out of resources collected by the influence-peddling system, the CPI was able to recall the checks and to prove the connection between the president and the kickback system. The CPI's reporter concluded, "The President received unlawful economic advantages that were in conflict with the rule of law and incompatible with the exercise of the presidency" (*Folha de São Paulo* 1992). One month later, 90 percent of Congress approved the impeachment charges against the president.

The role of public opinion was crucial to securing votes for impeachment in Congress. Every organized group positioned itself against the president. The press, every important social movement, and opposition parties all rejected any compromise that might have led to some other resolution short of impeachment. Middle-class associations, civil organizations, and student associations came out against the president. In two weeks, millions of people took to the streets of Brazil. Public opinion was clear: Nothing less than impeachment would guarantee governability. After the impeachment resolution was filed by the presidents of the Brazilian Bar Association and Brazilian Press Association in the name of civil society, the president constituted a fund of several billion dollars to be used to buy his way out of impeachment. Collor believed that he could follow the same patrimonial path that Sarney had used. This time, however, utilization of public resources for patrimonial purposes faced the check of organized civil society, acting in tandem with the judiciary. Federal judges prohibited the presidents of the two largest state banks from making loans in the face of accusations of political use of resources (*Veja* 1992b). A rebellion of public employees paralyzed the centers of patrimonial exchange. The president even had to type his last speech himself because he could not find anyone to do it for him.

The political alliance among public opinion, social movements, and the legal system proved stronger than the patrimonial forces the president mobilized on his own behalf. The impeachment showed that a new constellation of political forces was emerging in post-authoritarian Brazil, an alliance between the social actors constituted throughout the modernization process and more isolated sectors of civil society (the press and the judiciary). For the first time in the country's history, these groups had enough influence to pose the issue of control of the exercise of power. The impeachment of Collor represented the victory of public opinion and of modern actors over patrimonialism, underlining the constitutional principle that the exercise of power has legal limits. The impeachment represented the first successful attempt of the social movements and political forces that emerged in the late 1970s to influence the distribution of power at the level of political society.

THE IMPEACHMENT AND THE
NEW POLITICAL CULTURE IN BRAZIL

Even though Collor de Mello's fall did not lead to abolition of patrimonial practices in Brazil, his impeachment represented a watershed in the country's social actors' understanding of the modernization process. The impeachment fundamentally transformed the relationships among a rationalized legal system, a modern civil society, and the patrimonial sector of political society. After the impeachment, the most important cases of private utilization of public resources to build political clienteles led either to judicial proceedings or to congressional investigation committees. Certain members of Congress lost their mandates in some of these cases, the most important being the dismissal on corruption charges of several members of the Congressional Budget Committee (*Veja* 1993) and the recent CPI on the illegal emission of *precatórios*, public debt certificates. The latter has resulted in impeachment charges against the governor of Santa Catarina, as well as judicial investigation of the acts of two state governors and the former mayor of São Paulo.

Yet, it would be misleading to consider that actions taken thus far against patrimonial politics have led to fundamental changes in the dominant practices of political society. In its attempts to constitute a congressional super-majority in order to pursue constitutional and economic reforms, the Cardoso government has relied heavily on clientelism, and the president himself has been intellectually ambiguous as to such practices. After his election, Fernando Henrique Cardoso allied himself with two additional parties, the PMDB and the PPB. The latter counts among its major figures the former governor of São Paulo, Paulo Maluf. Cardoso's alliance with patrimonial politicians demanded his indifference to, if not complicity with, their actions, and several measures of his government indicate a willingness to condone patrimonial politics. These include his refusal to veto the self-amnesty conceded by the Senate to its President, Humberto Lucena. Early in Cardoso's presidency, he was faced with deciding whether to veto the amnesty Lucena had received from the Senate after the Electoral Tribunal suspended his mandate in February 1995 for using the Senate's printing facility to print material supporting his own Senate campaign. Cardoso's refusal to veto the amnesty indicated the importance of his alliance with the PMDB. He has also continued to distribute public jobs to clienteles of members of Congress known for patrimonial use of resources, appointing well-known patrimonial politicians to key administrative positions in the justice ministry and in the post office. Also reminiscent of patrimonial practices are charges by *Folha de São Paulo* that the minister of communication, one of the president's closest allies, purchased congressional votes for the approval of a constitutional amendment allowing the president's reelection. Despite the resignation of two members of Congress who admitted having received money to vote in favor of the reelection amendment, as of May 1998, no investigation of the charges had been initiated.

That patrimonialism still exists in national politics does not mean that Collor's impeachment had no important political consequences. The press and public opinion routinely criticize instances of illegal use of patrimonial resources. A poll published by *Jornal do Brasil* on the Lucena case revealed that 52 percent of the population supported the suspension of his mandate by the Electoral Tribunal, whereas 29 percent were against; 49 percent disapproved Cardoso's decision to refuse to veto the Senate's self-conceded amnesty, and only 24 percent approved (*Jornal do Brasil* 1995). The above-mentioned data reflect the new societal consensus being formed in Brazil on the importance of the rule of law and accountability. That Cardoso's government still utilizes support from patrimonial politicians demonstrates that the modernization it sponsors obeys the same paradoxical logic inaugurated by Vargas in the 1930s, in which modernization is advanced by nonmodern actors.

Notes

1. Clientelism is simply a form of exchange of favors, usually patronage, for political support.

2. It is important to understand fully the implication of such a decision in order to see the mistakes of authors like Linz and Cruz in their evaluation of its meaning. The authoritarian regime established a dual logic at the political level. If it allowed the operation of political institutions, it also disconnected them from the process of state control. In this sense, it instituted in Brazil more than an authoritarian situation, as Linz claims. It introduced an attempt permanently to disconnect the formation of political will from the decision of policies at the state level. This dissociation was so deep that it continued to operate after democratization. (See Linz 1978 and Cruz 1982.)

3. The decree-law first appeared in Vargas' 1937 Constitution. It reappeared in Article 58 of the 1967 Constitution, which authorized the president to issue decrees with the force of law only in matters involving national security and public finance, provided that they did not result in an increase in expenditures. Once published, such decree-laws had the force of law. Congress had 60 days in which to approve or reject a decree-law but could not modify its text. Article 55 of the 1969 Constitution expanded the subject matter of decree-laws to include creation of public positions and fixation of salaries. It also added a paragraph stating that rejection of a decree-law did not imply the nullity of any act performed while it was in force.

4. The concept of private space utilized here is an Arendtian one. According to Hannah Arendt, private means being "deprived of things essential to a truly human life." The sphere of work by being private leads to the loss of liberty and autonomy while work is being performed. (See Arendt 1958, 58-60.)

5. Modernization in Brazil was not authoritarian simply because it involved the possibility of radically interfering with the everyday lives of individuals by introducing them into structures of power and knowledge beyond their control. Every process of modernization encompassed such a possibility. The classic form of such analysis is still the writings of Karl Marx on primitive accumulation. (See Marx 1871.) In this sense, Brazilian modernization should not be considered more authoritarian than in other Western countries.

6. This discourse frightened both authoritarian power holders and the traditional left. The authoritarian regime based its strategy of repressing social movements by claiming that leftist forces had manipulated their constituencies. The state in this case was simply assuming the "paternalistic" position of defending a population that did not have the knowledge to understand what was at stake at a particular moment. This attitude was in accord with the whole conception of authoritarian modernization. The left, on the other hand, assumed the avant-garde role of showing to the "masses" the path of liberation. In his interview to *Cara-a-Cara* in 1978, Lula was pressed by interviewers to admit the role of union leadership in the movement, to admit the need for trade unions to assume an external coordination role, and so forth. The closer interpreters were to the traditional left, the more they rejected the movements as being social democratic or an expression of a workers' aristocracy.

7. I strongly reject the institutionalist perspective defended by Thomas Bruneau (1974). The Catholic Church was defending more than itself when it decided to face the Brazilian authoritarian government. It was defending, as José Casanova argues, ". . . the whole structure of Christian values upon which Western civilization is based . . . ," which were jeopardized in Brazil. (See Casanova 1994, 249.) On the Church transformation, see the excellent forthcoming book by José Casanova.

8. Constitutional Amendment No. 8 of April 14, 1977, provided that no state could have more than 55 deputies nor fewer than six.

9. In his interview to *Cara-a-Cara*, Lula made a clear contrast between the form of grassroots organization he was proposing and the rejection of the populist past: "Workers have ceased to believe in many things that deceived them for a long time. They had believed, for example, that governments could do many things for the working class, because the pseudo-benevolence of Getúlio Vargas was still firmly implanted in workers' minds. . . . Today the worker does not believe in that anymore. Today he believes more in his own strength." (See Lula, Luiz Inácio da Silva (Lula), 1978, Interview, *Latin American Perspectives*: 90-100.)

10. Those were basically northern states that had been granted the minimum number of six M.P.s (increased to eight by Constitutional Amendment No. 22 of June 29, 1982), whereas according to the previous proportional system, they should have between one and five M.P.s (one for Amapá and Acre; five to Amazonas). The northeastern states also had a net gain of 16 M.P.s due to the reduction of maximum M.P.s for São Paulo, Rio de Janeiro, and Minas Gerais.

11. I am drawing here on Alfred Stepan's definition of political society as an ". . . arena in which the polity specifically arranges itself for political contestation to gain control over public power and the state apparatus." (See Stepan 1988.)

12. Cardoso analyzes the conflict between social movements and the MDB in terms of a conflict between class and representation. He calls the members of the social movements "grassroots democrats" for whom ". . . the fundamental question is the autonomous organization of the population around concrete demands — almost always within the reach of and with direct consequences for the well-being of deprived groups of people. These demands should be made on public authority without the ostensive mediation of parties and, if possible, without the delegation of responsibility to elected representatives. The general will in this case is presented as the incarnation of a partiality which in its totality expresses a goal or a desire." (See Cardoso 1989, 314.) Cardoso fails to address the real issue: the incapacity of the PMDB to mediate between society and the state. The PMDB could not play this role because it viewed itself not as the representative of society but rather of particular constituencies who cared very little about societal organization. Hence, it was not the PMDB that would lead to the renewal of Brazilian politics.

CONCLUSION

Collor's Downfall in Comparative Perspective

RICHARD DOWNES AND KEITH S. ROSENN

The preceding analyses of the downfall of Fernando Collor de Mello and the ensuing efforts at political reform within Brazil highlight the turmoil and uncertainty marking Latin America's political development during the 1990s. The region began the 1990s attempting to recover from the economic debacle of the 1980s, the so-called "lost decade," in which personal and national income declined, country after country defaulted on its foreign debt, and inflation soared to record levels. As a consequence, electorates in many Latin American countries were unusually eager to believe the promises of salvation preached by a generation of new-age prophets trumpeting the gospel of privatization and neoliberalism.

In many ways, Collor characterized this genre of charismatic reformers who captured the imagination of people longing for democratic prosperity and economic stability. Collor persuaded a majority of voters that he was an economic messiah who would curb hyperinflation, eliminate widespread corruption, sharply reduce the gargantuan bureaucracy, and retake the path to rapid economic growth. Similarly, Carlos Saúl Menem of Argentina, Carlos Salinas de Gortari of Mexico, Alberto Fujimori of Peru, and Carlos Andrés Pérez of Venezuela all set out on a similar mission of leading their countries out of the morass of the 1980s and restoring them to economic health.

Their experiences demonstrate that such transformations do not occur easily. As the 1990s progressed, nearly simultaneous dramas engulfed these leaders in controversies that paralleled the tumultuous events of Collor's removal, the uncovering of new sources of corruption, and reformist efforts to craft mechanisms for effective governance of Brazil. Like Collor, many of his co-disciples of neoliberalism became the targets of corruption charges as they struggled with the hard realities of trying to retain their popularity while implementing painful economic reforms within political structures built upon clientelism, patronage, and personalism. Both Collor and Pérez were removed on corruption charges prior to finishing their terms in office. Yet, the others not only finished their terms, but two also managed to engineer reelection through high stakes political maneuvering that required amending constitutional prohibitions against second terms.

Within a year of Collor's fall, Venezuela's Pérez was removed from office amid charges of corruption after his popularity plummeted in the wake of his institution of austerity measures. As the Collor episode was beginning to unfold, Peru's Fujimori carried out an autogolpe, closed Congress, removed the entire

Supreme Court, and imprisoned journalists and opposition politicians. After international pressure forced him to explain his actions before the General Assembly of the Organization of American States, Fujimori released his opponents and restored some semblance of legitimacy by convoking a constitutional convention. Corruption charges have revolved around Argentina's Carlos Menem during much of his two terms, forcing him to defend himself in various forums and leading to defeat of his Peronist Party in the October 1997 congressional elections. After finishing his presidential term in 1994, Mexico's Salinas entered self-exile in Cuba and then Ireland amid mounting charges that corruption and illegality had been rampant during his administration.

Does this turbulent history indicate that corruption spread or intensified during these governments as a result of neoliberal reform? The answer to that question is quite complex. Privatization of a great many state enterprises and the opening of Latin American economies to foreign trade and investment occurred simultaneously with substantial increases in press freedom. Greater freedom permitted the media to "uncover corruption scandals aggressively in ways that would have been unthinkable in the past under authoritarian governments" (Manzetti 1994, 1). Press activism may have been responsible for uncovering old but previously concealed practices, as in the former Soviet Union, where a major study of contemporary corruption concluded, "The old structures which ruled Russia before are virtually all in place. They were corrupt before and still are" (von der Heydt 1995, 5). Experience in Eastern Europe has shown that incomplete reforms may actually strengthen corruption by creating monopolistic conditions and giving more discretionary power to bureaucrats (Kaufman 1997, 121). Regardless of whether corruption increases during transition phases, the perception that corruption is increasing may be produced because "rapid change produces strange new connections between wealth and power, and people are confronted with new values and problems, opportunities and temptations" (Johnston 1995, 2). Whether corruption actually increased in Latin America during this era of neoliberal reforms or whether public awareness of corruption increased is unclear. Neither those giving nor those taking bribes can be counted upon to fill out questionnaires honestly or to concede truthful interviews about their illicit activities. Moreover, the two questions are not mutually exclusive. It is quite possible that both real levels of corruption and people's perceptions of corruption actually increased. What is clear is that for all these neoliberal presidents, allegations of corruption and demands for reform became prominent political issues.

Why were Collor and Pérez removed from office while the others remained in power? A recent major study of Latin American presidentialism by Scott Mainwaring and Matthew Shugart suggests that presidential strength rests upon attributes conferred by the Constitution and the political party system. There is considerable similarity in Latin American constitutional provisions for removal of a president. These provisions generally require a finding of "criminal or anticonstitutional conduct," often supported by a judicial ruling and an extraordinary majority of one or both houses of Congress (Shugart and Mainwaring 1997, 13-18). The experiences of these contemporary neoliberal Latin American presidents suggest that the inability of the president to control either the Supreme Court or a substantial block in the legislature is the critical difference between remaining as president and being ousted on corruption charges. This implies that a major factor in controlling presidential corruption in the region is the level of development and independence of countervailing institutions, namely the judiciary and the legislature.

The experiences of Collor and his contemporaries show that a multiplicity of personal, institutional, and societal factors determine the ability of Latin American presidents to implement neoliberal agendas. In the case of Brazil, the power of top executives of state-owned enterprises and bureaucrats threatened by Collor's reforms may have influenced the impeachment process, but the lack of evidence to support this hypothesis, the practical difficulty of their influencing the votes of a majority of the Brazilian Chamber of Deputies, and the strength of popular support for Collor's ouster suggest that the real answer may lie elsewhere. While press and professional associations dedicated to transparency in government and legal and institutional restraints obviously influenced the political fates of Collor and his neoliberal colleagues, their ability to influence the judiciary may have played a central, if not determinant, role. Thus, this chapter offers observations from a comparative perspective about how some of Collor's contemporaries retained the presidency, while Collor and Pérez relinquished it.

THE ROLE OF THE BRAZILIAN SUPREME COURT IN COLLOR'S IMPEACHMENT

As Thomas Skidmore and others throughout this volume have amply demonstrated, Collor sought to utilize the nepotism, clientelism, personalism, and blatant corruption that had been so successful during his governance of the northeastern state of Alagoas. Early in his administration, Collor boldly eliminated the widespread use of bearer checks as part of his anticorruption crusade. Ironically, Collor was hoisted on his own petard because his own decree made it possible to trace a large trail of checks, uncovered by the parliamentary investigation, straight to bank accounts controlled by him. Curiously, Collor's harebrained plan for stopping inflation by seizing everyone's bank accounts for 18 months was never declared unconstitutional by the Supreme Court, although many of the lower courts eviscerated it on a case-by-case basis. Not only was it difficult to square with the Constitution's guarantee of private property [Art. 5 (22)], but its brazen disregard for property rights undermined his later efforts to rekindle economic growth by privatization and the promotion of private investment.

Collor apparently believed that the Supreme Court would shield him from impeachment. An effort to impeach his predecessor, José Sarney, had been rejected by a panel of the Supreme Court on February 9, 1990, on the theory that the Impeachment Law, Law No. 1079 of 1950, had been implicitly revoked by the 1988 Constitution.[1] As Professor Fábio Konder Comparato points out in Chapter 4 of this volume, the 1988 Constitution provides that the rules under which impeachable offenses are to be defined and tried must be defined by a special law, and if that special law were inconsistent with the 1988 Constitution, no Brazilian president could be impeached until the necessary legal rules were enacted. For some reason that Supreme Court decision remained unpublished for some two and one-half years. When Collor's attorneys attempted to make the same argument, the Supreme Court apparently changed its mind. Determining that the original reporter of that case had misconstrued the votes of the other justices in drafting the headnote that embodied the holding, the Court drafted a substitute headnote, concluding that the 1950 Impeachment Law had not been implicitly revoked by the 1988 Constitution and that a streamlined version of the rules contained therein could serve as a basis for Collor's impeachment.[2]

Collor tried several other procedural maneuvers before the Supreme Court in an effort to block his impeachment. When Minister Sydney Sánchez, who as president of the Supreme Court presided over the impeachment proceedings in the Senate, deferred the testimony of ex-Minister Marcílio Marques Moreira, who was in Europe, until after presentation of the final defense allegations, Collor unsuccessfully sought a preliminary injunction in the Supreme Court on the grounds that his defense was being curtailed. Subsequently, he raised that same issue by writ of security before the Supreme Court, along with a brazen claim that 28 senators should be disqualified for bias or interest, which would have made it impossible to muster the two-thirds vote necessary for conviction on the impeachment charges. In a 72-page decision, a majority of the Supreme Court decided to hear the case and rejected both claims on merits.[3] Finally, in a last-ditch effort to avert impeachment, Collor resigned just before his Senate trial. Rejecting his legalistic argument that his resignation deprived the Senate of the power to impeach, the Senate convicted Collor anyway, thereby preventing him from holding any public office for the next eight years. Collor continued to contest the legitimacy of his impeachment before the Supreme Court, claiming that his resignation precluded impeachment and that the 1950 Impeachment Law could not be applied under the 1988 Constitution (Braga 1997a). In December 1997, the Supreme Court unanimously refused to hear Collor's claims (Braga 1997b). The only solace that Collor received from the Brazilian Supreme Court was its lengthy, quixotic 4-3 decision acquitting him on criminal charges for his corrupt activities.[4]

Coming from a small political party with little representation in Congress, Collor tried to stave off impeachment by using public largesse to buy the necessary votes in Congress. This was a tactic employed successfully by Sarney to secure extension of his presidential mandate. This time, however, as Leonardo Avritzer explains in Chapter 6, federal judges prevented state banks from making loans because of accusations of political misuse of public funds.

Perhaps only Collor actually believed that a tribunal as independent as the Brazilian Supreme Court would bail him out. Surely only Collor could have truly believed that he could simultaneously denounce corruption, engage in extremely high levels of it, and then, when caught red-handed, expect the Brazilian populace to rise to his defense. Public tolerance for patrimonial practices had been swept away in the societal and political changes that accompanied the transition process.

Collor's removal for breaking the public trust, like the trial of members of Congress engaged in stealing directly from the treasury, may have come as a true shock to those accustomed to receiving personal benefits from public positions. Even several years thereafter, Collor refused to recognize publicly the role of his corrupt activities in his downfall. Writing from exile in Miami in February 1996, he judged that, aside from the opposition of statist entrepreneurs and bureaucrats, "several factors, that only now will begin to surface, could also have contributed to this fanatic release of passion and insanity." Remarkably, Collor dismisses the charges against him — the "ethical issue" — as part of a conspiracy marked by "judicial creations fed by emotional repulsion" that resulted in "destroying a legitimate presidency" (Collor 1996, 5). The Brazilian judiciary certainly did not by itself bring down the Collor presidency, but had it not greased the skids, the impeachment effort would probably never have left the launching pad.

VENEZUELA: THE ROLE OF THE SUPREME COURT IN PÉREZ' NON- IMPEACHMENT

Like Collor, Venezuela's Carlos Andrés Pérez attempted to instigate sweeping economic reforms. Pérez had strongly supported the statist development model during his first term as president from 1974 to 1979. He became a convert to neoliberalism after realizing the magnitude of the economic mess confronting his new administration. Petroleum prices had fallen sharply, foreign reserves were badly depleted, the foreign debt was close to $35 billion, and the annual inflation rate was nearing 100 percent. During the 1988 election campaign, he spoke about the need for profound changes but provided few details. His sumptuous inauguration on February 2, 1989, dubbed a "coronation," provided little warning for the announcement three weeks later that he was imposing a package of austerity measures suggested by the International Monetary Fund (IMF). These measures emphasized reliance on free market forces and removed a plethora of government subsidies and price controls, which created severe hardship for society's poorest sectors. These sectors were particularly hard hit by sharp increases in prices for food, gasoline, and public transportation.

Popular protests against these measures led to riots in several major cities on February 27, 1989, resulting in the deaths of more than 300 persons. Even though Pérez' reforms stimulated economic recovery, with the Venezuelan economy registering an impressive 9.2 percent growth in the gross national product (GNP) in 1991, the general public remained profoundly disturbed and disillusioned. The inability of the public sector to meet minimum expectations for services in urban transportation, health, housing, and education had "devastating consequences for government popularity" (Naim 1993, 159). More importantly, the real minimum wage level in 1992 was only 44 percent of its 1987 level. Pérez' signing of a letter of intent with the IMF, after he had campaigned against it in 1988, was to many Venezuelans an act of betrayal. Despite the impressive economic growth statistics, little trickled down to the lower classes. Consequently, Pérez' political support plummeted. This was reflected not only by two military coup attempts in 1992 but more importantly by the lack of any significant public outcry against the *golpistas*. A public opinion poll in late 1992 indicated an 87.5 percent rejection rate for the Pérez regime, the highest ever, as the government's deficiencies obscured any perception of progress (Romero 1993, 5; Camacho 1994, 106).

In the midst of generalized discontent with the government, political opponents and disillusioned former supporters focused on ways to force Pérez from
office. After efforts in Congress to shorten his mandate or to persuade him to resign
proved fruitless, political opponents and the press focused on corruption to
galvanize support for ousting Pérez. Brazil had set a precedent in impeaching
Collor, and many believed that Venezuela ought to follow Brazil's lead. They did
not need a Pedro Collor to uncover evidence of presidential corruption. Corruption
had permeated Venezuelan public life for decades (Perdomo 1995, 311-330). The
Venezuelan public was incensed by the legal system's failure to punish those
charged with wrongdoing in the series of scandals that had rocked the country. It was
widely known that Perez' predecessor, Jaime Lusinchi; his secretary and mistress,
Blanca Ibáñez; and former cabinet minister José Angel Ciliberto had fled to Miami
with large sums belonging to the country (Hillman 1994, 130). One of the biggest
corruption scandals involved RECADI (the National Preferential Exchange Office), which ultimately cost Venezuela about $11 billion by allowing preferred
individuals and businesses to buy foreign exchange at preferential rates between
1983 and 1989. Despite overwhelming evidence of massive corruption by government officials, politicians, and business owners, the only person who actually went
to jail in the fraud was a naturalized Chinese, Ho Fuk Wing, the so-called "expiatory
Chinaman" (Little and Herrera 1996, 270-285). Early in his administration Pérez
had begun an investigation of RECADI, which he labeled "a permanent source of
corruption" (Rodríguez-Valdés 1993, 157). Ironically, three days before he closed
down the operation in 1989, Pérez himself utilized RECADI to convert 250 million
bolivars taken from the foreign ministry at a highly preferential exchange rate (14.5
bolivars per dollar) into about $17.2 million that he allegedly used for his own
purposes. Such discretionary funds are traditionally provided to Venezuelan
presidents,[5] but converting the bolivars into dollars through RECADI while
claiming to fight corruption by shutting down RECADI had the same ring of
hypocrisy that characterized Collor's anticorruption campaign.

Pérez' private life and his use of this slush fund to meet highly questionable
expenses provided sufficient grist for the mill of a congressional investigation and
his subsequent removal from the presidency. Charges by opposition leaders of
widespread corruption in state contracts for public works were commonplace, as in
previous administrations. More explosive were press revelations in late 1992 that
Pérez had maintained a 25-year intimate relationship with Cecilia Matos, whose
ostentatious lifestyle included exorbitantly expensive jewels, private business deals
allegedly arranged through her relationship with Pérez, and frequent travels via
private jet between Caracas and New York, where she maintained a luxurious and
mysteriously financed apartment.[6]

A congressional committee's investigation led to a request by the nation's
Prosecutor General, Ramón Escovar Salóm, on March 11, 1993, that the Supreme
Court decide whether Pérez and two ex-ministers, Senator Alejandro Izaguirre and
Deputy Reinaldo Figueredo Planchart, should be tried for misusing the
$17,241,389.31 in proceeds from the RECADI transaction. In Venezuela, the
prosecutor general is elected by the Supreme Court rather than appointed by the
president (Venezuela Constitution, Art. 219). In an unprecedented decision on May
20, 1993, the Supreme Court, by a vote of nine to six, without giving Pérez an

opportunity to be heard, found sufficient cause for Pérez to stand trial for the crimes of misappropriation of public funds and embezzlement. The next day the opposition-controlled Senate, which also gave Pérez no opportunity to be heard, voted to authorize his impeachment. This vote had the effect of suspending his presidential functions.[7] The Senate invited the Chamber of Deputies for a joint session to swear in Octavio Lepage as acting president. On June 4, 1993, the Congress elected Ramón J. Velásquez as acting president for the duration of Pérez's suspension.

Curiously, Pérez never had an impeachment trial. Instead, on August 31, 1993, the Venezuelan Congress adopted an act declaring that since Perez's suspension exceeded 90 days, in accordance with Article 188 of the Constitution, it deemed his absence absolute. The act also declared that Velásquez was to serve out the rest of Perez's presidential term.[8] This act rested upon highly dubious constitutional interpretation. Article 187 permits the Congress to elect a new president if an absolute vacancy occurs after the president has taken office. By merely suspending Pérez, pending impeachment proceedings, and then declaring the suspension absolute, Venezuela's Congress circumvented any need for a trial to oust a sitting president for the balance of his mandate. Article 188 provides that:

> Temporary absences of the President of the Republic shall be filled by a Minister designated by the President himself, and in his default, by the person called upon to fill an absolute vacancy in accordance with the preceding article. If the temporary vacancy is prolonged for more than ninety consecutive days, the Chambers in joint session shall decide whether an absolute vacancy is considered to exist.

For good reason, Pérez challenged the constitutionality of this act, which deprived him of his presidential mandate without a trial and set a dangerous precedent for the future of democracy in Venezuela. The Venezuelan Supreme Court, which has itself been beleaguered by corruption charges, lacks the independence and the stature of the Brazilian Supreme Court. The president, with consent of the Senate, appoints members of the Brazilian Supreme Court for life terms with mandatory retirement at age 70. On the other hand, members of the Venezuelan Supreme Court are elected for nine-year terms by the Congress and are subject to political influence. It was not surprising, therefore, that the Political-Administrative Chamber of the Supreme Court, in a decision rendered September 14, 1993, declared itself incompetent to hear the *amparo* (summary remedy for protection of constitutional rights) action filed by Pérez.[9] Thus, an independent prosecutor general, a dependent Supreme Court, and the Congress, acting in tandem, eased Pérez from office by what might be termed a judicial-legislative *golpe*. A subsequent Supreme Court judgment placed him under house arrest, leaving Pérez, like Collor, to protest his innocence via the Internet while attempting to resurrect a political following.

As with Collor, a major factor in Pérez' downfall was his inability to control the Supreme Court or the prosecutor general. Had either president been able to secure a favorable decision from their Supreme Courts, they almost certainly would have been able to finish out their mandates.

Another major factor in the downfall of both these presidents was their loss of popular support through lack of political acumen. Despite the gravity of the domestic challenges facing Venezuela upon his inauguration, Pérez remained transfixed by a desire to secure his historical legacy by carrying out a vigorous foreign policy, hinting to some that he envisioned himself as a modern-day Simón Bolívar. Pérez believed that he had to strengthen coordination among Latin American countries beset by the dual perils of drug trafficking and the continuation of the Central American crisis. Pérez was deeply involved in providing support for Nicaragua's Violeta Chamorro, sending Venezuelan army forces in 1991 to assist in implementing the Central American peace plan. Activism in Central America was combined with attempts to serve as an intermediary in ongoing disputes in the Caribbean. During his first 11 months in office, Pérez traveled to Argentina, Bolivia, Brazil, Colombia, Hungary, Peru, Puerto Rico, Suriname, Trinidad and Tobago, the United States, and Yugoslavia. During his first two years in office, Pérez completed a total of 35 foreign trips, often with large entourages. Such conspicuous diplomatic tourism may have been compatible with Venezuela's oil-rich treasury during his first presidency, but it was totally inconsistent with his insistence that Venezuelans had to endure severe sacrifices in the name of economic reform.

Pérez' constant travels lent further credence to those within Venezuela who felt that he had lost touch with domestic political reality. His decision to shoulder virtually by himself the onerous political burden associated with the IMF-supported reforms cost him dearly. His responses to public misery and suffering were "distant from reality" and delivered in a boastful manner, reflecting indifference and unconcern. In the midst of protests and street demonstrations, Pérez reportedly mused, "What would be the rate of inflation and public hunger were I not the President?" (Rodríguez-Valdés 1993, 142).

Like Collor, Pérez refused to accept the validity of the charges of impropriety. His televised farewell speech of May 20, 1993, advised the nation that he had been the victim of a "repudiable campaign of lies, slanders, and distortions," that any mistakes were committed "in good faith," and that he remained convinced that his contributions would eventually be recognized "with equity and justice" (LaRoche 1993, 8). He has maintained a publicity campaign against his ouster, compiling extensive comments from political allies attacking the validity of the process and evidence presented against him.

ARGENTINA: SAVING ADAM SMITH FROM MY FRIENDS (AND RELATIVES)

The unsuccessful attempts by Collor and Pérez to portray themselves as victims of political conspiracies in the face of uncovered corruption are in sharp contrast to the experience of Carlos Saúl Menem, who has deftly fended off a variety of corruption charges in his two terms as president of Argentina. Although he has accepted a variety of expensive gifts from foreign and domestic businesses, Menem appears to be Teflon-coated. Thus far, no corruption charges have stuck to him. Moreover, Menem has cleverly deflected the political costs of his reforms upon his advisers and associates, maintaining his own image as the ultimate defender of Argentine national interests.

Menem's astute political skills enabled him to rise from the governorship of the obscure and impoverished province of La Rioja to the presidency of Argentina. Like Collor and Pérez, he implemented a series of radical economic reforms that returned the Argentine economy to fiscal solvency and economic stability (Manzetti 1993; Acuña 1994, 31-74). Unlike Collor and Pérez, however, Menem skillfully created political alliances to check the opposition and to maintain support for his reforms despite the substantial hardship they imposed on the Argentine lower and middle classes.

Menem's actions after he was elected also testify to his political shrewdness. Unlike Collor and Pérez, he moved quickly to control the judiciary. In 1990, he made a political deal with the Radical Party to enact a law increasing the number of justices on the Supreme Court from five to nine. Because one justice retired and another resigned in protest, Menem was able to pack the Supreme Court with six new pro-Menem justices. Despite life tenure, the new appointees have remained loyal to Menem. Indeed, the Supreme Court has been so responsive to the interests of the regime, a filed opinion was withdrawn and a new opinion secretly substituted, changing the result to save the government substantial sums.[10] In addition, Menem has packed the lower federal courts with his supporters. Thus, the Argentine judiciary has undergone a substantial loss of independence and prestige, and Menem's flank has been protected from judicial assault (Verbitsky 1993).

Menem has also been shrewd about his other flanks. He placated the military by pardoning the high-ranking officers convicted of human rights violations during Argentina's "dirty war" against terrorism. He also responded with overwhelming force when challenged by a military uprising in December 1990. To neutralize labor, he appointed pro-Menem unionists to key positions within the labor ministry and engineered agreements to curtail labor protests. Politically, he deflected criticism by emphasizing the absence of alternatives to his neoliberal reforms, backing non-Peronists willing to support the government's actions, frequently using executive orders to circumvent Congress when necessary, and establishing alliances in the House of Deputies with provincial and right-of-center parties.

Menem also distinguished himself from Collor and Pérez by foisting the challenges of economic reform onto the shoulders of economic advisers whom he unhesitatingly dismissed when conditions so warranted. Just before assuming the presidency, Menem explained that if he could not initially overcome Argentina's overwhelming economic difficulties, he would employ "other teams, and if these fail, I will try others. . . . I would change all teams necessary to move Argentina ahead" (Menem 1989, 4). His high-profile consultations with the Bunge and Born group only a few weeks into his administration correctly implied that economy ministers would follow policies they had advised. The demise of "Plan BB" later that year was soon followed by Plan BONEX, and then by "course corrections" closely associated with a new Economy Minister, Ermán González. Ultimately, Menem was able to claim credit for finally eliminating Argentina's chronic severe inflation when his former Finance Minister, Domingo Cavallo, pegged the Argentine peso to the U.S. dollar, made it fully convertible, and prohibited new currency emissions unless backed by gold or foreign currency (Smith 1992, 41-51).

Menem's political craftiness has allowed him to shift the blame for alleged corruption onto other members of his cabinet, the discredited system of state-sponsored industries, and even the generally corrupt nature of society, all the while calling for adoption of major features of his program as an antidote. Menem considered Collor's major failings to have been his political naiveté and lack of a political support structure. In Menem's opinion, Collor failed to understand that he had been elected by "35 million Brazilians" to terminate corruption and that "the direct management [of corruption] by Collor and his collaborators left open his weakest flank, which accelerated the growth of his discredit throughout society" (Baizán 1993, 81). In the midst of surveys showing that concern about corruption in Argentine society had grown exponentially during his administration (Ocampo 1993, 131-138), Menem made it clear that he considered corruption was "more than anything else, a cultural system," to be combated not only by attacking individual cases but especially by "dismantling of the structures of corruption encysted into the structures of state intervention in the economy." Just as combating domestic corruption required adoption of Menem's programs, the fight against international crime and corruption required Argentina to adopt new international relationships, since there was "no other road than international cooperation with the powers who have been confronting these *mafiosos* for years" (Baizán 1993, 82-84).

Menem's handling of corruption charges leveled by U.S. Ambassador Terrence Todman in late 1990 typified his uncanny ability to duck corruption charges and to preserve, or even enhance, his political position. In January 1991, details surfaced in the press of a December 1990 letter from Todman to the Minister of the Economy, complaining that a government official (later identified as Emir Yoma, the president's brother-in-law and adviser) had requested a bribe to process long-pending paper-work submitted by the Swift Corporation. Todman also cited seven cases of irregularities in bid procedures encountered by other U.S. companies.

News of the impropriety heightened the crisis atmosphere generated by Menem's unsuccessful search for an economic plan to curtail inflation and to restore growth. Menem reacted rapidly to the charges, which soon became known as "Swiftgate," by dissolving the Ministry of Public Works and Services, a symbol of corruption within the administration, and making sweeping changes in his cabinet. Brother-in-law Yoma and Álvaro Alsogaray, another prominent adviser, conveniently resigned, and the ministers of Public Works and Services, Defense, and Social Action were replaced. To placate the United States, Menem ordered Argentine naval vessels participating in the naval blockade against Iraq to enter into battle if the coalition effort escalated to war. Meanwhile, government pressure on Swift clouded the accusations. A judicial investigation of whether crimes had been committed closed the case for "lack of proof," but it criticized the U.S. ambassador for failing to collaborate with the investigation. As in previous situations, Menem's associates bore the brunt of the corruption charges. Menem was able to claim that he acted promptly and properly in defending the state against corrupt subordinates (Gilbert 1991, 140-149; Cerruti 1993, 362-266). More important for Menem's long-term survival, his promulgation of a new and successful economic plan substantially strengthened his political standing. In contrast with Collor and Pérez, Menem's political popularity enabled his Peronist Party to maintain solid control of both houses of Congress until the 1997 congressional elections, when the Peronistas finally lost control of the lower chamber. Moreover, Menem never lost control over the Supreme Court.

PERU: ADAM SMITH AND THE STEEL FIST

In Peru, charges of corruption also contributed to intense political maneuvering that resulted in an authoritarian regime quite different from democratic regimes in Brazil, Venezuela, and Argentina. By 1990, three decades of successive failures of both military and civilian politicians had left Peru's next political leader with the seemingly insurmountable challenges of saving the country from terrorism and bankruptcy. While Collor, Pérez, and Menem were seeking to implant a modern state, Peru's Alberto Fujimori was confronted with the monumental task of reviving a state under siege from internal and external forces that threatened its very existence. In 1990, per capita income was less than it had been in 1966; tax collections were less than 5 percent of gross domestic product; and the general price level had increased by a factor of 27 million in the past 30 years (World Bank). Along with a raging insurgency, hyperinflation, and a huge foreign debt many years in arrears, Fujimori inherited a state apparatus riddled with endemic corruption, including a judiciary that regularly released known terrorists or drug traffickers for "insufficient evidence."

Fujimori's embrace of neoliberal reform occurred only after he had secured the presidency, prompting some to proclaim his actions an example of "bait and switch" neoliberalism (Drake 1991, 36). Like Collor, Fujimori had risen to political prominence from obscurity and had mentioned few specifics about his reform program prior to election. Son of a Japanese immigrant, Fujimori, a professor of agronomy, and then a university rector, obtained a majority in the second round of the 1990 presidential elections over novelist Mario Vargas Llosa, after heavily criticizing Vargas Llosa's proposed neoliberal reform program. With support from civilian technocrats, the international financial community, domestic business, and especially the military, Fujimori attempted to overcome Peru's desperate economic straits by measures designed to reverse over two decades of disastrous statist economics. Terming his action "major surgery without anesthesia," Fujimori announced reforms to free the exchange rate, simplify taxes, cut bureaucratic red tape, privatize state companies, and reduce the government's workforce.

Congressional intransigence soon caused Fujimori to take drastic measures. Congress, led by former President and would-be opposition leader Alan Garcia, refused to incorporate Fujimori's economic and security proposals into the 1992 budget, opposed his antiterrorist campaign, and engaged Fujimori in an acrimonious contest of wills concerning the direction of reforms. Fujimori responded with an autogolpe. On April 5, 1992, Fujimori suspended substantial parts of the Constitution of 1979, dissolved Congress, removed the entire Supreme Court and many other members of the judiciary, and assumed complete control of the government. Substantial international pressure eventually forced Fujimori to restore some semblance of democratic rule. In late 1992, he permitted election of a constituent assembly and promulgation of a new Constitution, approved by plebiscite in 1993. While nominally democratic, the Constitution's provisions for a weak unicameral legislature and presidential reelection and its conversion of regional and municipal governments into mere extensions of the presidency strengthened executive power immensely. Fujimori shrank the state while expanding the powers of the presidency far beyond those enjoyed by any of his neoliberal contemporaries (Boloña 1996, 183-264; Wise 1994, 75-126; Mauceri 1995, 7-33; Radu 1992).

Fujimori's demolition of Peru's political and institutional structure and his neoliberal reforms have received high marks in public polls and have turned around Peru's foundering economy. The inflation rate declined from 7,649 percent in 1990, to 40 percent in 1993, and to 11 percent in 1995. Gross domestic product grew very rapidly, increasing by an average of 8.5 percent a year in the 1993-1995 period. Foreign investment has soared, and Peru's international credit has been largely restored. Unemployment is still high (about 40 percent), but the poverty level declined from 55 to 50 percent of the population between 1991 and 1994. Analysts have coined the term "Fujipopulism" to describe Fujimori's "executive philanthropy bankrolled by a liberal state" (Kay 1996, 56; Palmer 1996, 70-75; Roberts 1996, 82-116). Similar to previous versions of populism, Fujimori's brand embraces the "politics of anti-politics" through an anti-elitist and anti-ideological orientation that identifies Fujimori personally with improvements in living conditions. To sustain support for his program, Fujimori used the windfalls of the privatization process to portray himself as the advocate of Peru's forgotten masses. "Fujipopulism," in the view of Bruce Kay, results from radical changes in the power of the Peruvian state and voter approval of concentration of authority in the office of the presidency, thereby making Peru an example of "delegative democracy" (Kay 1996, 55-98; O'Donnell 1994, 55-69).

Fujimori has been the only neoliberal reformer to politicize the military and to convert it into an instrument of oppression to guarantee the success of his reform program. Collor had established his authority over the armed forces by working through the military ministers, chosen because of their apolitical orientation, and these ministers were content to allow the civilian legal processes to deal with the fate of their commander-in-chief. In Venezuela, the frequent rotation of the senior officers of the armed forces and their reluctance to become politically involved, with the exception of dissident nationalist factions who challenged Pérez in 1992, prevented politicization of the armed forces. The Argentine armed forces' enthusiasm for Menem's global activism, the trauma of the Dirty War of the 1970s, and their defeat at the hands of the British in the Falklands/Malvinas war of 1982 adequately inoculated them against engaging in domestic oppression in the 1990s (de Oliveira 1994m 201-204; Pala 1994).

Fujimori, on the other hand, has blatantly used Peru's military as a secure institutional base to sustain and extend his rule. Peru's armed forces have gradually assumed an increasingly prominent role in presidential politics. Decrees promulgated by Fujimori in late 1991 gave the military increased authority over the press, the right to confiscate property for national security reasons, authority to try suspected terrorists in military courts, and a guarantee that civil courts would not try military officers for human rights violations. After the 1992 autogolpe, Fujimori employed military forces to perform house-to-house searches in Lima's slums for suspected guerrilla leaders, to occupy universities, and even to pass out campaign literature (Mauceri 1995, 23-24; Kay 1996, 74-77). The military's capture of Abimael Guzmán, leader of the feared terrorist organization, Sendero Luminoso (Shining Path), in September 1992 boosted Fujimori's political popularity, as did the military's successful resolution of the Tupac Amaru Revolutionary Movement's seizure of the Japanese ambassador's residence in late 1996.

In 1995, Fujimori was reelected to a second five-year term. Although the 1993 Constitution restricts the president to two terms, the unicameral Congress, which is controlled by Fujimori's Cambio 90/Nueva Mayoría Party, adopted an interpretive law allowing Fujimori to run for a third term. The interpretation was that Fujimori's third term would only be his second under the 1993 Constitution. The constitutionality of this law was promptly challenged before the seven-judge Constitutional Tribunal created by the 1993 Constitution. This tribunal requires six votes to declare a statute unconstitutional. Three of the seven members appointed to this Tribunal were so ideologically tied to Fujimori that their independence has been seriously questioned from the beginning of the Tribunal's activities. Three judges held that the law was not necessarily unconstitutional, but that it did not apply to Fujimori's situation. These judges held a press conference to explain their votes. In May 1996, a congressional committee charged these three members of the Tribunal with exceeding their authority, and the president of the Tribunal with failure to restrain his colleagues. Although it is not clear whether the Constitution requires a two-thirds vote or a simple majority to remove a member of the Constitutional Tribunal, an ample majority of Congress voted to remove the three dissenters. The president of the Tribunal resigned in protest, vividly underscoring the lack of judicial independence of the Constitutional Tribunal. The Supreme Court has also been kept in a dependent position; 16 of its 32 members have provisional or temporary appointments, increasing their susceptibility to outside influence. Moreover, only 403 of the 1,473 judges have permanent appointments (U.S. Department of State 1998). Thus, Fujimori has effectively insulated himself from both judicial challenge and congressional impeachment.

The economic and political challenges faced by Fujimori on the surface were similar to those confronted by Collor. Both were challenged by the need to adopt a coherent and stabilizing economic policy that would generate sufficient political support to become effective. Both lacked a strong political party that could have lent support to controversial programs within political systems characterized by weak political parties and legislatures interested in asserting institutional prerogatives. Fujimori's authoritarian approach distinguished the Peruvian experience from that of Collor and other disciples of neoliberalism in the region. Peru's Congress, press, judiciary, dissident military officers, and ordinary citizens have endured the weight of his authoritarian rule. While the economic results have been largely positive and public opinion polls regularly expressed support for Fujimori's program, especially during the initial phases of implementation, his tactics of suppression, manipulation, and intimidation are more reminiscent of the darker days of Latin America's history than of modern precepts of liberal democracy.

MEXICO: THE BUREAUCRATS RETAIN CONTROL

The problems confronting the two largest countries in Latin America, Brazil and Mexico, at the end of the 1980s had numerous similarities. Both had enormous bureaucracies and inefficient state enterprises that were relics of failed state capitalism and *dirigiste* policies, and both were staggering under the burden of huge foreign debts that were in default. Their very size seemed to make recovery that much more difficult. Both suffered from a scarcity of new investment capital and intense social pressures from rapid urbanization growth and rampant underemployment. Even more so than in Brazil, corruption in Mexico was institutionalized (Morris 1991; Knight 1996, 219-236). Mexico's presidents had ample opportunity to enrich themselves while in office, generally on a level far surpassing other countries in the region. One estimate put the total take of José López Portillo, Mexico's president from 1976 to 1982, at between $1 and $3 billion (Rosenn 1987-1988, 97).

The task of reforming Brazil and Mexico fell to two presidents with little in common: Fernando Collor de Mello and Carlos Salinas de Gortari. While Collor had been educated solely in Brazil and had limited political experience as governor of a small rural state, Salinas had advanced degrees in economics from Harvard and two decades of increasingly powerful positions within Mexico's federal bureaucracy. Prior to being tapped as the presidential candidate of the Partido Revolucionario Institucional (PRI), Mexico's dominant political party, Salinas had served as the Minister of Programming and Budgeting and guided economic policy for the de la Madrid regime. As one Brazilian business owner explained, "While Salinas was studying economics at Harvard, Collor was chasing girls and learning frontier politics in Alagoas" (*The Economist* 1991, 17). While Collor had gained national prominence through media appearances without the backing of an established political party, Salinas had been handpicked by the region's most powerful political machine. Collor plainly defeated his opponents in an honest election, while Salinas entered office under a cloud of allegations that he had been elected only because of massive fraud in counting the ballots.[11] Even though both instituted revolutionary programs to overcome severe economic challenges, Collor was ignominiously deprived of his presidential mandate, while Salinas skillfully completed his term of office.

Salinas astutely managed to implement a series of major reforms during his six-year term. He developed a model of "State Paternalism" to stimulate modernization, economic growth, efficiency, deregulation, and trade liberalization. He quickly pushed through reforms that cut corporate, personal, and value-added taxes and relaxed price controls. He opened up the Mexican economy to foreign investment, eliminated import restrictions, lowered tariff barriers, accelerated privatization of state companies, reduced the public sector deficit, and promoted further reduction in government regulation of business. He also negotiated an "economic solidarity pact" among government, business, and labor to slow rises in the cost of living. New laws allowed farmers on communal lands, known as *ejidos*, to own, sell, rent, or mortgage their land. Salinas made reduction of Mexico's $100 billion foreign debt his highest priority, and his government signed a "Brady Plan" agreement a little more than two months after his inauguration that reduced annual debt service by $4 billion. He helped engineer ratification of the North American Free Trade Agreement (NAFTA) to make these reforms exceedingly difficult to reverse (North-South Center 1992, 4-5; *El Financiero* 1993, 16; Teichman 1995, 87-93).

Salinas's political agenda complemented his economic reforms by cushioning their impact among the poor and garnering support from economic and social sectors critical to sustaining his reform program. He moved quickly to divide and weaken the Left, reenergize the governing party, and fortify his image as an economic reformer with a heart, proclaiming his adherence to "social liberalism." He sought to establish his credibility (and settle political scores) by lashing out against corruption through the arrest of several prominent labor and political figures. He reacted strongly to labor strife and asserted presidential prerogatives when challenges arose to the PRI's predominance in several state elections. He forged a historic rapprochement with the Roman Catholic Church, alienated from the state by anticlerical legal provisions dating from the mid-nineteenth century, by inviting six prelates to attend his inauguration ceremony. After Mexico's bishops and the Pope expressed support for Salinas's government, the PRI-dominated legislature allowed clerics to vote, legitimized public religious celebrations, expanded alternatives for religious education, and allowed church groups to hold property. To counter perennial charges of electoral fraud, he instituted reforms that promoted intraparty competition, increased opposition-party representation in Congress, and decreased the likelihood of fraud in the election process, including the issuance of high-tech voter identification cards to all 42.6 million eligible voters (Morris 1992a, 30-33; Morris 1992b, 4; Reding 1989, 687-689; Cornelius 1994, 55-56).

By far the most innovative of Salinas's programs was the Programa Nacional de Solidaridad (PRONASOL), a popular public works, rural credit, and social mobilization program initiated in 1989 and administered during its early phases directly from the office of the presidency. PRONASOL not only brought health facilities, schools, water, roads, and electricity to the country's poorer regions, it also improved the political standing of the president and the PRI by targeting geographic areas threatened by opposition political gains. The program's massive budgets — US$680 million in 1989, $950 million in 1990, $1.7 billion in 1991, and $2 billion in 1992 — attest to Salinas's pragmatic willingness to combine traditional forms of patronage, corporatism, and caudillo-like largesse with an emphasis on austerity. The decision by Salinas's successor to continue the program and increase funding by over 45 percent for PRONASOL's community projects program following the 1994 Chiapas uprising testifies to the leadership's faith in its durability as a policy instrument. As in Peru, this neopopulist program benefited significantly from the proceeds of the privatization process (Ward 1993, 626-628; Craske 1994, 43-46; Teichman 1995, 177).

Politically, Salinas created new sources of support for the presidency and his party through PRONASOL and similar programs, first certified by an impressive midterm victory in the 1991 elections. The PRI won 60 percent of the vote and all six governorships being contested and increased its control in the 500-seat Chamber of Deputies from 266 in 1988 to 310 in 1991. The PRI victory in the 1994 presidential elections, in a contest widely monitored by domestic observers and international "visitors," was another indication that Salinas had contributed to sustaining the PRI's traditional role in Mexican politics.

While electoral abuses by the PRI were by no means eliminated by the observation process, exit polls indicated that more than 40 percent of those voting felt that their economic situation had improved during the previous six years, and support from large segments of the urban and rural populations suggested that Salinas's PRONASOL and similar programs had been effective in generating political support. Aside from restoring his party's position, Salinas contributed to the recovery of presidential power and helped to prevent "Mexico from slipping down the slope of chaotic readjustment and political disorganization" (Cavarozzi 1994, 323). While criticism abounds concerning the need for effective political reform within Mexico, Salinas was clearly able to maneuver effectively within the confines of a highly centralized and authoritarian presidential system (Morris 1992b, 4; Dresser 1996, 162; Dresser 1997, 49; Conger 1995).

The role of corruption in the Salinas regime is subject to intense debate. All the facts have not emerged with respect to his role or involvement, if any, with the drug-related activities of his brother Raúl and the huge sums that his brother had deposited in foreign bank accounts. The corrupt and inefficient Mexican judiciary has been unable or unwilling to resolve unanswered questions about the assassination of presidential candidate Donaldo Colosio in March 1994 as well as the possible role of Carlos Salinas in his brother's criminal activities. While commendably forcing the PRI to forego subsidies from the public treasury, Salinas saw nothing improper in utilizing his office to raise an average of US$25 million apiece from 30 of Mexico's wealthiest men at a private dinner party on February 23, 1993. Many of the state enterprises Salinas privatized were purchased by a select group of his friends and supporters, who became billionaires in the process. While these companies were not sold for bargain prices, Salinas did reward purchasers with subsidies, substantial rate increases, and monopoly protection for substantial periods (Oppenheimer 1996).

Salinas's personal desire to become head of the World Trade Organization when his term ended beclouded his economic judgment. He postponed devaluation of the Mexican peso and failed to institute needed austerity measures, leaving an economic debacle of major proportions for his successor, Ernesto Zedillo. The economic disaster was also related to the January 1, 1994, guerrilla uprising in Chiapas. This rebellion, which dramatically called the world's attention to the enormous socioeconomic disparities and political unrest in Mexico, occurred on Salinas's watch and has continued to fester.

Salinas never had any real concern about impeachment. Mexican presidents have traditionally been untouchable for any misdeeds in office. Indeed, the Mexican presidency is usually regarded as a six-year license to become rich at public expense. With a Congress and a judiciary subservient to the executive, Salinas was never in any danger as long as he remained in office. Mexico is, however, in the process of changing the political system. One of Zedillo's earliest actions was to secure a constitutional amendment on December 31, 1994, enabling him to force the entire Supreme Court to retire, to reduce its size from 21 to 11, to reduce the term of office from life to a nonrenewable 15-year term, and to change the manner of appointment from presidential selection to election by a two-thirds vote of the Senate from a slate proposed by the president. Zedillo has also embarked on a serious campaign to root out the deeply entrenched corruption that has led to the imprisonment of Raúl Salinas. Carlos Salinas, concerned that the law of impunity for former presidents would be revoked and that he could be dragged into the ongoing corruption investigation, left the country.

LOOKING TO THE FUTURE

The preceding comparative perspective suggests that the likelihood of presidential removal from office in Latin America is not a function of the level of corruption that surrounds the president. Rather, it is a function of the ability of the president to maintain control over the Congress and the Supreme Court. The ability to maintain control over Congress depends upon a number of factors, including the president's personal popularity, his control over his political party, his party's control over the Congress, and the political party's control over its membership. The ability to control the Supreme Court depends upon how independent the court is, which is a function of tradition, the manner of appointment, the caliber of the appointments, and who has made the appointments.

It is quite possible that Brazil's impeachment of Collor de Mello was a fluke and that Venezuela's quasi-impeachment of Carlos Andrés Pérez was merely a desperate effort at imitation. Certainly, evidence of Collor's peculation came to light by chance, and Pérez' opponents were so anxious to get him out of office that reliable evidence that he misused the $17.2 million slush fund may never come to light. Significant economic and political reform has been implemented by presidents who, if the truth be known, were at least as corrupt as Collor or Pérez. Yet the truth will probably never be known because the political and judicial systems have been co-opted in a way that will ensure that the truth about presidential corruption will never surface. While the Collor and Pérez cases show that Latin American presidents can be removed by impeachment, it is a weapon unlikely ever to be fired against strong presidents with the political acumen to protect their judicial and legislative flanks. Nevertheless, there are clear signs that public tolerance for corruption is diminishing not only in Latin America but also in other parts of the world.[12]

Notes

1. Mandado de Segurança No. 20,941 of February 9, 1990. A part of this case is reported in 141 Revista Trimestral de Jurisprudência 803-810 (Agravo Regimental, decision of the Full STF of May 3, 1989).

2. Mandado de Segurança No. 21.564-DF of September 23, 1992, original reporter Gallotti, substitute reporter Velloso.

3. Mandado de Segurança No. 21,623 of December 17, 1992, Rel. Min. Carlos Velloso, 192 Revista de Direito Administrativo 212-284 (1993).

4. Penal Action No. 307-3, December 13, 1994, reported in *Revista Forense*, (335), 183-438.

5. "Epilogue," in Goodman, 1995, 400.

6. A year later, both she and Pérez remained embroiled in legal proceedings over the contents of bank accounts they reportedly shared in New York and Switzerland. See *El Universal* [Caracas] 1996.

7. This action was taken pursuant to Article 150 (8) of the Constitution, which grants the Senate the power "To authorize, by majority vote of its members, the trial of the President of the Republic following a ruling by the Supreme Court of Justice that there are grounds therefor. If the trial is authorized, the President of the Republic is thereby suspended from office."

8. The text of the act is reproduced in Sánchez, Perdomo, Mora, and Monteverde 1994, 31-32.

9. Decision of September 14, 1993, reproduced in 1994, *Revista de la Facultad de Ciencias Jurídicas y Políticas* 91: 378-406.

10. See Verbitsky 1993, 445-455. Copies of the original and substituted opinions are reproduced at the end of the book just prior to the index.

11. A week-long interruption of the computerized vote count, after early indications that the opposition was ahead, led to a widespread belief that the PRI had resorted to electoral fraud to retain control of the presidency. Salinas was "elected" with the lowest PRI vote ever recorded and the highest-ever rate of voter abstention; only 30 percent of the Mexican electorate actually supported Salinas. Craske 1994, 1.

12. One can see evidence of this diminution of tolerance in the adoption on March 29, 1996, at Caracas of the Inter-American Convention against Corruption. Perhaps even more significant was the signing of the Organization for Economic Cooperation and Development (OECD) Convention on Combatting Bribery of Foreign Officials in International Business Transactions in Paris on December 17, 1997. This convention commits the OECD nations to adopt legislation similar to the U.S. Foreign Corrupt Practices Act by the end of 1998, criminalizing bribery of foreign officials and denying tax deductions for bribes. Although Mexico is the only Latin American member of the OECD, this convention was also signed by Argentina, Brazil, and Chile.

References

Abramo, Lois. 1988. "Greve Metalúrgica em São Bernardo: Sobre a Dignidade do Trabalho." In *As Lutas Sociais e a Cidade*, ed. L. Kowarick. São Paulo: Passado e Presente.

Abranches, Sérgio H.H. 1988. "Presidencialismo de Coalizão: O Dilema Brasileiro." *DADOS* 31(1): 5-34.

Abranches, Sérgio H.H. 1993. "Strangers in a Common Land: Executive/Legislative Relations in Brazil." In *Political Constraints on Brazil's Economic Development*, ed. Siegfried Marks. New Brunswick, N.J.: Transaction Publishers.

Abrucio, Fernando Luiz. 1994. "Os Barões da Federação." *Lua Nova* 33: 165-183.

Acuña, Carlos H. 1994. "Politics and Economics in the Argentina of the Nineties (Or, Why the Future No Longer Is What It Used to Be)." In *Democracy, Markets, and Structural Reform in Contemporary Latin America: Argentina, Bolivia, Brazil, Chile, and Mexico*, eds. William C. Smith, Carlos H. Acuña, and Eduardo A. Gamarra. Coral Gables, Fla.: North-South Center Press.

Aguiar, Roberto. 1989. "O Custo das Campanhas Eleitorais." *Cadernos de Estudos Sociais* 5 (1): 5-13.

Alfonso, Mariza Resende. 1987. "Cidade, Poder Público e Movimento de Favelados." In *Movimentos Sociais em Minas Gerais,* ed. M. Pompermayer. Belo Horizonte: Editora da Universidade Federal de Minas Gerais.

Alves, Maria Helena. 1985. *State and Opposition in Military Brazil.* Austin: University of Texas Press.

Ames, Barry. 1995a. "Electoral Rules, Constituency Pressures, and Pork Barrel: Bases of Voting in the Brazilian Congress." *Journal of Politics* 57: 2 (May): 324-343.

Ames, Barry. 1995b. "Electoral Strategy under Open-List Proportional Representation." *American Journal of Political Science* 39 (2): 406-433.

Andrade, Régis de Castro. 1991. "Presidencialismo e Reforma Institucional no Brasil." *Lua Nova* 24.

Arendt, Hannah. 1958. *The Human Condition.* Chicago: University of Chicago Press.

Avritzer, Leonardo. 1993. "Modernity and Democracy in Brazil: An Interpretation of the Brazilian Path of Modernization." Ph.D. dissertation, New School of Social Research.

Avritzer, Leonardo. 1995. "Cultura Política, Atores Sociais e Democratização." *Revista Brasileira de Ciências Sociais* 28: 109-122.

Azevedo, Luiz, and Adacir Reis. 1994. *Roteiro da Impunidade: Uma Radiografia dos Sistemas de Corrupção.* São Paulo: Scritta Editorial.

Baaklini, Abdo I. 1993. *O Congresso e o Sistema Político do Brasil.* São Paulo: Editora Paz e Terra.

Bagehot, Walter. 1978 [1872]. *The English Constitution.* New York: Garland Publications [London: Henry S. King & Co., 2nd ed.].

Baizán, Mario. 1993. *Conversaciones con Carlos Menem: Colección Testimonios de Actualización Política.* Buenos Aires: Fundación de la Integración Americana.

Baltazar, Ricardo. 1997. "Parlamentares Tentam Evitar Error da CPI do Esquema PC." *O Estado de São Paulo,* March 23.

Barbosa, Maria Lúcia Vitor. 1988. *O Voto da Pobreza e a Pobreza do Voto.* Rio de Janeiro: Zahar.

Barbosa, Rui. 1933. *Commentários a Constituição Federal Brasileira, Colligidos e Ordenados por Homero Pires,* vol. III. São Paulo: Saraiva.

Barbosa, Rui. 1992. *Obras Completas,* vol. 134. Rio de Janeiro: Casa de Rui Barbosa.

Barbosa, Vivaldo. 1980. "Law and the Authoritarian State." Ph.D. dissertation, Harvard University.

Bates, Robert. 1990. "Macropolitical Economy in the Field of Development." In *Perspectives on Positive Political Economy,* eds. James Alt and Kenneth Shepsle. New York: Cambridge University Press.

Benevides, Maria Victoria de Mesquita. 1991. *A Cidadania Ativa - Referendo, Plebiscito e Iniciativa Popular.* São Paulo: Atica.

Black, Charles L., Jr. 1974. *Impeachment — A Handbook.* New Haven, Conn., and London: Yale University Press.

Black, Jan Knippers. 1992. "Brazil's Limited Redemocratization." *Current History* 91: 85-99.

Black's Law Dictionary. 1951. 4th ed. St. Paul, Minn.: West Publishing Co.

Boloña, Carlos. 1996. "The Viability of Alberto Fujimori's Economic Strategy." In *The Peruvian Economy and Structural Adjustment: Past, Present and Future,* ed. Efraín Gonzales de Olarte. Coral Gables, Fla.: North-South Center Press.

Bortot, I.J., and E. Silva. 1992. "SDR Privilegia Governistas." *Folha de São Paulo,* August 14, 5.

Boschi, Renato. 1987. *A Arte da Associação.* Rio de Janeiro: Vértice.

Braga, H.S. 1990. *Sistemas Eleitorais do Brasil (1821-1988).* Brasília: Senado Federal.

Braga, Isabel. 1997a. "Ação de Collor Deverá Ser Adiada." *O Estado de São Paulo,* December 3.

Braga, Isabel. 1997b. "STF Rejeita Pedido de Collor por Unanimidade." *O Estado de São Paulo,* December 4.

Brasil de Lima Júnior, Olavo. 1993. "A Reforma das Instituições Políticas: A Experiência Brasileira e o Aperfeiçoamento Democrático." *Dados* 36 (1): 89-117.

Bresser Pereira, Luiz Carlos. 1996. "Managerial Public Administration: Strategy and Structure for a New State," Latin American Program Working Paper Series, July. Washington, D.C.: Woodrow Wilson Center.

Brito, Eduardo. 1993. "Congresso Vai Mudar Relação entre Poderes." *Correio Braziliense,* April 25, 9.

Brito e Policarpo Jr., O. 1992. "As Floridas Cachoeiras da Corrupção." *Veja,* September 9, 16-25.

Brody, Richard A. 1991. *Assessing the President: The Media, Elite Opinion, and Public Support.* Stanford, Calif.: Stanford University Press.

Brooke, James. 1992. "Looting Brazil." *New York Times Magazine,* November 8.

Brossard, Paulo. 1992. *O Impeachment — Aspectos da Responsabilidade Política do Presidente da República,* 2nd ed. São Paulo: Saraiva.

Brossard, Paulo. 1993. "Depois do Impeachment." *Folha de São Paulo,* January 7.

Bruneau, Thomas. 1974. *The Political Transformation of the Brazilian Catholic Church.* Cambridge, U.K.: Cambridge University Press.

Bruzzi Castello, José Carlos. 1989. *Os Crimes do Presidente (117 Dias no CPI da Corrupção)*. Porto Alegre: L&PM Editores.

Burdeau, Georges, Francis Hamon, and Michel Trope. 1991. *Droit Constitutionnel*, 22nd ed. Paris: Librairie Générale de Droit et de Jurisprudence.

Bursztyn, Marcel. 1990. *O País das Alianças: Elites e Continuísmo no Brasil*. Petrópolis, Brazil: Ed. Vozes.

Caldera, Rafael. 1996. "Remarks at Opening of the Specialized Conference for Consideration of the Draft Inter-American Convention Against Corruption." March 27, at <www.oas.org>.

Camacho, Francisco Barrios. 1994. *La Memoria Fértil: Crónicas Periodísticas sobre Cinco Presidentes Venezolanos Vivos*. Caracas: Centauro.

Camargo, Aspasia, and Eli Diniz, eds. 1989. *Continuidade e Mudança no Brasil da Nova República*. São Paulo: Vertice.

Cardoso, Fernando Henrique. 1989. "Associated-Dependent Development and Democratic Theory." In *Democratizing Brazil*, ed. Alfred Stepan. New York: Oxford University Press.

Cardoso, Fernando Henrique. 1993a. "Breve Resposta aos Presidencialistas." *Folha de São Paulo,* January 31.

Cardoso, Fernando Henrique. 1993b. *A Construção da Democracia: Estudos sobre Política*. São Paulo: Editora Siciliano.

Cardoso, Fernando Henrique, and Enzo Faletto. 1969. *Dependency and Development in Latin America*. Berkeley, Calif.: University of California Press.

Carmagnani, Marcello, ed. 1995. *Federalismos Latinoamericanos: México/Brasil/Argentina*. Mexico City: Fondo Cultura Económica.

Carneiro, Cláudia. 1997. "Impasse Jurídico Mantem 'Anões' Impunes." *O Estado de São Paulo,* June 15.

Carvalhosa, Modesto, ed. 1995. *O Livro Negro da Corrupção*. Rio de Janeiro: Paz e Terra.

Casanova, José. 1994. *Public Religions in the Modern World*. Chicago: University of Chicago Press.

Cavalcanti, João Barbalho Uchoa. 1924. *Constituição Federal Brasileira - Commentários*, 2nd ed. Rio de Janeiro: F. Briguiet e Cia.

Cavarozzi, Marcelo. 1994. "Mexico's Political Formula, Past and Present." In *The Politics of Economic Restructuring: State-Society Relations and Regime Change in Mexico*, eds. María Lorena Cook, Kevin J. Middlebrook, and Juan Molinar Horcasitas. San Diego, Calif.: University of California at San Diego Center for U.S.-Mexican Studies.

CEBRAP. 1994. *O Desafio do Congresso Nacional: Mudanças Internas e Fortalecimento Institucional*. São Paulo: Cadernos do CEBRAP, No. 3.

Cerruti, Gabriela. 1993. *El Jefe: Vida y Obra de Carlos Saúl Menem*. Buenos Aires: Planeta.

Coelho, Argus de Faro. 1994. *A Proposta Monarquista na Assembleia Nacional Constituinte de 1987 e o Plebiscito de 1993*. M.A. thesis, University of Brasília.

Coelho, J.G., and David Fleischer. 1988. *Modificações do Sistema Eleitoral e Suas Conseqüências para as Eleições de 1988-1990*. Águas de São Pedro, Brazil: Anpocs.

Cohen, Jean L., and Andrew Arato. 1992. *Civil Society and Political Theory*. Cambridge, Mass.: MIT Press.

Collor de Mello, Fernando. 1989. *O Fenômeno Collor*. 1989. São Paulo: M. Claret Editores.

Collor de Mello, Fernando. 1996. "Impeached Brazilian President Tells His Side of the Story." *Business News* (Miami) 15 (February): 5.

Collor de Mello, Pedro. 1993. *Passando a Limpo: A Trajetória de um Farsante*. Rio de Janeiro: Editora Record.

Comissão de Estudos para a Reforma da Legislação Eleitoral. 1995. *Relatórios das Subcomissões Temáticas*. Brasília: Tribunal Superior Eleitoral.

Comissão Especial. 1994. *A Comissão Especial e a Corrupção na Administração Pública Federal*. Brasília: Presidência da República.

Conger, Lucy. 1995. "Power to the Plutocrats." *Institutional Investor* (February), at <daisy.uwaterloo.ca>.

Cornelius, Wayne A. 1994. "Mexico's Delayed Democratization." *Foreign Policy* 95: 55-56.

Cotrim, Fernando da Silveira. 1990. *A Geografia do Voto no Brasil*. Rio de Janeiro: IBASE.

Craske, Nikke. 1994. *Corporatism Revisited: Salinas and the Reform of the Popular Sector*. London: Institute of Latin American Studies, University of London.

Cruz, Sebastião, and Carlos Estevan Martins. 1983. "De Castelo a Figueiredo." In *Sociedade e Política no Brasil Pos-64*, eds. B. Sorj and M.H. Tavares. São Paulo: Brasiliense.

da Fonseca, Annibbal Freire. 1981[1916]. *O Poder Executivo na República Brasileira*. Brasília: Chamber of Deputies and University of Brasília.

Dagnino, Evelina, ed. 1994. *Os Anos 90: Política e Sociedade no Brasil*. São Paulo: Editora Brasiliense.

Dahl, Robert. 1971. *Poliarchy: Participation and Opposition*. New Haven, Conn.: Yale University Press.

da Silva, Luiz Inácio Lula. 1978. Interview. *Latin American Perspectives*, 90-100.

de Assis, José Carlos. 1984. *Os Mandrins da República: Anatomia dos Escândalos da Administração Pública*. Rio de Janeiro: Paz e Terra.

de Azevedo, Marcelo. 1987. *Basic Ecclesiastical Communities in Brazil: The Challenge of a New Way of Being Church*. Washington, D.C.: Georgetown University Press.

de Lima, Olavo Brasil, Jr. 1993. *Democracia e Instituições Políticas no Brasil dos Anos 80*. São Paulo: Edições Loyola.

de Lima, Olavo Brasil, Jr. 1995. "As Eleições Gerais de 1994: Resultados e Implicações Político-Institucionais." *DADOS* 38 (1): 93-146.

de Lima, Venício Artur. 1993. "Brazilian Television in the 1989 Presidential Elections: Constructing a President. In *Television, Politics and the Transition to Democracy in Latin America*, ed. Thomas Skidmore. Baltimore: The Johns Hopkins University Press.

de Oliveira, Eliézer Rizzo. 1994. *De Geisel a Collor: Forças Armadas, Transição e Democracia*. São Paulo: Papirus Editorial.

de Oliveira, Francisco. 1990. "O Marajá Superkitsch." *Novos Estudos* 26 (March): 5-14.

de Souza, Amaury. 1992a. "Sistema Político-Partidário." In *Sociedade, Estado e Partidos na Atualidade Brasileira*, ed. Helio Jaguaribe. São Paulo: Paz e Terra.

de Souza, Amaury. 1992b. "Depois do Plebiscito: O Congresso Nacional e a Operacionalização dos Sistemas do Governo." *Agenda de Políticas Públicas* 2. Rio de Janeiro: IUPERJ.

de Souza, Amaury, and Bolívar Lamounier. 1990. "A Feitura da Nova Constituição: Um Reexame da Cultura Política Brasileira." In *De Geisel a Collor: O Balanço da Transição*, ed. Bolívar Lamounier. São Paulo: Editora Sumaré.

de Souza, Maria do Carmo Campello. 1976. *Estado e Partidos Políticos no Brasil (1930-1964)*. São Paulo: Alfa-Omega.

de Souza, Hamilton Dias, ed. 1995. *A Reengenharia do Estado Brasileiro*. Rio de Janeiro: Diário de Rio de Janeiro.

Diamond, Larry, ed. 1993. *Political Culture and Democracy in Developing Countries*. Boulder, Colo.: Lynne Rienner Publishers.

Dimenstein, Gilberto. 1988. *A República dos Padrinhos*. São Paulo: Brasiliense.

Dimenstein, Gilberto. 1992. "Mapa da Fisiologia Mostra Ação do BB para Barrar Impeachment." *Folha de São Paulo*, September 12, 1.

Dimenstein, Gilberto, and Josias de Souza. 1994. *A História Real — Trama de uma Sucessão*. São Paulo: Editorial Atica.

Domínguez, Jorge I., and Jeanne Kinney Giraldo. 1996. "Conclusion: Parties, Institutions, and Market Reforms in Constructing Democracies." In *Constructive Democratic Governance: Latin America and the Caribbean in the 1990s*, eds. Jorge I. Domínguez and Abraham F. Lowenthal. Baltimore: The Johns Hopkins University Press.

dos Santos, Wanderley Guilherme. 1986. *Sessenta e Quatro: Anatomia da Crise*. São Paulo: Editores Vértice.

dos Santos, Wanderley Guilherme. 1994a. *Regresso: Máscaras Institucionais do Liberalismo Oligárquico*. Rio de Janeiro: Opera Nostra Editora.

dos Santos, Wanderley Guilherme. 1994b. *Máscaras Institucionais do Liberalismo Oligárquico*. Rio de Janeiro: Opera Nostra Editora.

Drake, Paul. 1991. "Comment." In *The Macroeconomics of Populism in Latin America*, eds. Rudiger Dornbush and Sebastian Edwards. Chicago: University of Chicago Press.

Dresser, Denise. 1996. "Mexico: The Decline of Dominant-Party Rule." In *Constructing Democratic Governance: Latin America and the Caribbean in the 1990s*, eds. Jorge I. Domínguez and Abraham F. Lowenthal. Baltimore: The Johns Hopkins University Press.

Dresser, Denise. 1997. "Mexico: Uneasy, Uncertain, Unpredictable." *Current History* 96 (February): 49.

Duarte, Néstor. 1939. *A Ordem Privada e a Organização Política Nacional*. São Paulo: Editora Nacional.

Duverger, Maurice. 1954. *Political Parties: Their Organization and Activity in the Modern State*. New York: Wiley & Sons.

El Financiero. 1993. *Sucesión Pactada: La Ingeniería Política del Salinismo*. Mexico: Plaza y Valdés Editores.

El Universal [Caracas]. 1996. "Cecilia Matos Será Informada sobre Rogatoria Enviada a EUA," September 19.

Faoro, Raimundo. 1975. *Os Donos do Poder*. São Paulo: Editora Nacional.

Farrand, Max, ed. 1937. *The Records of the Federal Convention of 1787*, vol. 2. New Haven, Conn.: Yale University Press.

Ferreira, José de Castro. 1995. *Itamar: O Homen que Redescobriu o Brasil - A Trajetória Política de Itamar Franco e os Bastidores do Seu Governo*. Rio de Janeiro: Record.

Figueiredo, Argelina Cheibub. 1993. *Democracia ou Reformas? Alternativas Democráticas à Crise Política*. Rio de Janeiro: Paz e Terra.

Figueiredo, Rubens. 1993. "Parlamentarismo x Presidencialismo: A Elite Influência as Massas?" *Opinião Pública* 1:13-18.

Finley, Moses I. 1983. *Politics in the Ancient World*. New York: Cambridge University Press.

Fiorina, Morris P. 1981. *Retrospective Voting in American Elections.* New Haven, Conn.: Yale University Press.

Fleischer, David. 1983. "'Ingeniería' Política en Suramérica: Brasil en Perspectiva Comparada." *Revista de Estudios Políticos* 36.

Fleischer, David. 1990a. "The Constituent Assembly and the Transformation Strategy: Attempts to Shift Political Power from the Presidency to the Congress." In *The Political Economy of Brazil*, eds. Larry Graham and Robert Wilson. Austin: University of Texas Press.

Fleischer, David. 1990b. "Comportamento Eleitoral Brasileiro na Eleição Presidencial de 1990: Transferência de Votos do 1 para o 2 Turno - uma Análise de Dados Agregados." *Revista de Ciências Humanas* (Florianópolis, S.C.) 5 (9): 9-35.

Fleischer, David. 1992. "Reforma do Sistema Eleitoral Brasileiro: Análise das Alternativas Frente às Experiências e Casuísmos Recentes." In *Reforma Eleitoral e Representação Política no Brasil (anos 90)*, ed. Hélgio Trindade. Porto Alegre: Editora da UFRGS.

Fleischer, David. 1993. "Financiamento de Campanhas Políticas no Brasil." In *Sistemas Eleitorais e Processos Políticos Comparados: A Promessa de Democracia na América Latina e Caribe*, ed. Luiz Pedone. Brasília: UnB/OAS/CNPq.

Flynn, Peter. 1993. "Collor, Corruption and Crisis." *Journal of Latin American Studies* 25: 351-371.

Folha de São Paulo. 1990, October 29, special edition, 1-4.

Folha de São Paulo. 1992a. "PF Aposta em Disquete Que PC Nega," September 3, 7.

Folha de São Paulo. 1992b. "O Relatório: Leia o Documento Que Envolve o Presidente," August 25, special edition, 1-18.

Folha de São Paulo. 1992c. "Reforma Não Melhora Imagem de Collor," April 5.

Folha de São Paulo. 1992d. "Para 65 Percent, Collor Está Envolvido," June 25.

Folha de São Paulo. 1992e. "Ibsen Está Pronto para o Impeachment," July 26.

Folha de São Paulo. 1992f, September 25.

Folha de São Paulo. 1993a. "Empreiteiro Revela Rede de Corrupção," November 8, A1.

Folha de São Paulo. 1993b. "CPI Acha Cartel de Empreiteiras para Desviar Verbas," December 2, A1.

Folha de São Paulo. 1993c. "Conheça os Documentos Que Revelam o Tráfico de Influência das Empreiteiras," December 3, special edition, E1.

Folha de São Paulo. 1993d. "Alves Culpa José Carlos e Empreiteiras," November 13, A6.

Folha de São Paulo. 1993e. "Documentos Permitem Cassação de Alves," November 3, A6.

Folha de São Paulo. 1993f. "Depósitos de Ibsen Superam US$1 Bi," November 13, A1.

Folha de São Paulo. 1993g. "Ex-Assessor Expõe Esquema de Corrupção," October 21, A1.

Folha de São Paulo. 1993h. "Moreira Fez Emendas de Hospitais Fantasmas," November 16, A1.

Folha de São Paulo. 1993i. "50 Mil Entidades Receberam Verbas em 30 Anos," October 20, A7.

Folha de São Paulo. 1993j. "Documento Contradiz Defesa de Fiuza," November 15, A1.

Folha de São Paulo. 1993k. "Acusados Aprovam Mais de 840 Emendas," October 21, A8.

Folha de São Paulo. 1993l, April 25, 1-6.

Folha de São Paulo. 1993m, December 15, 4.

Folha de São Paulo. 1994a. "Collor Fez Acordo com 'Anões' do Orçamento," January 3, A1.

Folha de São Paulo. 1994b. "Relatório Lista 26 Políticos no Caso do Orçamento," January 1, A1.

Folha de São Paulo. 1994c, January 7, 1-9.

Freedman, Eric M. 1992. "The Law as King and the King as Law: Is a President Immune from Criminal Prosecution before Impeachment?" *Hastings Constitutional Law Quarterly* 29: 7-68.

Garner, Lydia M. 1992. "Unresolved Issues in Brazil: Challenges to the Political Leadership in the 1990s." *Journal of Third World Studies* 9: 59-79.

Gaviria, César. 1996. "Latin America Toward the 21st Century, Beyond Miracles and Stereotypes: The Quest for Sustainability and Long-Term Growth." Speech delivered at the Fifth Annual Latin American Conference organized by ING-Barings, Miami, Florida, April 17 at <www.oas.org>.

Gay, Robert. 1988. "Political Clientelism and Urban Social Movements in Rio de Janeiro." Ph.D. dissertation, Brown University.

Gay, Robert. 1990. "Popular Incorporation and Prospects for Democracy: Some Implications of the Brazilian Case." *Theory and Society* 19: 447-463.

Geddes, Barbara. 1991. "A Game-Theoretic Model of Reform in Latin American Democracies." *American Political Science Review* 85 (1): 371-392.

Geddes, Barbara, and Artur Ribeiro Neto. 1992. "Institutional Sources of Corruption in Brazil." *Third World Quarterly:* 13, 341-361.

Gilbert, Isodoro. 1991. *El Largo Verano del 91: De la Ilusión Menemista a la Realidad Todmania.* Buenos Aires: Editorial Legasa.

Gohn, Maria da Glória. 1982. *Reivindicações Populares Urbanas.* São Paulo: Editora Cortez.

Goldenstein, Lidia. 1990. "Rambo Vem Aí." *Novos Estudos* 26 (March): 39-43.

Gomes, Angela. 1977. "Confronto e Compromisso no Processo de Constitucionalização." In *História Geral da Civilização Brasileira,* ed. Sérgio Buarque de Hollanda. São Paulo: Difel.

Granato, Fernando. 1994. *Sociedade de Ladrões (ou como um desconhecido funcionário transformou-se no pivô do escândalo que abalou o país).* São Paulo: Scritta Editorial.

Gurgel, Antônio, and David Fleischer. 1990. *O Brasil Vai as Urnas: Retrato da Campanha Presidencial.* Brasília: Ed. Thesaurus.

Habermas, Jürgen. 1984. *Theory of Communicative Action,* trans. Thomas McCarthy. Boston: Beacon Press.

Hagopian, Frances. 1990. "Democracy by Undemocratic Means?: Elites, Political Pacts and Regime Transition in Brazil." *Comparative Political Studies* 23 (2): 147-170.

Hagopian, Frances, and Scott Mainwaring. 1987. "Democracy in Brazil: Problems and Prospects." *World Policy Journal* 4: 485-514.

Hansen, Mogens Herman. 1991. *Saint-Just.* Worcester, England: Billing and Sons.

Hansen, Mogens Herman. 1992. "Pouvoirs Politiques du Tribunal du Peuple à Athènes au IVe. Siècle." In *La Cité Grecque d'Homère à Alexandre,* eds. Oswyn Murray and Simon Rice. Paris: Editions La Dècouverte.

Hillman, Richard S. 1994. *Crisis and Transition in Venezuela.* Boulder, Colo.: Lynne Rienner Publishers.

Hirschman, Albert. 1958. *The Strategy of Economic Development.* New Haven, Conn.: Yale University Press.

Humphrey, John. 1982. *Capitalist Control and Workers' Struggle in the Brazilian Auto Industry.* Princeton, N.J.: Princeton University Press.

Huntington, Samuel P. 1968. "Modernization and Corruption." In *Political Order in Changing Societies.* New Haven, Conn.: Yale University Press.

Institute of Latin American Studies. 1993. *Brazil: The Struggle for Modernization.* London: University of London/ILAS.

Instituto Brasileiro de Geografia e Estatística. 1991. *Anuário Estatística do Brasil.* Rio de Janeiro: IBGE.

Istoé. 1994. "CPI do Orçamento: A História e os Resultados," January 26, 39-54.

Jobim, Melson. 1994. "Pareceres sobre as Emendas Apresentadas." *Revisão da Constituição Federal,* January 12.

Johnston, Michael. 1995. "Corruption, Markets, and Reform." Paper presented at the Seventh International Anti-Corruption Conference, Beijing, China, October.

Jones, Mark P. 1995. *Election Laws and the Survival of Presidential Democracies.* Notre Dame, Ind.: University of Notre Dame Press.

Jornal do Brasil. 1992. "Viva o Presidencialismo!" October 7.

Jornal do Brasil. 1993, January 31, 4.

Jornal do Brasil. 1995, September 2.

Kaufman, Daniel. 1997. "Corruption: The Facts." *Foreign Policy* 107:121.

Kaufman Purcell, Susan, and Riordan Roett, eds. 1997. *Brazil Under Cardoso.* Boulder, Colo.: Lynne Rienner Publishers.

Kay, Bruce H. 1996. "'Fujipopulism' and the Liberal State in Peru, 1990-1995." *Journal of Interamerican Studies and World Affairs* 38 (4): 55-98.

Keck, Margaret E. 1992. "Brazil: Impeachment." *Report on the Americas* 26 (December): 4-7.

Key, V.O. 1936. "The Techniques of Political Graft in the United States." Ph.D. dissertation, University of Chicago, 5-6.

Kinzo, Maria D'Alva. 1989. "O Papel dos Partidos." *O Estado de São Paulo,* October 28.

Kinzo, Maria D'Alva, ed. 1993. *Brazil: The Challenges of the 1990s.* London: A. Tauris/ILAS.

Kinzo, Maria D'Alva, and Victor Bulmer-Thomas. 1995. *Growth and Development: Cardoso's 'Real' Challenge.* London: University of London/ILAS.

Klitgaard, Robert E. 1988. *Controlling Corruption.* Berkeley, Calif.: University of California Press.

Knight, Alan. 1996. "Corruption in Twentieth Century Mexico." In *Political Corruption in Europe and Latin America,* eds. Walter Little and Eduardo Posada-Carbo. London: Institute of Latin American Studies, Macmillan Press.

Krieger, Gustavo. 1992. "Procuradoria Apura Liberação de Cruzados." *Folha de São Paulo,* September 3, 9.

Krieger, Gustavo, Luiz A. Novaes, and Tales Faria. 1992. *Todos os Sócios do Presidente.* São Paulo: Scritta Editorial.

Krieger, Gustavo, Fernando Rodrigues, and Elvis Cesar Bonassa. 1994. *Os Donos do Congresso: A Farsa na CPI do Orçamento.* São Paulo: Editora Ática.

Krueger, Anne. 1980. "The Political Economy of the Rent-Seeking Society." In *Toward a Theory of the Rent-Seeking Society,* eds. J. Buchanan, R. Tollison, and G. Tullock. College Station, Texas: Texas A&M Press.

Labovitz, John R. 1978. *Presidential Impeachment*. New Haven, Conn.: Yale University Press.

Lamounier, Bolívar. 1991. *Depois da Transição: Democracia e Eleições no Governo Collor.* São Paulo: Edições Loyola.

Lamounier, Bolívar. 1992a. "Institutional Structure and Governability in the 1990s." In *Brazil: Economic, Social, and Political Challenges of the 1990s*, ed. Mario D'Alva G. Kinzo. London: British Academic Press.

Lamounier, Bolívar. 1992b. "Bagatela sobre uma Lorota." *Jornal da Tarde*, December 5.

Lamounier, Bolívar. 1994a. "Brazil at an Impasse." *Journal of Democracy* 5 (3):72-87.

Lamounier, Bolívar. 1994b. "Brazil: Towards Parliamentarism?" In *The Failure of Presidential Democracy: The Case of Latin America*, eds. Juan Linz and Arturo Valenzuela. Baltimore: The Johns Hopkins University Press.

Lamounier, Bolívar. 1995a. "And Yet It Does Move: Formation and Evolution of the Democratic State in Brazil, 1930-1994." In *Fifty Years of Brazil*, eds. Bolívar Lamounier, Marcelo Abreu, and Dionísio Cameiro. Rio de Janeiro: Editora da Fundação Getúlio Vargas.

Lamounier, Bolívar. 1995b. "Agenda Mínima para a Reforma Político-Institucional." In *A Reengenharia do Estado Brasileiro*, ed. Hamilton Dias de Souza. São Paulo: Editora Revista das Tribunais.

Lamounier, Bolívar. 1996. "Pact-making and the Brazilian South African Transitions." In *Comparing Brazil and South Africa: Two Transitional States in Political and Economic Perspectives*, eds. Steven Friedman and Riaan de Villers. Capetown: CPS, FGD, and IDESP.

Lamounier, Bolívar, and Fernando Henrique Cardoso. 1975. *Partidos e Eleições no Brasil.* São Paulo: Paz e Terra.

Lamounier, Bolívar, and Amaury de Souza. 1990. *As Elites Brasileiras e a Modernização do Setor Público.* São Paulo: IDESP.

Lamounier, Bolívar, and Amaury de Souza. 1991. *O Congresso Nacional e a Crise Brasileira.* São Paulo: IDESP.

Lamounier, Bolívar, and Amaury de Souza. 1992. *A Opinião Pública Frente ao Plebiscito.* São Paulo: IDESP.

Lamounier, Bolívar, and Amaury de Souza. 1993. "Changing Attitudes Toward Democracy and Institutional Reform in Brazil." In *Political Culture and Democracy in Developing Nations*, ed. Larry Diamond. Boulder, Colo.: Lynne Rienner Publishers.

LaRoche, Nelson Chitty. 1993. *250 Millones: La Historia Secreta.* Caracas: Editorial Pomaire.

Latin American Regional Report: Brazil Report. 1995, January 12, 7.

Latin American Weekly Report. 1993. "Congress Begins Corruption Inquiry." WR93-43, November 4, 508.

Leal, Victor Nunes. 1949. *Coronelismo: The Municipality and Representative Government in Brazil.* Cambridge, U.K.: Cambridge University Press.

Leff, Nathaniel H. 1978. "Economic Development Through Bureaucratic Corruption." In *Political Corruption: Readings in Comparative Analysis*, ed. Arnold J. Heidenheimer. New Brunswick, N.J.: Transaction Publishers.

Limongi, Fernando, and Argelina Cheibub Figueiredo. 1994. "O Processo Legislativo e a Produção Legal no Congresso." *Novos Estudos CEBRAP* 38: 24-37.

Linz, Juan. 1978. *The Breakdown of Democratic Regimes.* Baltimore: The Johns Hopkins University Press.

Little, Walter, and Antonio Herrera. 1996. "Political Corruption in Venezuela." In *Political Corruption in Latin America*, eds. Walter Little and Eduardo Posada-Carbo. New York: St. Martin's Press.

Little, Walter, and Eduardo Posada-Carbo, eds. 1996. *Political Corruption in Europe and Latin America.* London: Institute of Latin American Studies.

Loewenstein, Karl. 1957. *Political Power and Governmental Process.* Chicago: University of Chicago Press.

Lowi, Theodore J. 1985. *The Personal President: Power Invested, Promise Unfulfilled.* Ithaca, N.Y.: Cornell University Press.

Maciel, Marco. 1993a. "Presidencialismo e Renovação." *O Estado de São Paulo,* January 28.

Maciel, Marco. 1993b. "Proposta de Emenda Constitucional Republicana Presidencialista." In *Cara ou Coroa,* ed. Álvaro Pereira. Rio de Janeiro: Editora Globo.

Mainwaring, Scott. 1986. "The Transition to Democracy in Brazil." *Journal of Interamerican Studies and World Affairs* 18 (1).

Mainwaring, Scott. 1991a. "Politicians, Parties, and Electoral Systems: Brazil in Comparative Perspective." *Comparative Politics* 24 (1): 21-44.

Mainwaring, Scott. 1991b. "Clientelism, Patrimonialism and Economic Crisis: Brazil Since 1979." Paper presented at LASA conference.

Mainwaring, Scott. 1993. "Democracia Presidencialista Multipartidária: O Caso do Brasil." *Lua Nova* (São Paulo) 28/29.

Mainwaring, Scott, and Timothy R. Scully, eds. 1995. *Building Democratic Institutions: Party Systems in Latin America.* Stanford, Calif.: Stanford University Press.

Manfredini, Noely, and Fernando José Santos. 1994. *Crimes Eleitorais e Outras Infringências.* São Paulo: Ed. Juruá.

Manzetti, Luigi. 1993. "Argentina: The Costs of Economic Restructuring." *North-South Focus* 2 (1).

Manzetti, Luigi. 1994. "Economic Reform and Corruption in Latin America." *North-South Issues* 3 (1): 1.

Manzetti, Luigi. 1997. "Combatting Corruption." Conference paper prepared for "Monitoring the Summit of the Americas," North-South Center, Washington, D.C., September 29-30.

Marchal, Odile, Hervé Théry, and Philippe Wainez. 1992. "La Géographie Électorale du Brésil aprés l'Election Présidentielle de 1989." *Cahiers des Sciences Humaines* 28: 535-554.

Marks, Siegfried, ed. 1993. *Political Constraints on Brazil's Economic Development.* New Brunswick, N.J.: Transaction Publishers.

Martines, Temistocle. 1986. *Diritto Costituzionale,* 4th ed. Milan: Giuffré.

Martínez-Lara, Javier. 1994. "Building Democracy in Brazil: The Politics of Constitutional Change, 1985-1993." Ph.D. dissertation, St. Antony's College, Oxford University.

Martins, Luicano. 1975. *Estado Capitalista e Burocracia no Brasil Pos-64.* Rio de Janeiro: Paz e Terra.

Marx, Karl. 1871. *The Capital.* London: Penguin Books.

Mauceri, Philip. 1995. "State Reform, Coalitions, and the Neo-liberal *Autogolpe* in Peru." *Latin American Research Review* 30 (1): 7-33.

McDonald, Ronald, and Mark Ruhl. 1989. *Party Politics and Elections in Latin America.* Boulder, Colo.: Westview Press.

Mendes, João Batista Peterson, ed. 1992. *A CPI do PC e os Crimes do Poder.* Rio de Janeiro: Foglio Editora Ltda.

Menem, Carlos Saúl. 1989. *Yo, Carlos Menem.* San Isidro, Argentina: Editorial Ceyne.

Michigan Law Review. 1987. "In Defense of the Constitution's Judicial Impeachment Standard." 86:420-463.

Moises, José Alvaro. 1993. "Elections, Political Parties and Political Culture in Brazil: Changes and Continuities." *Journal of Latin American Studies* 25(3): 575-595.

Morris, Stephen D. 1991. *Corruption and Politics in Contemporary Mexico.* Tuscaloosa, Ala.: University of Alabama Press.

Morris, Stephen D. 1992a. "Political Reformism in Mexico: Salinas at the Brink." *Journal of Interamerican Studies and World Affairs* 34 (1): 30-33.

Morris, Stephen D. 1992b. "Economic and Political Change." *Journal of Interamerican Studies and World Affairs* 34 (1): 4.

Mossri, S., and Gustavo Krieger. 1992. "BB Distribui Verbas a Parlementares." *Folha de São Paulo*, August 13, 1.

Moulin, Richard. 1978. *Le Présidentialisme et la Classification des Règimes Politiques.* Paris: Librairie Générale de Droit et de Jurisprudence.

Naim, Moises. 1993. "The Political Management of Radical Economic Change: Lessons from the Venezuelan Experience." In *Venezuela in the Wake of Radical Reform*, eds. Joseph Tulchin and Gary Bland. Boulder, Colo.: Lynne Rienner Publishers.

Nascimento, Elimar Pinheiro do. 1992. *Renúncia e Impeachment no Presidencialismo Brasileiro - l'Affaire Collor de Mello.* Paris: Cahiers du Centre d'Etudes Politiques Brésiliennes, No. 15/16, July-October.

Nery, Sebastião. 1990. *A História da Vitória: Porque Collor — Ganhou.* Brasília: Dom Quixote Editora.

Neumane, José. 1992. *A República na Lama: Uma Tragédia Brasileira.* São Paulo: Geração Editorial.

Noblat, Ricardo. 1990. *Céu dos Favoritos: O Brasil de Sarney a Collor.* Rio de Janeiro: Rio Fundo Editora.

North-South Center. 1992. "Economic and Political Change in Mexico: In Sequence or Out of Sync?" *North-South Focus* (June): 4-5.

Novaes, Carlos Alberto Marques. 1994. "Dinâmica Institucional da Representação." *Novos Estudos CEBRAP* 38: 99-147.

Nunes, Edson. 1984. "Bureaucratic Insulation and Clientelism in Contemporary Brazil: Uneven State-building and the Taming of Modernity." Ph.D. dissertation, University of California at Berkeley.

Ocampo, Luis Moreno. 1993. *En Defensa Propria: Como Salir de la Corrupción.* Buenos Aires: Editorial Sudamericana.

O'Donnell, Guillermo. 1994. "Delegative Democracy." *Journal of Democracy* 5 (1): 55-69.

O'Donnell, Guillermo. 1988. "Challenges to Democratization in Brazil." *World Policy Journal* 5: 281-300.

O'Donnell, Guillermo, and Philippe C. Schmitter. 1986. "Tentative Conclusions about Uncertain Democracies." In *Transitions from Authoritarian Rule: Prospects for Democracy*, eds. Guillermo O'Donnell, Philippe C. Schmitter, and Laurence Whitehead. Baltimore: The Johns Hopkins University Press.

O Estado de São Paulo. 1996. "Congresso se Mobiliza para Limitar o Uso de MPs," October 27.

Oeuvres. 1957. "Principes de Politique." 1:173.

O Globo. 1986. "Pequenos Partidos Só Pensam en 90." November 2, 12.

Oliveira, Alberto, and Leonardo Avritzer. 1992. "El Concepto de Sociedad Civil en el Estudio de la Transición Democrática." In *Revista Mexicana de Sociología* No. 4.

Oppenheimer, Andrés. 1996. *Bordering on Chaos — Guerrillas, Stockbrokers, Politicians and Mexico's Road to Prosperity.* Boston: Little, Brown.

Pala, Antonio L. 1994. "The Increased Role of Latin American Armed Forces in UN Peacekeeping: Opportunities and Challenges," at <www.cdsar.af.mil>.

Palmer, David Scott. 1996. "'Fujipopulism' and Peru's Progress." *Current History* 95 (February): 70-75.

Perdomo, Rogelio Pérez. 1995. "Corruption and Political Crisis." In *Lessons of the Venezuelan Experience*, eds. Louis W. Goodman, Johanna Mendelson Forman, Moisés Naim, Joseph S. Tulchin, and Gary Bland. Baltimore: The Johns Hopkins University Press.

Pertence, José Paulo Sepúlveda. 1994. "A Lei É Hipócrita." *Istoé*, January 19, 5-7.

Petersen Mendes, João Batista, ed. 1992. *O CPI do PC e os Crimes do Poder.* Rio de Janeiro: Foglio Editora.

Polybius. 1922-1927. *The Histories*, vol. 6. London: W. Heinemann. New York: G.P. Putnam's Sons.

Pompeu de Toledo, Roberto. 1994. "A Era da Corrupção." *Veja*, January 5, 80-93.

Porto, Mauro. 1993. "Meios de Communicação e Hegemonia: O Papel da Televisão na Eleição de 1992 para Prefeito de São Paulo." M.A. thesis, University of Brasília.

Power, Timothy J. 1994. "The Pen is Mightier Than the Congress: Presidential Decree Power in Brazil." Paper presented at the Eighteenth International Congress of the Latin American Studies Association (LASA), Atlanta, Georgia, March 10-12.

Power, Timothy J. 1991. "Politicized Democracy: Competition, Institutions and 'Civil Fatigue' in Brazil." *Journal of Interamerican Studies and World Affairs* 33 (3): 75-112.

Prudente, Antônio Souza. 1992. *A Corrupção e a Imunidade no Brasil: Remédios Institucionais.* Brasília: Cartilha Jurídica No. 18.

Radu, Michael. 1992. "Can Fujimori Save Peru?" *Bulletin of Atomic Scientists*, January, at <www.bullatomsci.org>.

Redig, Andrew. 1989. "Mexico Under Salinas: A Facade of Reform." *World Policy Journal* 6 (4): 687-689.

Reis, Fábio Wanderley. 1995. "Governabilidade, Instituições e Partidos." *Novos Estudos CEBRAP* 41: 40-59.

Ribeiro, Flávia. 1988. *Abuso do Poder no Direito Eleitoral.* Rio de Janeiro: Ed. Forense.

Roberts, Kenneth M. 1996. "Neo-liberalism and the Transformation of Populism in Latin America: The Peruvian Case." *World Politics* 48 (1): 82-116.

Rochon, Thomas R., and Michael Mitchel. 1989. "Social Bases of the Transition to Democracy in Brazil." *Comparative Politics* 21 (3): 307-322.

Rodrigues, Cássia Maria. 1994. *Operação 7 Anões: Um Brasileiro Descobre a Rota Oficial da Corrupção em Brasília.* Porto Alegre, Brazil: L&PM Editorial.

Rodrigues, Leôncio Martins. 1987. *Quem É Quem na Constituinte.* São Paulo: Oesp-Maltese.

Rodrigues, Leôncio Martins. 1995a. "Eleições, Fragmentação Partidária e Governabilidade." *Novos Estudos CEBRAP* 41: 78-90.

Rodrigues, Leôncio Martins. 1995b. "As Eleições de 1994: Uma Apreciação Geral." *DADOS* 38 (1): 71-92.

Rodríguez-Valdés, Angel. 1993. *La Otra Muerte de CAP*. Caracas: Alfadil Ediciones.

Roett, Riordan. 1992. *Brazil: Politics in a Patrimonial Society*. New York: Praeger.

Romero, Aníbal. 1993. "Corruption as Political Myth and Symbol: The Case of Venezuela." Conference paper, North-South Center, University of Miami.

Rose-Ackerman, Susan. 1978. *Corruption: A Study in Political Economy*. New York: Academic Press.

Rosenn, Keith S. 1987-1988. "Corruption in Mexico: Implications for U.S. Foreign Policy." *California Western International Law Journal* 18 (1): 97.

Rosenn, Keith S. 1990. "Brazil's New Constitution: An Exercise in Transient Constitutionalism for a Transitional Society." *American Journal of Comparative Law* 38: 773-802.

Rossiter, Clinton. 1987. *The American Presidency*. Baltimore: The Johns Hopkins University Press.

Roxborough, Ian. 1997. "Citizenship and Social Movements under Neo-liberalism." In *Politics, Social Change, and Economic Restructuring in Latin America*, eds. William C. Smith and Roberto Patricio Korzeniewicz. Coral Gables, Fla.: North-South Center Press.

Rubio, Delia Ferreira, and Matteo Goretti. 1995. "La Reforma Constitucional Argentina: Un Presidente Menos Poderoso?" *Contribuciones* 12 (1): 69-89.

Sader, Eder. 1988. *Quando Novos Personagens Entraram em Cena*. São Paulo: Paz e Terra.

Sader, Emir, and Ken Silverstein. 1991. *Without Fear of Being Happy: Lula, the Workers' Party and the 1989 Elections in Brazil*. New York: Verso.

Sánchez, Alberto Arteaga, Rafael Pérez Perdomo, Héctor Pérez Mora, and Henrique Irribarren Monteverde. 1994. *El Juicio Político al Presidente Carlos Andrés Pérez*. Caracas: Centauro.

Santori, Giovanni. 1994. *Comparative Constitutional Engineering: An Inquiry into Structures, Incentives and Outcomes*. London: Macmillan.

Sartori, Giovanni. 1993. "Nem Presidencialismo, Nem Parlamentarismo." *Novo Estudos CEBRAP* 35: 3-20.

Schlesinger, Arthur M., Jr. 1973. *The Imperial Presidency*. Boston: Houghton Mifflin.

Schlesinger, Arthur M., Jr. 1975. "The Runaway Presidency." In *Watergate and the American Political Process*, ed. Ronald E. Pynn. New York: Praeger.

Schneider, Ben Ross. 1991. "Brazil Under Collor: Anatomy of a Crisis." *World Policy Journal* 8: 321-347.

Schneider, Ronald M. 1991. *"Order and Progress": A Political History of Brazil*. Boulder, Colo.: Westview Press.

Schneider, Ronald M. 1995. *Brazil: Culture and Politics in a New Industrial Powerhouse*. Boulder, Colo.: Westview Press.

Serra, José. 1994. *Orçamento no Brasil: As Raízes da Crise*. São Paulo: Atual Editora.

Shugart, Matthew Soberg, and Scott Mainwaring. 1997. "Presidentialism and Democracy in Latin America: Rethinking the Terms of the Debate." In *Presidentialism and Democracy in Latin America*, eds. Scott Mainwaring and Matthew Soberg Shugart. New York: Cambridge University Press.

Smith, William C. 1992. "Hyperinflation, Macroeconomic Instability, and Neo-liberal Restructuring in Democratic Argentina." In *The New Argentine Democracy: The Search for a Successful Formula*, ed. Edward C. Epstein. Westport, Conn.: Praeger.

Soares, Gláucio Ary Dillon. 1973. *Sociedade e Política no Brasil*. São Paulo: Difusão Européia do Livro.

Somarriba, Maria das Mercedes. 1987. "Movimentos Urbanos e Estado." In *Movimentos Sociais em Minas Gerais*, ed. M. Pompermayer. Belo Horizonte: Editora da Universidade Federal de Minas Gerais.

Stepan, Alfred. 1988. *Rethinking Military Politics*. Princeton, N.J.: Princeton University Press.

Suassuna, Luciano, and Luiz Antônio Novaes. 1994. *Como Fernando Henrique Foi Eleito Presidente — Os Acordos Secretos, o PT de Salto Alto*. São Paulo: Contexto Editorial.

Suassuna, Luciano, and Luiz Costa Pinto. 1992. *Os Fantasmas na Casa da Dinda*. São Paulo: Contexto Editorial.

Tavares de Almeida, Maria Hermínia. 1995. "Federalismo e Políticas Sociais." *Revista Brasileira de Ciências Sociais* 28:88-108.

Teichman, Judith A. 1995. *Privatization and Political Change in Mexico*. Pittsburgh, Pa.: University of Pittsburgh Press.

The Economist. 1991, December 7, 17.

"The TI Source Book," at <www.transparency.de>.

Transparency International. 1997. "Report on Progress and Recommendations Toward Implementing the 1994 Summit Anticorruption Commitments." Conference paper prepared for "Monitoring the Summit of the Americas," North-South Center, Washington, D.C., September 29-30.

Tribe, Laurence H. 1988. *American Constitutional Law,* 2nd ed. Mineola, N.Y.: Foundation Press.

Trindade, Hélgio, ed. 1992. *Reforma Eleitoral e Representação Política no Brasil dos Anos 90*. Porto Alegre: Editora da UFRGS.

Uricochea, Fernando. 1980. *The Patrimonial Foundations of the Brazilian Democratic State*. Berkeley, Calif.: University of California Press.

U.S. Department of State. 1998. *Peru Country Report on Human Rights Practices for 1997*. Released January 30.

Uslaner, Eric M., and M. Margaret Conway. 1985. "The Responsible Congressional Electorate: Watergate, the Economy, and Vote Choice in 1974." *American Political Science Review* 79 (3): 788-803.

Valente, Luiz Ismaelino. 1992. *Crimes na Propaganda Eleitoral*. Belem: CEJUP.

Valenzuela, Arturo, and Juan Linz, eds. 1995. *Presidentialism and Parlamentarism: Does It Make a Difference?* Baltimore: The Johns Hopkins University Press.

Vargas, Getúlio. 1938. *A Nova Política do Brasil*, vol. I. Rio de Janeiro: José Olímpio.

Vasconcellos, Gilberto. 1989. *Collor: A Cocaína dos Pobres, a Nova Cara da Direita*. São Paulo: Icone.

Veja. 1991, April 9.

Veja. 1992a. "Os Jardins da Casa da Dinda," September 1, 16-18.

Veja. 1992b. "O Jogo Sujo da Retaliação," July 15, 13.

Veja. 1992c, May 27.

Veja. 1992d, September 30.

Veja. 1993, October 27.

Veja. 1994a. "O Congresso Dá a Volta por Cima," January 26, 28-35.

Veja. 1994b. "Devagar e Sempre," October 19, 29-30.

Velho, Gilberto. 1990. "A Vitória de Collor: Uma Análise Antropológico." *Novos Estudos* 26 (March): 44-47.

Velloso, João Paulo dos Reis, ed. 1990. *Modernização Política e Desenvolvimento.* Rio de Janeiro: José Olympio.

Velloso, João Paulo dos Reis. 1994. *Governabilidade, Sistema Político e Violência Urbana.* Rio de Janeiro: José Olympio.

Venturi, Gustavo. 1993. "Presidencialismo, Parlamentarismo ou Muito pelo Contrário?" *Opinião Pública* 1:50-54.

Verbitsky, Horacio. 1993. *Hacer La Corte: La Construcción de un Poder Absoluto sin Justicia ni Control.* Buenos Aires: Planeta.

von der Heydt, Barbara. 1995. "Corruption in Russia: No Democracy without Morality." Heritage Committee Brief No. 13 (June 21): 5.

von Mettenheim, Kurt. 1996. *The Brazilian Voter: Mass Politics in Democratic Transition, 1974-1986.* Pittsburgh, Pa.: Pittsburgh University Press.

Ward, Peter M. 1993. "Social Welfare and Politics in Mexico." *Journal of Latin American Studies* 25 (3): 626-628.

Weaver, D.H., M.E. McCombs, and C. Spellman. 1975. "Watergate and the Media: A Case Study of Agenda-Setting." *American Politics Quarterly* No. 3: 458-472.

Weber, Max. 1946. *From Max Weber.* New York: Oxford University Press.

Weber, Max. 1967. *On Law in Economy and Society,* ed. Max Rheinstein. New York: Simon & Schuster.

Weffort, Francisco. 1978. *O Populismo na Política Brasileira.* São Paulo: Paz e Terra.

Weyland, Kurt. 1993. "The Rise and Fall of President Collor and Its Impact on Brazilian Democracy." *Journal of Interamerican Studies and World Affairs* 35 (1): 1-38.

Whitehead, Laurence. 1983. "Presidential Graft: Latin American Evidence." In *Corruption: Causes, Consequences and Control.* New York: St. Martin's Press.

Wise, Carol. 1994. "The Politics of Peruvian Economic Reform: Overcoming the Legacies of State-Led Development." *Journal of Interamerican Studies and World Affairs* 36 (1): 75-126.

Wohlcke, Manfred. 1994. *Brasilien: Diagnose einer Krise.* Munich: Ebenhausen Institute.

Woodrow Wilson International Center for Scholars. 1997. "The Cardoso Administration at Midterm." Rapporteur's Report, Washington, D.C.

World Bank Group. "Peru: Country Overview," at <www.worldbank.org>.

Contributors

Thomas Skidmore is the director of the Center for Latin American Studies at the Watson Institute and Céspedes Professor of Modern Latin American History and Portuguese and Brazilian Studies at Brown University. He received his master's degree in philosophy, politics, and economics from Oxford University and his Ph.D. in modern European history from Harvard University. He has written extensively on Brazilian political history and recently published *Television, Politics, and the Transition to Democracy in Latin America* (Baltimore: Johns Hopkins University Press, 1993, as editor) and *Modern Latin America* (New York: Oxford University Press, 1989, with Peter H. Smith).

Barbara Geddes is professor of political science at the University of California, Los Angeles. She received her Ph.D. from the University of California, Berkeley. Dr. Geddes has been the recipient of numerous grants. Her publications include "A Game Theoretical Model of Administrative Reform in Latin American Democracies," *American Political Science Review* 85:2(1991); "Building 'State' Autonomy in Brazil, 1930-1964," *Comparative Politics*, 22:2 (January 1990); and *Politicians' Dilemma: Building State Capacity in Latin America* (Berkeley: University of California Press, 1994).

Artur Ribeiro Neto is an associate with Booz-Allen & Hamilton, a management consulting firm, focusing primarily on mergers and acquisitions. He has worked as managing editor of politics and the editorial pages at the *Folha de São Paulo* daily newspaper. He holds a master's degree in political science and an MBA in finance from the University of California, Los Angeles, and has written extensively on Brazilian politics.

David Fleischer is professor of political science at the University of Brasília and a member of the State University of New York-Brazil program. He received his master's degree in Latin American Studies, his Ph.D. in political science from the University of Florida, and has done post-doctoral work at the State University of New York's Comparative Development Studies Center. His most recent publications include *Brazil's Economic Future* (Boulder, Colo.: Westview Press, 1988); *O Brasil vai as urnas: retrato da companha presidencial* (Brasília: Thesaurus, 1990); *Perfil Parlamentar Brasileiro* (São Paulo: Editora Tres, 1991); *Las consecuencias políticas del sistema electoral brasileño: partidos políticos, poder leglislativo y gobernabilidad* (San José, Costa Rica: Instituto Interamericano de Derechos Humanos, 1995); and numerous journal articles and book chapters on Brazil's political development.

Fábio Konder Comparato is a distinguished Brazilian jurist and legal scholar. As a member of the Brazilian Bar Association, Konder Comparato was one of the authors of the impeachment request used as the basis for removing President Collor. He is the author of *O poder de controle na sociedade anônima* (São Paulo: NP, 1975); *Comentários às disposições transitórias da nova Lei de sociedades por ações* (Rio de Janeiro: Forense, 1978); *Muda Brazil! Uma constiuição para o* *desenvolvimento democrático* (São Paulo: Brasiliense, 1986); *Educação, estado e poder* (São Paulo: Brasiliense, 1987); *Para viver a democracia* (São Paulo: Brasiliense, 1989); and *Direito empresarial* (São Paulo: Saraiva, 1990), among other works.

Amaury de Souza is senior research fellow at the Instituto de Estudos Econômicos, Sociais e Políticas de São Paulo (IDESP) and senior partner at the consulting firm of Techne Informática e Recursos Humanos, Ltda., in Rio de Janeiro. He holds a Ph.D. in political science from the Massachusetts Institute of Technology, is the former editor of *Dados: Revista de Ciências Sociais*, and served as a visiting professor in political science at Duke University and the University of North Carolina, Chapel Hill. Among his publications is "Changing Attitudes towards Democracy and Institutional Reform in Brazil" (with Bolívar Lamounier) in Larry Diamond, ed., *Political Culture and Democracy in Developing Countries* (Boulder, Colo.: Lynne Rienner, 1993).

Leonardo Avritzer is associate professor of political science and director of the master's degree in political science program at the Universidade Federal de Minas Gerais, in Belo Horizonte, Minas Gerais. He earned a Ph.D. in political science from the New School for Social Science Research in 1993 and is the author of *Sociedade Civil e Democratizição* (Editorial del Rey, 1994) and *A Moralidade da Democracia* (Editorial Perspectiva, 1996).

Richard Downes is an adjunct senior research associate at the North-South Center with extensive research and experience related to Brazil and Portugal. As a career Air Force officer with a Ph.D. in history from the University of Texas, he served as the political adviser for the U.S. Forces, Azores, and as the Pentagon's Joint Staff desk officer for Brazil and liaison officer with the Brazilian Armed Forces Staff. His dissertation focused on the changing political and economic relationships between the United States and Brazil's Old Republic. He is the author of "Autos Over Rails: How U.S. Business Supplanted the British in Brazil, 1910-1928," *Journal of Latin American Studies* (24), and of various articles on inter-American relations.

Keith S. Rosenn is professor of law at the University of Miami School of Law, where he is also director of the Foreign Graduate Law Program and the Master's Program in Inter-American Law. He holds a B.A. from Amherst College and an LLB from Yale Law School. He has written extensively on legal systems in Latin America. Among his publications are *Foreign Investment in Brazil* (Boulder, Colo.: Westview Press, 1991)*; A Panorama of Brazilian Law (*Coral Gables, Fla.: North-South Center, 1992)*, editor with Jacob Dollinger; and "Federalism in the Americas in Comparative Perspective," *University of Miami Inter-American Law Review* (26).

Index

W

Y